Welcome to the East of England

The Official Guide to the East of England provides you with hundreds of ideas for great days out. Historic houses, museums, gardens, animal collections, country parks and a host of other things are included, as well as some good suggestions for shopping and places to eat.

Whether you are on a short break or holiday, visiting friends or family or just planning to explore your neighbourhood the Guide gives you all the information you need to explore this beautiful region.

Contents

Cover picture: Snape Maltings, Suffolk

This picture: Dedham, Essex

GW00707746

There are so many places to go and things to see in the East of England you'll find it hard to fit it all in!

Each of the region's counties has its very own unique character, and all of them have a wealth of places to explore, treasures to discover and places to eat and shop. Take time out to leisurely tour round the region, whether you know where you want to go or just want some useful ideas to help you plan your visit, this Guide has all the information you need.

Each county section is packed with general information on the main towns and cities to visit, as well as providing details for many of the places to visit, which are listed alphabetically by town name under the following categories:

- **History & Heritage**
- **Bloomin' Beautiful**
- **Family Fun**
- **Countryside Activities and Sport**
- **Food & Drink**
- **Stop & Shop**

You will find all places to visit are listed alphabetically by town name. Each has a map reference, shown in brackets at the end of the listing, to help you locate them on the relevant map (found at the beginning of each county section).

Norfolk Shire Horse Centre, West Runton, Cromer, Norfolk

If you want a few ideas to help you plan your d out, don't miss our **'Discovery Tours'**, featured the end of each county section. These tours gi you a few suggestions on what to see and how fit it all in! Of course these are only a selection the places you can visit in the East of England why not use the Guide to plan your own tou Please remember to contact all establishmen before visiting, to check their opening times ar prices.

Important Information

All **prices** for attractions appear in the order of **Adults / Child / Senior Citizen** - in some instances prices were not available at the time of going to press. We always advise that before visiting any of the attractions/establishments listed in this Guide, you contact them in advance, just to confirm both the prices and opening times, as the information may have altered since production of this Guide.

All of the attractions in this guide have signed the **National Code of Practice for Visitor Attractions** and many are **members** of the East of England Tourist Board. You will recognise them by the Rose symbol ⊛ shown alongside entries in this guide.

In addition, you will find some attractions participate in the **Visitor Attraction Quality Assurance Service**. These attractions have all been independently assessed and offer an assured level of quality for the visitor. You will recognise these attractions by the Ⓠ shown alongside **Quality Assured Visitor Attractions**.

Access for visitors with disabilities - we strongly advise visitors to check with the individual attractions for specific information about their facilities before visiting.

PLEASE NOTE

All information contained in this Guide is given in good faith, based on the information supplied by the individual establishments listed. Whilst every care has been taken to ensure the accuracy of the information published herein, the East of England Tourist Board cannot accept responsibility in respect of any error or omission which may have occurred.

Visitors are always advised to check details of opening times, admission prices etc, as changes do occur following the publication date.

EAST OF ENGLAND
TOURIST BOARD

Compiled and published by:
The East of England Tourist Board
Toppesfield Hall, Hadleigh, Suffolk IP7 5DN
Tel: (01473) 822922 Fax: (01473) 823063
Email: eastofenglandtouristboard@compuserve.com
Web: www.eastofenglandtouristboard.com

Blickling Hall, Norfolk

Editor and Production Manager: Emma Cross
Production Assistants:
Sam Emptage & Lyn Mowat
Editorial Contribution:
Stephen Rampley
Graphic Design: PRS, Ipswich, Suffolk
Maps: ©Maps in Minutes™2001. ©Crown Copyright, Ordnance Survey 2001
Printed: in the UK by Acorn, Normanton, West Yorkshire

ISBN: 1 873246 560

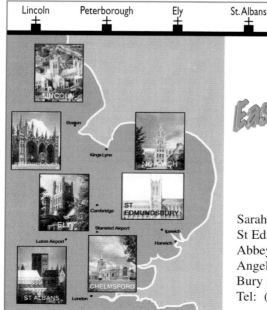

Lincoln   Peterborough   Ely   St. Albans   Chelmsford   St. Edmundsbury   Norwich

Follow the Eastern Cathedral Trail

Further details of the cathedrals, opening times and facilities can be found in the relevant County section. For more information on the trail, please contact:

Sarah Friswell, Visitors' Officer
St Edmundsbury Cathedral
Abbey House
Angel Hill
Bury St Edmunds IP33 1 LS
Tel: (01284) 748726

Braintree District Museum

Braintree, Essex

Offer: Half price entry with Guide. Non-residents of Braintree District all qualify for half price entry.

Closing Date: 31 December 2002
(See page 128)

The Fitzwilliam Museum

Cambridge

Offer: 5% discount at the Museum Shop.

Closing Date: December 2002
(See page 88)

Bressingham Steam Experience & Gardens

Norfolk

Offer: Two adults paying full entrance fee can take one child free. Cannot be used on event days.

Closing Date: 31 July 2002
(See page 183)

Flag Fen Bronze Age Excavations

Fengate, Cambridgeshire

Offer: 20% discount off admission price.

Closing Date: 31 December 2002
(See page 86)

Bure Valley Railway

Aylsham, Norfolk

Offer: 50p off standard adult return ticket. Cannot be used in conjunction with boat/train tickets.

Closing Date: October 2002
(See page 184)

Henry Watsons Pottery

Wattisfield, Suffolk

Offer: Free gift on purchases over £10 with this voucher. (Limited to one gift per family).

Closing Date: Valid during 2002
(See page 258)

Colchester Castle

Colchester, Essex

Offer: 2 for 1 - One free entry with one full paying adult (excluding Bank Holidays).

Closing Date: 31 December 2002
(See page 129)

Hylands House

Writtle, nr Chelmsford, Essex

Offer: A free cup of tea when you visit Hylands House, Chelmsford on a Sunday.

Closing Date: 31 December 2002
(See page 123)

Ecotech Centre

Norwich, Norfolk

Offer: £1.00 off a family ticket.

Closing Date: 31 October 2002
(See page 175)

Inspire Discovery Centre

Norwich, Norfolk

Offer: Adults can enter at the children's price.

Closing Date: 31 December 2002
(See page 177)

The Fitzwilliam Museum

Cambridge

Offer: 5% discount at the Museum Shop.

Closing Date: December 2002
(See page 88)

Braintree District Museum

Braintree, Essex

Offer: Half price entry with Guide. Non-residents of Braintree District all qualify for half price entry.

Closing Date: 31 December 2002
(See page 128)

Flag Fen Bronze Age Excavations

Fengate, Cambridgeshire

Offer: 20% discount off admission price.

Closing Date: 31 December 2002
(See page 86)

Bressingham Steam Experience & Gardens

Norfolk

Offer: Two adults paying full entrance fee can take one child free. Cannot be used on event days.

Closing Date: 31 July 2002
(See page 183)

Henry Watsons Pottery

Wattisfield, Suffolk

Offer: Free gift on purchases over £10 with this voucher. (Limited to one gift per family).

Closing Date: Valid during 2002
(See page 258)

Bure Valley Railway

Aylsham, Norfolk

Offer: 50p off standard adult return ticket. Cannot be used in conjunction with boat/train tickets.

Closing Date: October 2002
(See page 184)

Hylands House

Writtle, nr Chelmsford, Essex

Offer: A free cup of tea when you visit Hylands House, Chelmsford on a Sunday.

Closing Date: 31 December 2002
(See page 123)

Colchester Castle

Colchester, Essex

Offer: 2 for 1 - One free entry with one full paying adult (excluding Bank Holidays).

Closing Date: 31 December 2002
(See page 129)

Inspire Discovery Centre

Norwich, Norfolk

Offer: Adults can enter at the children's price.

Closing Date: 31 December 2002
(See page 177)

Ecotech Centre

Norwich, Norfolk

Offer: £1.00 off a family ticket.

Closing Date: 31 October 2002
(See page 175)

Kelvedon Hatch Nuclear Bunker

Kelvedon Hatch, Essex

Offer: 50p reduction on entry.

Closing Date: 31 December 2002
(See page 128)

The Original Great Maze

Braintree, Essex

Offer: 1 child free with 2 adults.

Closing Date: 31 October 2002
(See page 148)

Mark David Cooking Experience

Hadleigh, Suffolk

Offer: 5% discount per person on all courses.

Closing Date: September 2002
(See page 257)

The Raptor Foundation

Woodhurst, Cambs

Offer: Two for the price of one. (excluding Bank Holidays)

Closing Date: 31 October 2002
(See page 96)

The National Horseracing Museum

Newmarket, Suffolk

Offer: 10% off admission to Museum.

Closing Date: 30 September 2002
(See page 234)

RHS Garden

Rettendon, Essex

Offer: Two for the price of one. (excluding Weekends & Bank Holidays)

Closing Date: 31 October 2002
(See page 144)

National Trust - Shaw's Corner

Ayot St Lawrence, Herts

Offer: Two for One. Valid when accompanied by a full paying adult or NT member - except bank holidays.

Closing Date: October 2002
(See page 52)

Shepreth Wildlife Park Willersmill

Shepreth, Hertfordshire

Offer: Free guide book.

Closing Date: 31 December 2002
(See page 111)

Oliver Cromwell's House

Ely, Cambridgeshire

Offer: 10% off admission.

Closing Date: 31 December 2002
(See page 83)

Woburn Safari Park

Woburn, Bedfordshire

Offer: One child free with one paying adult. Cannot be combined with any other discount or offer.

Closing Date: 27 October 2002
(See page 68)

The Original Great Maze
Braintree, Essex

Offer: 1 child free with 2 adults.

Closing Date: 31 October 2002
(See page 148)

ONE CHILD FREE

Kelvedon Hatch Nuclear Bunker
Kelvedon Hatch, Essex

Offer: 50p reduction on entry.

Closing Date: 31 December 2002
(See page 128)

50p

The Raptor Foundation
Woodhurst, Cambs

Offer: Two for the price of one.
(excluding Bank Holidays)

Closing Date: 31 October 2002
(See page 96)

2 FOR 1

Mark David Cooking Experience
Hadleigh, Suffolk

Offer: 5% discount per person on all courses.

Closing Date: September 2002
(See page 257)

5%

RHS Garden
Rettendon, Essex

Offer: Two for the price of one.
(excluding Weekends & Bank Holidays)

Closing Date: 31 October 2002
(See page 144)

2 FOR 1

The National Horseracing Museum
Newmarket, Suffolk

Offer: 10% off admission to Museum.

Closing Date: 30 September 2002
(See page 234)

10%

Shepreth Wildlife Park Willersmill
Shepreth, Hertfordshire

Offer: Free guide book.

Closing Date: 31 December 2002
(See page 111)

GUIDE BOOK

National Trust - Shaw's Corner
Ayot St Lawrence, Herts

Offer: Two for One. Valid when accompanied by a full paying adult or NT member - except bank holidays.

Closing Date: October 2002
(See page 52)

2 FOR 1

Woburn Safari Park
Woburn, Bedfordshire

Offer: One child free with one paying adult. Cannot be combined with any other discount or offer.

Closing Date: 27 October 2002
(See page 68)

ONE CHILD FREE

Oliver Cromwell's House
Ely, Cambridgeshire

Offer: 10% off admission.

Closing Date: 31 December 2002
(See page 83)

10%

ifree|art

take something home
to remember

Babylon Gallery	t: 01353 669022	Focal Point Gallery	t: 01702 612621
Bircham Contemporary Arts	t: 01263 713312	Haddenham Studios & Gallery	t: 01353 749188
Bromham Mill Art Gallery	t: 01234 824330	Kettle's Yard Gallery	t: 01223 352124
Buckenham Galleries	t: 01502 725418	Lynne Strover Gallery	t: 01223 295264
Bury St Edmunds Art Gallery	t: 01284 762081	Margaret Harvey Gallery	t: 01707 285376
Byard Art	t: 01223 560400	Norwich Gallery	t: 01603 610561
Cambridge Contemporary Art	t: 01223 324222	Pam Schomberg Gallery	t: 01206 769458
Chapel Gallery	t: 01234 708604	Primavera	t: 01223 357708
Collections of Harpenden	t: 01582 620015	UH Gallery	t: 01707 285376
Elm Hill Contemporary Art	t: 01603 617945	Wingfield Arts	t: 01379 384505
Field Dalling Gallery	t: 01328 830518	Wolsey Art Gallery	t: 01473 433554
Firstsite	t: Q1206 577067	Wysing Arts	t: 01954 718881

east england|arts

The East of England offers a range of exciting and varied events to suit all tastes, from air shows to arts festivals, from historical re-enactments and cheese rolling contests to craft fairs and agricultural shows. Or for the more unusual, try the World Snail Racing and Pea Shooting Championships, all held in the region throughout the year. On the following pages we have brought together a selection of events taking place during the year 2002. For information on the events listed or other events taking place during 2002, please call the East of England Tourist Board on (01473) 822922.

* - Provisional

January

9-13 Jan	Whittlesey Straw Bear Festival, various venues, Whittlesey, Cambs
25-27 Jan	Woburn Abbey Elegant Homes and Garden Show, Woburn Abbey, Woburn, Beds

February

5-11 Feb	Beryl Cook Art Exhibition, Elstree Golf Club, Herts
14-26 Feb	King's Lynn Mart, Tuesday Market Place, King's Lynn, Norfolk
16-24 Feb	Primrose and Spring Plant Festival, Capel St Mary, Ipswich, Suffolk
17 Feb-24 Mar	Lambing Sundays and Spring Bulb Days, Kentwell Hall, Long Melford, Suffolk
27 Feb*	Lowestoft Pancake Race, The Triangle Market Place, Lowestoft, Suffolk

March

2 Mar-9 Oct	Bedfordshire Festival of Music, Speech and Drama, Corn Exchange, Bedford, Beds
3 Mar	Bedfordshire Spring Craft Show at Woburn Safari Park, Woburn Abbey, Woburn, Beds
9-10 Mar	Towerlands Home Spring Fair, Towerlands Centre, Panfield Road, Braintree, Essex
15 Mar	Fakenham Races, Fakenham Racecourse, Norfolk
16-17 Mar	National Shire Horse Show, East of England Showground, Alwalton, nr. Peterborough, Cambs
23-24 Mar	The 34th Thriplow Daffodil Weekend, various venues, Thriplow, Cambs
29 Mar-1 Apr	A Day Out With Thomas, East Anglian Railway Museum, Chappel Station, Colchester, Essex
29 Mar-1 Apr	Aldeburgh Easter Music Festival, Aldeburgh, Suffolk
29 Mar-1 Apr	Blickling Craft Show, Blickling Hall, Blickling, Norfolk
29 Mar-1 Apr	Great Easter Egg Hunt Quiz and Re-Creation of Tudor Life, Kentwell Hall, Long Melford, Suffolk
29 Mar-7 Apr	Early Spring Flowers, Fairhaven Garden Trust, School Road, South Walsham, Norfolk
31 Mar-1 Apr	Anglo-Saxon Activity Day, West Stow Country Park and Anglo Saxon Village, West Stow, Suffolk
31 Mar-1 Apr	Easter Steam Up 2002, Barleylands Farm Museum and Visitor Centre, Billericay, Essex
31 Mar-1 Apr	Gamekeeper and Countryman's Fair, Hertfordshire Agricultural Society, Redbourn, Herts

April

Apr-Oct	Racing and Royalty National Horseracing Museum, Newmarket, Suffolk
Apr-Oct	Racing & Writing of Dick Francis, The National Horseracing Museum, Newmarket, Suffolk
1-30 Apr	Lambing Weekends, Wimpole Hall and Home Farm, Arrington, Cambs
20-21 Apr	St. George's Festival, Wrest Park Gardens, Silsoe, Beds
22-27 Apr	Hertford Theatre Week, Hertford Castle, Hertford, Herts
24-27 Apr	Bury St Edmunds Beer Festival, The Corn Exchange, Cornhill, Bury St Edmunds, Suffolk
25-26 Apr	Gamekeeper and Countryman's Fair, Hertfordshire Agricultural Society, Redbourn

May

May-Oct	The Shuttleworth Collection Flying Displays, Old Warden, Beds
1 May	King's Lynn May Garland Procession, Town Centre, King's Lynn, Norfolk
1-12 May	Norfolk & Norwich Festival, various venues, Norwich, Norfolk
2-3 May	Norfolk Game and Country Fair, Bircham Newton, Norfolk
3,4,5 May*	Newmarket Guineas Festival of Racing, Music & Heritage, Town Centre, Newmarket, Suffolk
4 -6 May	Tudor May Day Celebrations, Kentwell Hall, Long Melford, Suffolk
5 May	Heritage Coast Run or Walk, Thorpeness Sports Ground, Suffolk
5 May*	Historic Vehicle Run, Felixstowe, Suffolk
5-6 May	Mendlesham Street Fayre and Art Exhibition, Mendlesham, Suffolk
5 May	Spring Airshow, Imperial War Museum, Duxford, Cambs
5-6 May	Suffolk Game and Country Fair, Glemham Hall, Little Glemham, Suffolk
5-6 May	Truckfest 2002, East of England Show Ground, Peterborough, Cambs
6 May	Dunstable Carnival, Bennett Memorial Recreation Ground, Dunstable, Beds

6 May	Ickwell May Festival, Ickwell Green, Biggleswade, Beds
6 May	Woodbridge Horse Show, Suffolk Showground, Ipswich, Suffolk
9-12 May	Living Crafts at Hatfield House, Hatfield House, Hatfield, Herts
10-12 May	East of England Garden Show, East of England Showground, Alwalton, Peterborough, Cambs
10-26 May	Bury St. Edmunds Festival, various venues, Bury St. Edmunds, Suffolk
11-12 May	Norfolk Food and Gardening Festival, Blickling Park, Norfolk
11-18 May	Chelmsford Cathedral Festival, Chelmsford, Essex
11 May - 4 Jun	Norfolk Visual Arts Festival, various venues, Norwich, Norfolk
11 May	Rickmansworth Week 2002, Bury Grounds, Bury Lane, Rickmansworth, Herts
12 May*	The Colchester Classic Vehicle Show, Colchester Institute, Colchester, Essex
12 May	South Suffolk Show, Ampton Park, Ingham, nr. Bury St. Edmunds, Suffolk

18 May	Hadleigh Farmer's Agricultural Association May Show, Holbecks Park, Hadleigh, Suffolk
18-19 May*	Hertfordshire Garden Show, Knebworth House, Knebworth, Herts
19 May	Tour de Tendring (Cycle Race), various venues, Tendring district, Essex
19-20 May	BMF Bike Show, East of England Show Ground, Alwalton, nr. Peterborough, Cambs
25-26 May*	Air Fete, RAF Mildenhall, Mildenhall, Suffolk
25-26 May	Hertfordshire County Show, Hertfordshire County Showground, Dunstable Road, Redbourn, Herts
25-26 May	Long Melford Garden Show, Melford Hall Park, Suffolk
25-26 May	Woolpit Steam Rally, Warren Farm, Wetherden, nr. Stowmarket, Suffolk

June

Jun-Sep	Gardens of the Rose 'Summer Season', The Gardens of the Rose, Chiswell Green, Herts
1-2 Jun	The Prom Fantasia, Promenade Park, Maldon, Essex
1-2 Jun	World War II Re-creation, Kentwell Hall, Long Melford, Suffolk
1-4 Jun	Birthday Gala, Leighton Buzzard Railway, Page's Park Station, Leighton Buzzard, Beds
1-4 Jun	Felbrigg Coast & Country Show, Felbrigg Hall, Felbrigg, Norfolk
1-4 Jun	Re-Creation of Tudor Life at Whitsuntide, Kentwell Hall, Long Melford, Suffolk
1-8 Jun	Downham Market Carnival & Festival, various venues, Downham Market, Norfolk

1-8 Jun	Felixstowe Drama Festival, Spa Pavillion Theatre, Seafront, Felixstowe, Suffolk
2 Jun	Bury in Bloom Spring Flower Market, The Buttermarket, Bury St Edmunds, Suffolk
2 Jun	Woolpit Street Fair, Woolpit, nr. Bury St Edmunds, Suffolk
2-3 Jun*	Knebworth Country Show, Knebworth House, Knebworth, nr. Stevenage, Herts
2-3 Jun	Southend Air Show, Seafront, Southend-on-Sea, Essex
3 Jun	Luton International Carnival, Luton Town Centre and Wardow Park, Luton, Beds
3 Jun	Stilton Cheese Rolling Contest, Stilton, Peterborough, Cambs
3-6 Jun	Wisbech Rose Fair, St. Peter's Parish Church, Wisbech, Cambs
6-7 Jun	Suffolk Show, Suffolk Showground, Ipswich, Suffolk
7-9 Jun	Festival of Gardening, Hatfield House, Hatfield, Herts
7-23 Jun	Aldeburgh Festival of Music and Arts (55th), Snape Maltings, Snape, Suffolk
7 Jun- 7 Jul *	Multi-Arts Festival, various venues, Broxbourne, Herts
7-9 Jun	Thaxted Festival, Thaxted Parish Church and various venues, Essex
8-9 Jun	Thaxted Morris Ring Meeting, various venues in Thaxted and surrounding villages, Essex

8 Jun-7 Jul	Harwich Festival, various venues, Harwich, Essex
8-30 Jun*	Leigh Folk Festival, various venues, Southend-on-Sea, Essex
9 Jun	Luton Festival of Transport, Stockwood Country Park, Farley Hill, Luton, Beds
9 Jun	12th Euston Park Rural Pastimes Show, Euston Hall, Euston, nr. Thetford, Norfolk
16 Jun	Nowton Park Country Fair, Nowton Park, Bury St Edmunds, Suffolk
14-16 Jun	The Pearl East of England Show, East of England Showground, Alwalton, Peterborough, Cambs
14-16 Jun	Woburn Garden Show, Woburn Abbey, Woburn, Beds

15 Jun	Strawberry Fair, Midsummer Common, Cambridge, Cambs
15 Jun	Strawberry Fair, Shenfield Common, Ingrave Road, Brentwood, Essex
16 Jun	The Hidden Gardens of Bury St Edmunds, various venues, Bury St Edmunds, Suffolk
17 Jun	Flitwick Carnival, Recreation Ground, Flitwick, Beds
19-24 Jun*	Cambridge Midsummer Fair, Midsummer Common, Cambridge, Cambs

DID YOU KNOW

The village of Stilton in Cambs, is where the famous cheese was first distributed from (not made). This is celebrated each May Bank Holiday, by rolling wooden 'cheeses' down the High Street!

19-30 Jun	15th Ampthill Music Festival, Saint Andrew's Parish Church, Ampthill, Beds
23-24 Jun	20 Eye Gardens Open in Aid of Eye Church Appeal, Eye, Suffolk
26-27 Jun	Royal Norfolk Show, Norfolk Showground, Norwich
28-30 Jun	East Anglian Garden and Flower Show, Bourn Airfield, Bourn, Cambs
28-30 Jun	Sandringham Country Show & Horse Driving Trials, Sandringham Estate, Norfolk
29 Jun	Concert in the Park, Priory Park, Southend-on-Sea, Essex
29-30 Jun	National Garden Party Weekend, Sponsored by The Horticultural Trades Assoc. Various Garden Centres Participate
29-30 Jun	Wings & Wheels Model Spectacular, North Weald Airfield, Epping, Essex
29 Jun-14 Jul	Hitchin Festival, various venues, Hitchin, Hertfordshire
29 Jun-14 Jul	Peterborough Festival, Peterborough, Cambs
30 Jun	Chelsworth Open Gardens Day, various venues, Chelsworth, Suffolk

July

Jul-Aug	Theatre in the Parks, various venues, Norwich, Norfolk
1 Jul*	Ipswich Music Day, Christchurch Park, Ipswich, Suffolk
1 Jul*	Newmarket Carnival, Suffolk
1 Jul-6 Aug*	Southend Jazz Festival, various venues, Southend-on-Sea, Essex
5-6 Jul	PFA International Air Rally, Cranfield Airfield, Cranfield, Beds

6 Jul	Meadow Park Families Day, Meadow Park, Borehamwood, Herts
6 Jul	Pin Mill Barge Match, River Orwell, Pin Mill, Suffolk
6-7 Jul	Essex Garden Show, Brentwood Centre Showground, Doddinghurst Road, Brentwood, Essex
7 Jul	Aquafest, Riverside (Willow Walk/Maltings area), Ely, Cambs
7 Jul	Clacton Classic Vehicle Show, West Road, Clacton-on-Sea, Essex
7 Jul	Hunstanton Rotary Carnival, The Green, Hunstanton, Norfolk
7 Jul	Model Railway Mania, Leighton Buzzard Railway, Page's Park Station, Leighton Buzzard, Beds
7-13 Jul	Ashton Graham East of England Tennis Championships, Felixstowe Lawn Tennis Club, Suffolk

| 7-8 Jul | Ely Folk Weekend, various venues, Ely, Cambs |
| 12 Jul | Great Annual Re-creation of Tudor Life, Kentwell Hall, Long Melford, Suffolk. |

12-14 Jul	Hacheston Rose Festival, All Saints Church, Hacheston, Suffolk
12-14 Jul	Lord Mayor's Weekend Celebrations, various venues, Norwich, Norfolk
12-14 Jul	Summer in the City 2002, 'Pop in the Park' (12th), 'The Big Day Out' (13th), 'Party on the Piece (14th), Parker's Piece, Cambridge, Cambs
13 Jul	The Big Day Out, Parker's Piece, Cambridge
13 Jul	Tendring Hundred Show, Lawford House Park, Lawford, nr. Manningtree, Essex

13 Jul	World Pea Shooting Championships, Village Green, Witcham, Cambs
13-14 Jul	Flying Legends Air Show, Imperial War Museum, Duxford Cambs
13 Jul-4 Aug	24th East Anglian International Summer Music Festival, The Old School, Bridge Street, Hadleigh, Suffolk
14 Jul	Pre-50 American Auto Club "Rally of the Giants", Knebworth House, Gardens & Park, Knebworth, nr. Stevenage, Herts.
17-29 Jul	Beccles Carnival, The Quay, Beccles, Suffolk
18-21 Jul	Cressing Temple Festival, Cressing Temple Barns, Cressing, Braintree, Essex
19-21 Jul	Weeting Steam Engine Rally, Fengate Farm, Weeting, Brandon, Suffolk

20 Jul	Framlingham Horse Show, Castle Meadow, Framlingham, Suffolk
20 Jul	Pop Picnic Concert, Blake Hall, Ongar, Essex
20 Jul	World Snail Racing Championships, The Cricket Field, Grimston, nr. King's Lynn, Norfolk
20-21 Jul	Basildon Festival, Wat Tyler Country Park, Pitsea, Basildon, Essex
21 Jul	Summer Festival 2002, Needham Lake and Nature Reserve, Needham Market, Suffolk
25-26 Jul	Eye Show, Eye Show Ground, Dragon Hill, Eye, Suffolk
25 Jul-3 Aug	King's Lynn Festival, various venues, King's Lynn, Norfolk
26-28 Jul	Worstead Festival, various venues, Worstead, Norfolk
27 Jul	Classical Concert in Christchurch Park, Ipswich, Suffolk
27 Jul-7 Aug	Hunstanton & District Festival of Arts, various venues, Hunstanton, Norfolk
28 Jul*	Annual British Open Crabbing Championship, Ferry Car Park, Walberswick, Suffolk
28 Jul*	London to Southend Classic Car Run, Southend-on-Sea Pier, Western Esplande, Southend-on-Sea, Essex
31 Jul	Sandringham Flower Show, Sandringham Park, Sandringham, Norfolk

DID YOU KNOW

The annual Air Fete at RAF Mildenhall, Suffolk is the largest air display organised by the military anywhere in the world, the best attended in Europe and NATO's biggest public event.

August

1-2 Aug	Lowestoft Seafront Air Festival 2002, Seafront, Lowestoft, Suffolk
1-4 Aug	38th Charles Wells Cambridge Folk Festival, Cherry Hinton Hall Grounds, Cherry Hinton, Cambs
1-31 Aug	Snape Proms, Snape Maltings Concert Hall, Snape, Suffolk
3 Aug	Proms in the Park 2002, Bedford Park, Park Ave, Bedford, Beds
3-4 Aug*	NSRA Hot Rod Supernationals, Knebworth House, Gardens & Park, Knebworth, nr. Stevenage, Herts
4 Aug	Duxford Military Vehicle Show, Duxford, Cambs
4 Aug	Lifeboat Day Cromer, The Promenade, Cromer, Norfolk
4-10 Aug	18th Mundesley Festival, Coronation Hall, Cromer Road, Mundesley-on-Sea, Norfolk
7 Aug	Sheringham Carnival, various venues, Sheringham, Norfolk
9-11 Aug	100 Years Ago Craft Fair, Aldenham Country Park, Elstree, Herts
10 Aug	Felixstowe Carnival, various venues, Felixstowe, Suffolk
11 Aug	Family Fun Day, Leighton Buzzard Railway, Page's Park Station, Leighton Buzzard, Beds
11 Aug	Lowestoft Carnival Procession, various venues, Lowestoft, Suffolk
16-17 Aug	Blickling Fireworks & Laser Concert, Blickling Hall, Blickling, Norfolk
17 Aug	Illuminated Carnival Procession & Firework Spectacular, Seafront, Southend-on-Sea, Essex
17-18 Aug*	De-Havilland Tiger Moth Club, Woburn Abbey, Woburn, Beds
17-18 Aug*	Hertfordshire Craft Fair, Knebworth House, Gardens & Park, Knebworth, nr. Stevenage, Herts
17-18 Aug*	V2002, Hylands Park, Chelmsford, Essex
18 Aug	Westleton Barrel Fair, Westleton, Suffolk
19 Aug	Aldeburgh Olde Marine Regatta and Carnival, High Street and Seafront, Aldeburgh, Suffolk
20-25 Aug	Peterborough Beer Festival, The Embankment, Bishop's Road, Peterborough, Cambs
21 Aug	Cromer Carnival, various venues, Cromer, Norfolk
22-23 Aug	The 11th Clacton Air Show, Marine Parade, Clacton-on-Sea, Essex
23 Aug	Thorpeness Regatta & Fireworks, Thorpeness, Suffolk

DID YOU KNOW

An unusual 'trial' takes place every four years in the town of Great Dunmow, Essex, whereby married couples have to prove, before a bewigged judge, that they "haven't had a brawl for the last 12 months and a day". The winners are awarded with a "Flitch of bacon".

23-26 Aug	Clacton Jazz Festival, various venues, Clacton-on-Sea, Essex
23-26 Aug	High Summer Re-Creation of Tudor Life, Kentwell Hall, Long Melford, Suffolk
24-26 Aug	Mildenhall Cycling Rally, Jubilee Fields, Recreation Way, Mildenhall, Suffolk
24 Aug	Southend Sailing Barge Race, Seafront, Southend-on-Sea, Essex
24-25 Aug	Ely Horticultural Society Show, Ely, Cambs
25-26 Aug	Eye Show, Eye Showground, Dragon Hill, Eye, Suffolk
25-26 Aug	Fenland Country Fair, Quy Park, Stow Cum Quy, Cambs
25-26 Aug*	Knebworth 2002 - The Classic Car Show, Knebworth House, Gardens & Park, Knebworth, nr. Stevenage, Herts
25-26 Aug*	The Countess of Warwick's Country Show, Little Easton, nr Dunmow, Essex
26 Aug	Aylsham Agricultural Show, Blickling Hall, Blickling, Norfolk
26 Aug	Gorleston Carnival, Gorleston, Norfolk
26 Aug*	Oulton Broad Charity Gala Day, Nicholas Everitt Park, Oulton Broad, nr. Lowestoft, Suffolk
26 Aug	St. Albans Carnival, various venues, St. Albans, Herts
27-28 Aug	The National Show for Miniature Roses, The Gardens of the Rose, Chiswell Green, nr. St. Albans, Herts

September

1 Sep	Herring Festival, Hemsby Beach, nr. Great Yarmouth, Norfolk
2 Sep	Great Yarmouth Carnival, Great Yarmouth, Norfolk
7-8 Sep	Duxford 2002 Airshow, Duxford, Cambs
7-8 Sep	English Wine Festival and Country Craft Fair, New Hall Vineyards, Purleigh, Essex
7-8 Sep	Haddenham Steam Engine Rally, Haddenham, nr. Ely, Cambs

14-15 Sep	Bedfordshire Steam & Country Fayre, Shuttleworth Park, Old Warden, nr. Biggleswade, Beds
14-15 Sep	Essex Steam Rally & Country Fair, Barleylands Farm Museum, Barleylands Road, Billericay, Essex
14-15 Sep	Somerleyton Horse Trials, Somerleyton Hall & Gardens, Somerleyton, nr. Lowestoft, Suffolk
21-22 Sep	Great Henham Steam Rally, Henham Park, nr Blythburgh, Suffolk
21-24 Sep*	Re-creation of Tudor Life at Michaelmas, Kentwell Hall, Long Melford, Suffolk
22-28 Sep	Quaker Walden, Various Venues, Saffron Waldon, Essex
28 Sep	Soham Pumpkin Fayre, Recreation Ground, Soham, Cambs

October

2-5 Oct	Bedford Beer Festival, Corn Exchange, Bedford, Beds
13 Oct	Duxford Autumn Airshow, Duxford, Cambs
13 Oct	World Conker Championships 2002, The Village Green, Ashton, Cambs
28 Oct-2 Nov	24th CAMRA Beer Festival, St. Andrews & Blackfriars Hall, Norwich, Norfolk

November

1 Nov	34rd Big Night Out, Melford Hall Park, Long Melford, Sudbury, Suffolk
2-4 Nov	The Craft Show, Marks Hall Estate, nr. Coggeshall, Essex
2 Nov	Annual Firework Display, Christchurch Park, Ipswich, Suffolk
2 Nov*	Luton Fireworks Spectacular, Popes Meadow, Old Bedford Road, Luton, Beds
2 Nov*	Gala and Fireworks Celebration at St Albans, Verulamium Park, St. Albans, Herts
5 Nov	'Grafton Centre' Fireworks 2002, Midsummer Common, Cambridge, Cambs
16 Nov-23 Dec	The Thursford Collection Christmas Spectacular, The Thursford Collection, Thursford, Norfolk
16 Nov	Southend Christmas Fayre, Southend-on-Sea, Essex

December

5-7 Dec*	Bedford Victorian Christmas Fayre, various venues, Bedford, Beds
5-12 Dec	Victorian Christmas in Maldon, High Street, Maldon, Essex

13-15 Dec	Christmas Craft Fair, Blickling Hall, Blickling, Norfolk
8 Dec	Hitchin Winter Gala, various venues, Hitchin, Herts

Horseracing
(Contact relevant racecourse for events list)
Fakenham - (01328) 862388
Great Yarmouth - (01493) 842527
Huntingdon - (01480) 453373
Newmarket - (01638) 663482

Motor Racing
(Contact relevant venue for events list)
Santa Pod Raceway, Santa Pod, Beds - Europe's premier drag racing strip.
Tel: (01234) 782828
Snetterton Circuit, Snetterton, Norfolk - motorcar and bike racing events.
Tel: (01953) 887303

The National Trust & English Heritage
Both organise a wide and varied range of special events at their properties in the East of England. Contact:
The National Trust - (01263) 733471
English Heritage - (020) 7973 3396

The Classic Car Show, Knebworth House, Hertfordshire

Lights, Camera, action

Discover the scenes of your favourite films and television programmes in the East of England. From Chariots of Fire, Lovejoy, Dad's Army and Vanity Fair to James Bond, Eastenders and Star Wars, you'll find them all here, plus lots more.

Eastern Screen - is the film Commission for the East of England. Since the organisation was formed in 1993, the Commission's staff have assisted many film and television production companies with finding locations in the region. Eastern Screen is proud to have assisted a number of prestigious productions - some of which are featured here - and endeavours to bring the East of England to cinema and television screens around the world.

The Tourist Board would like to thank Eastern Screen for their help with this special feature.

Below:
James Bond-Goldeneye

Bedfordshire & Hertfordshire

Film

Batman (1990) - directed by Tim Burton, and starring Jack Nicholson and Michael Keaton. Wayne Manor in the film was Knebworth House in Herts.

Boston Kickout (1998) - gritty youth drama shot on location in Stevenage, Herts. Barclays School was one location.

Chitty Chitty Bang Bang (1968)
- classic family film starring Dick van Dyke. Scenes were filmed at Cardington in Beds.

Empire of the Sun (1987) - war drama, directed by Steven Spielberg. Scenes shot at Luton Hoo in Beds.

Eyes Wide Shut (1999) - erotic drama, directed by Stanley Kubrick, starring Tom Cruise and Nicole Kidman. Partly filmed at Woburn Abbey in Beds.

First Knight (1995) - romantic King Arthur adventure with Sean Connery and Richard Gere. Scenes were filmed at the Ashridge Estate in Herts (where a complete hill village was built), and the Cathedral and Abbey Church in St. Albans, Herts.

Four Weddings and a Funeral (1994)
- romantic comedy, with scenes shot at Luton Hoo in Beds, starred Hugh Grant.

The Great Escape (1963) - classic wartime drama. Scenes were filmed at Luton Hoo in Beds.

Haunted Honeymoon (1986) - comedy with Gene Wilder. Filmed at Knebworth House in Herts.

Lair of the White Worm (1988)
- Ken Russell horror film shot at Knebworth House in Herts. Starred Hugh Grant.

Lara Croft: Tomb Raider (2001) - action/ adventure based on the popular computer game, starring Angelina Jolie. Exterior shots for Lara's home were filmed at Hatfield House, Herts.

Lucky Break (2001) - comedy starring James Nesbitt and Olivia Williams. An empty psychiatric hospital near St. Albans, Herts doubles as a prison.

The Mummy Returns (2001) - action/adventure starring Brendan Fraser. An exterior set used for filming was constructed at Bovingdon Airfield in Herts.

My Brother Tom (2002) - story of two teenagers escaping suburban childhood. Shot around Watford, St. Albans and Hatfield in Herts.

Never Say Never Again (1983)
- James Bond film with scenes shot at Luton Hoo in Beds. Starred Sean Connery.

Peter's Friends (1992) - drama directed by Kenneth Brannagh, and filmed at Wrotham Park in Herts.

Princess Caraboo (1994) - comedy with scenes shot at both Luton Hoo in Beds and Wrotham Park in Herts.

James Bond -Tomorrow Never Dies

Behind the Scenes, Vanity Fair

Revelation (2002) - supernatural thriller which was filmed at two locations in Herts. Stars Terence Stamp and Derek Jacobi.

Saving Private Ryan (1998) - directed by Steven Spielberg, this wartime epic was shot on vast sets constructed on the former British Aerospace facility at Hatfield in Herts. Starred Tom Hanks.

Spygame (2001) - spy thriller starring Robert Redford and Brad Pitt. The exteriors of a major pharmaceutical company's research centre in Herts, doubled as the entrance to the CIA headquarters in Washington, USA.

Those Magnificent Men in their Flying Machines (1965) - classic film which used many of the planes now displayed at The Shuttleworth Collection, Old Warden in Beds. A scene from the film was shot on the former railway line between Cardington and Old Warden. This is where a plane lands on top of a moving train.

The Wings of the Dove (1997) - drama by Henry James. Filmed at Luton Hoo in Beds.

Television

The Alchemist (Channel 5) - four part thriller filmed at Leavesden Studios, and throughout Herts.

Band of Brothers (UStv/BBC) - major wartime mini-series. A number of spectacular sets were built on the former British Aerospace airfield/factory site at Hatfield, Herts. The village of Wilstone, nr. Tring replicated the area around Brecourt Manaor in Normandy, whilst The Ayot Estate, nr. Welwyn Garden City (saw a major tank battle, also for Normandy). A large area within the pine woodland of Hatfield House was cleared to build the concentration camp at Landsberg.

Bugs (BBC) - hi-tech adventure series which filmed at locations throughout Herts.

The Canterville Ghost (ITV) - two versions of this tale have been filmed at Knebworth House in Herts. The most recent (1998) starring comedian Rik Mayall.

Eastenders (BBC) - soap opera, filmed at the BBC Elstree Studios in Borehamwood, Herts. Storylines are sometimes filmed at outside locations, such as Shenley (Michelle and Lofty's marriage) and Watford (where Arthur Fowler is buried). Hatfield Courthouse, Herts was used for the court appearance of Grant Mitchell.

Hertfordshire - Britain's very own Hollywood

The southeast of Hertfordshire has developed as a focal point for film and television production, particularly the town of Borehamwood, better known as Elstree. The first studio opened in 1914, and six more followed. Elstree became known as the 'British Hollywood', as it had the greatest number of production facilities outside Hollywood itself. Elstree gave us the first talkie to be made in Britain, the first British musical, the first colour talking film, and the first film to use Dolby sound. During the 1980's Borehamwood could boast six out of the top ten box office hits of all time. The MGM Studios (closed in 1970) played host to major stars such as Elizabeth Taylor, Stewart Granger and Clark Gable. The Dirty Dozen and 2001: A Space Odyssey were made here. Today only three studios remain:-

BBC Elstree Centre - opened in 1914, as the historic Neptune Studio. Over the years it has played host to many different owners. In the 1960's it became part of ATV Television, home of big entertainment specials with Shirley Bassey and Tom Jones. Then in the 1980's it became part of the BBC, with the sets of EastEnders, Grange Hill, Holby City and Top of the Pops based here.
Elstree Film Studios - opened in 1926, and home to over 500 feature films, including the Star Wars and Indiana Jones trilogies, The Shining, The Dambusters, Moby Dick and Who Framed Roger Rabbit? Famous directors to have passed through the doors include Steven Spielberg, Stanley Kubrick and Alfred Hitchcock. George Lucas recently filmed part of Episode 2 of Star Wars here, and in recognition 'Stage One' has been named after him. Popular television shows past and present has also been made here, including The Saint, The Avengers, The Muppet Show, The Tweenies, Silent Witness and Who Wants to be a Millionaire? The studios are owned by Hertsmere Borough Council.
Millennium Studios - opened in 1995, and has played host to Bliss (ITV) and Bugs (BBC).

You can discover Borehamwood/Elstree's film heritage, by following a special signposted walk. This includes 'Shenley Road' with its plaques commemorating many famous stars.

Just to the north, (beside the M25) at Abbots Langley, is Leavesden Studios, Britain's most exciting film making complex. Here a former wartime plane factory, once owned by Rolls Royce, has been transformed into over one million square feet of studio space and hundreds of acres of back lot. It has been used for **GoldenEye (James Bond)**, Mortal Kombat Annihilation, The Beach, Sleepy Hollow, Star Wars 'The Phantom Menace' and Harry Potter and the Sorcerer's Stone.

The Gentlemen Thief (BBC) - 'Raffles' drama, starring Michael French and Nigel Havers. Scenes were shot at the Langleybury Campus, nr. Watford, Herts.

A Great Deliverance (BBC) - a large, empty Elizabethan house in Hatfield, Herts was used. The interiors double for the main location in Yorkshire.

Hope and Glory (BBC) - school drama starring Lenny Henry. Filmed at the former Langleybury School, nr. Watford, Herts (just off junction 19 of M25).

In Deep (BBC) - police drama with scenes shot around St. Albans and Watford, Herts.

Jane Eyre (ITV) - the recent adaptation of this Charlotte Bronte novel, filmed scenes at Knebworth House in Herts.

Kavanagh QC (ITV) - courtroom drama starring John Thaw. Scenes were shot at Hatfield Courthouse in Herts.

Lady Chatterley (BBC) - recent version of D.H. Lawrence novel, shot at Wrotham Park in Herts.

Merlin (UStv) - Camelot adventure set in AD800, and partially shot at the Ashridge Estate in Herts.

Scene from Lady Audley's Secret, Ingatestone Hall

Murder in Mind (BBC) - drama series of psychological thrillers, filmed at several locations in Hertfordshire, including Langleybury Campus, nr. Watford, Herts.

Murder Rooms (BBC) - series of dramas looking at Sherlock Holmes' creator Sir Arthur Conan Doyle, and the people/places which inspired his stories. A large, empty Georgian house in Elstree, Herts was used for filming.

Pie in the Sky (BBC) - comedy drama with Richard Griffiths. The restaurant exterior used can be found at Hemel Hempstead Old Town in Herts.

Playing the Field (BBC) - drama about a woman's football team, filmed in the Herts area.

Porridge (BBC) - classic 70's comedy set in Slade Prison, and starring Ronnie Barker. The opening shot features the gatehouse of the old prison in Victoria Road, St. Albans in Herts.

Randall and Hopkirk Deceased (BBC) - two properties in Hertford and Watford (Herts) were used for episodes of this comedy drama, starring Vic Reeves and Bob Mortimer.

Some Mothers do have em' (BBC)
- classic 70's comedy, with scenes filmed at Short Street in Bedford, Beds. Starred Michael Crawford.

The Shooting Party (1995) - drama starring James Mason and Edward Fox. Scenes shot at Knebworth House in Herts.

Station Jim (BBC) - an empty mansion house in Herts, became a Victorian railway station for this television film starring George Cole.

Trial and Retribution II (ITV) - Lynda La Plante drama filmed in South Herts.

Topsy-Turvy (1999) - Mike Leigh drama/musical based on the story of Gilbert and Sullivan. Scenes shot at the former Langleybury School, nr. Watford, Herts (just off junction 19 of M25).

The Vice (ITV) - hard-hitting drama series which filmed locations around the Watford, Herts area

Cambridgeshire

Film

Chariots of Fire (1981)
- oscar-winning film based on the true story of the Olympic runners Harold Abrahams and Eric Liddell, and the 1924 games. Street scenes were filmed in Cambridge. The famous race around the college precinct was based on the actual event at Trinity College, but filmed at Eton College in Berkshire.

Dad Savage (1998) - kidnap and revenge film starring Patrick Stewart (Star Trek). Scenes shot in the Fens.

GoldenEye (1995) and Octopussy (1983) - two James Bond adventure's with scenes filmed at the Nene Valley Railway at Peterborough in Cambs.

Peter's Friends (1992) - scenes filmed at the Nene Valley Railway at Peterborough in Cambs.

Waterland (1992) - intense and intriguing drama starring Jeremy Irons, filmed in the Fens.

Television

An Unsuitable Job for a Lady (ITV) - detective drama with an episode filmed in Cambridge. Starred Helen Baxendale.

Bliss (ITV) - set in Cambridge, Simon Shepherd takes the lead as a scientific investigator.

Cold Enough for Snow (BBC) - drama with Maureen Lipman. Scenes filmed in Cambridge.

David Copperfield (BBC) - adaptation of Dickens novel starring Bob Hoskins and Nicholas Lyndhurst. Areas of Wisbech (The Crescent, Castle and Peckover House) were used in the filming.

Honey for Tea (BBC) - Clare College in Cambridge provided scenes for this comedy series.

London's Burning (ITV) - fire fighting drama series. Scenes filmed at the Nene Valley Railway at Peterborough in Cambs.

Micawber (ITV) - drama series based on Dickens' character from 'David Copperfield'. Filmed in Wisbech (including Peckover House), which depicted London in the 1820's. Stars David Jason.

A Sense of Guilt (BBC) - controversial drama with Trevor Eve, featuring scenes of Cambridge.

Silent Witness (BBC) - drama set in Cambridge, with Amanda Burton as pathologist Sam Ryan.

The Student Prince (BBC) - drama with Robson Green. Filmed at Queens' College, Cambridge.

Wings (UStv) - 80s American mini-series set during the war, and starring Robert Mitcham. Scenes were filmed at the Cambridge American Cemetery.

Essex

Film

Clockwork Mice (1995) - poignant drama starring Art Malik and Ian Hart. Shot at Chipping Ongar.

Essex Boys (2000) - gangland thriller starring Sean Bean and Alex Kingston. Filming took place at Brightlingsea, Jaywick, Clacton and Southend.

The Fourth Protocol (1987) - spy thriller starring Michael Caine and Pierce Brosnan. Shot in Essex at Colchester and Chelmsford (where there is a memorable car chase scene).

Four Weddings and a Funeral (1994) - romantic comedy, with scenes shot at St. Clement's Church, West Thurrock.

GoldenEye (1995) - James Bond adventure, with scenes shot at Stansted Airport.

Killing Dad (1989) - drama starring Richard E. Grant. Filmed at the Pier and Palace Hotels in Southend.

Television

Brothers in Trouble (BBC) - immigration drama shot at Clacton and Mistley Quay.

EastEnders (BBC) - soap opera, which has featured both Southend-on-Sea and Clacton-on-Sea in past episodes.

Hi-de-Hi (BBC) - comedy series centred around Maplin's Holiday Camp. Scenes for the show were filmed on the Essex Sunshine Coast at Dovercourt.

Ivanhoe (BBC) - classic adventure tale, filmed at Hedingham Castle, Castle Hedingham.

Jonathan Creek (BBC) - comedy drama. One episode featured Stansted Airport.

Lady Audley's Secret (ITV) - scandalous Victorian tale of a man's obsession with a woman. Ingatestone Hall became Audley House, which is where the novel was actually written.

Jonathan Creek -
Caroline Quentin and Alan Davies.

Lovejoy (BBC) - based on the books by Essex writer Jonathan Gash, this comedy drama was set around the adventures of antiques rogue 'Lovejoy' played by Ian McShane. Filmed throughout Essex including Braintree, Chelmsford, Coggeshall, Colchester, Finchingfield, Gosfield Hall, Halstead, Hedingham Castle, Ingatestone Hall, Kelvedon, Layer Marney Tower, Maldon, Moyns Park, Saffron Walden, Thaxted and Wakes Colne.

Plotlands (BBC) - 1920's drama filmed at Wivenhoe.

Sharpe's Regiment (ITV) - military adventure starring Sean Bean. Scenes filmed at Tilbury Fort.

Norfolk

Film

The Beach (1999) - although the film was not shot in the region, it is worth noting that the video for the related No.1 single by the girl group 'All Saints' was filmed on Holkham Beach in Norfolk.

The Care of Time (1990) - with Christopher Lee. Hemsby in Norfolk became Miami Beach USA.

Dad Savage (1998) - kidnap and revenge film shot in Norfolk at Hunstanton and Wells.

The Dambusters (1955) - classic film which used Langham Airfield in Norfolk for some scenes.

Eyes Wide Shut (1999) - erotic drama directed by Stanley Kubrick, and starring Tom Cruise and Nicole Kidman. Filmed partly at Elveden Hall and Thetford Forest.

The Go Between (1970) - with Alan Bates. Used Melton Constable Hall and Norwich.

The Grotesque (1997) - starring Sting and Alan Bates. Filmed at Heydon Hall.

Julia (1977) - filmed at Winterton, which doubled as an 1930's Cape Cod, USA.

Out of Africa (1985) - oscar-winning film, starring Robert Redford and Meryl Streep. The opening shots which seem to show Denmark, were actually filmed at Castle Rising.

Shakespeare in Love, Holkham Beach, Norfolk

Revolution (1985) - King's Lynn became 18th C. New York for this film starring Al Pacino, and set against the background of the American War of Independence.

Shakespeare in Love (1998)
Romantic comedy starring Gwyneth Paltrow. Scenes based around a dramatic shipwreck were filmed at Holkham Beach.

Tarka the Otter (1979) - classic family film, which follows the life of a real otter, and its adventures in the wild. Scenes were filmed at Bintree Mill in Norfolk.

Television

The Adventures of Sherlock Holmes (ITV) - drama series based on the Baker Street detective. Part of 'The Sign of Four' story was filmed at Burgh Castle.

A Fatal Inversion (BBC) and Gallowglass (BBC) - two chilling tales from East Anglian writer, Ruth Rendall. Both were filmed at locations in Norfolk.

Allo Allo (BBC) - comedy series set in France during the Second World War. Scenes were filmed in Thetford Forest, and at 19th C. Lynford Hall, nr. Mundford. A cobbled courtyard at the back of the hall was used as the Nouvion town square, complete with the 'Café Rene' in the corner.

All the King's Men (BBC) - First World War drama starring David Jason and Maggie Smith. Filmed on the royal estate at Sandringham and other locations in the area (Blickling, Cromer, West Newton, Sheringham, Burnham Deepdale and Holkham).

Campion (BBC) - 1930's based detective drama starring Peter Davidson. Scenes for a two-part story were filmed at Bintree Mill in Norfolk.

The Chief (ITV) - drama set around the head of the regional police and filmed throughout the area.

Dad's Army (BBC) - comedy classic, following the exploits of the Home Guard. Eighty episodes were filmed over nine years during the 1960/70's, and nearly all featured locations in Norfolk, including:- The MoD's Stanford Training Ground, nr. Thetford; High Lodge in Thetford Forest; Lynford Hall, nr. Mundford; North Norfolk Railway, Sheringham; Oxburgh Hall, Oxborough and Winterton beach. Bressingham Steam Experience and Gardens (nr. Diss) is home to the Dad's Army Museum, featuring vehicles used in the show, including Cpl. Jones' butcher van, a Leyland fire engine, "Birtha" the tractor engine and a threshing machine. There is also a reconstructed street scene of Walmington-on-Sea.

Dangerfield (BBC) - medical/police drama, which for two episodes used the North Norfolk coast. Starred Nigel Le Valliante.

David Copperfield (BBC) - adaptation of Dickens novel starring Bob Hoskins and Nicholas Lyndhurst. Areas of King's Lynn, (King Street) were used in the filming.

Eastenders (BBC) - soap opera which featured episodes filmed in the Norfolk Broads.

Great Expectations (BBC) - the recent adaptation of this Dickens novel recreated the Essex marshes (where Pip is caught by Magwitch) at Thornham in Norfolk.

Gullivers Travels (UStv) - lavish US mini-series of classic tale, starring Ted Danson. Some scenes shot at Elveden Hall.

Kavanagh QC (ITV) - courtroom drama starring John Thaw. Scenes shot at Norwich.

Keeping up Appearances (BBC) - comedy series which in 1995 filmed scenes in Great Yarmouth. Starred Patricia Routledge.

Love on a Branch Line (BBC) - nostalgic drama, filmed at Oxburgh Hall, nr. Oxborough and on the North Norfolk Railway at Sheringham.

Martin Chuzzlewit (BBC) - classic Dicken's tale brought to life in 1996, and filmed in the town of King's Lynn (which was designed to represent London at the time).

The Mill on the Floss (BBC) - latest adaptation of George Eliot novel, filmed at Bintree Mill, nr. Dereham.

The Moonstone (BBC) - costume detective drama, filmed at Heydon and Elveden Halls. Starred Greg Wise.

Mill on the Floss - 'Maggie' Emily Watson

Murder Rooms (BBC) - series of dramas looking at Sherlock Holmes' creator Sir Arthur Conan Doyle, and the people/places which inspired his stories. Filming took place at Cromer, including the beach, pier and North Lodge Park council offices.

P.D. James Mysteries (ITV) - drama series based on the novels written by East Anglian writer P.D. James, and featuring detective Adam Dalgiish. Filmed throughout Norfolk including the coastline, Norfolk Broads and Norwich.

September Song (ITV) - comedy drama starring Russ Abbot. Filmed at Cromer.

The Uninvited (ITV) - sci-fi drama starring Leslie Grantham, and filmed throughout Norfolk

Up Rising (ITV) - saucy comedy starring Michelle Collins and Anton Rogers. Heydon in Norfolk was transformed to become the village of 'Rising' for the series.

Vanity Fair (BBC) - the latest adaptation of William Thackeray's tale. Filmed at Rainthorpe Hall, nr. Flordon; Barningham Hall, nr. Holt and Thelveton Hall, nr. Diss. These three though appear on screen as one property, the grand Elizabethan Queens Crawley.

Suffolk

Film

The Bridge (1993) - drama with scenes filmed at Walberswick and Yoxford. Stars Saskia Reeves and Geraldine James.

Defence of the Realm (1985) - drama starring Denholm Elliot. Scenes filmed at RAF Lakenheath.

Drowning by Numbers (1987) - drama starring Bernard Hill and Joan Plowright. Scenes filmed at Thorpeness and Southwold.

The Fourth Protocol (1987) - spy thriller with Michael Caine. Scenes shot in Ipswich (wet dock) and along the River Orwell (Orwell bridge).

The Golden Bowl (1999) - Merchant/Ivory costume drama starring Uma Thurman and Anjelica Huston. Scenes shot at Helmingham Hall.

Iris (2002) - bio-pic of the novelist/philosopher Iris Murdoch. Starring Dame Judi Dench and Kate Winslet. Scenes were filmed on Southwold beach, and at St. Lawrence's Church in South Cove.

Lara Croft: Tomb Raider (2001) - action/adventure based on the popular computer game, starring Angelina Jolie. Some of the scenes were shot at Elveden Hall, nr. Thetford.

The Lost Son (1999) - detective drama starring Natassja Kinski. Scenes were shot at Landguard Point, Felixstowe.

Tomorrow Never Dies (1997) - James Bond adventure with Pierce Bronsan. Scenes were shot at RAF Mildenhall, which doubled as the US airbase at Okinawa in Japan, complete with fake palm trees. RAF Lakenheath was transformed into an Afghan arms dump.

The Wind in the Willows (1995) - Kentwell Hall at Long Melford became Toad Hall for the latest film adaptation of Kenneth Cranham's animal adventures.

The Witchfinder General (1968) - story of Matthew Hopkins, starring Vincent Price. Filmed throughout Suffolk, mainly in the fields/country lanes around Debenham and Eye.

Yangste Incident (1957) - wartime drama starring Richard Todd. Scenes filmed on the River Orwell (which doubled for China).

Yesterday's Hero (1979) - football drama starring Ian McShane. Scenes filmed in Ipswich.

Television

A Fatal Inversion (BBC) and Gallowglass (BBC) - two chilling tales from East Anglian writer, Ruth Rendall. Both were filmed at locations in the Suffolk area.

Between the Lines (BBC) - police series, mainly based in London. One storyline had scenes filmed in the town of Felixstowe and at the riverside hamlet of Pin Mill.

The Chief (ITV) - drama set around the head of the regional police and filmed throughout the area.

Dark Ages (ITV) - comedy starring Phil Jupitus and Alistair McGowan. The programme used the West Stow Anglo-Saxon village (nr. Bury St Edmunds) for its location shots.

David Copperfield (BBC) - adaptation of Dickens novel starring Bob Hoskins and Nicholas Lyndhurst. Areas of Southwold were used in the filming.

Deceit (BBC) - thriller based on Clare Francis novel. Various locations were used around the Rivers Deben and Orwell.

Great Expectations (BBC) - Ramsholt Church featured in the recent adaptation of this Dickens novel.

It's a Wonderful Life (ITV) - relationship drama which filmed scenes at Walberswick.

A Line in the Sand (ITV) - thriller starring Ross Kemp. Scenes were filmed at Walberswick.

Jonathan Creek (BBC) - one of the episodes from the first series of this comedy drama was filmed at The Bell pub in Middleton, and at locations in Wangford and Wrentham.

A scene from David Copperfield

Lovejoy (BBC) - based on the books by Essex writer Jonathan Gash, this comedy drama was set around the adventures of antiques rogue 'Lovejoy' played by Ian McShane. Filmed throughout Suffolk including Bury St. Edmunds, Hadleigh, Kersey, Lindsey, Lavenham, Long Melford, Old College, Wingfield and Pin Mill. Felsham Hall (home of Lady Jane) can be found in the village of Belchamp Walte

P.D. James Mysteries (ITV)
- drama series based on the novels written by East Anglian writer P.D. James, and featuring detective Adam Dalglish. Filmed throughout Suffolk, including Ipswich.

Cycling *in the* East of England

Why not leave your car behind, and discover the East of England on two wheels? The area is perfect for cycling, with its gently rolling landscape ideal for the occasional cyclist and families.

Where else can you explore a 'church within a church', climb the world's most efficient wind turbine, visit a unique Swiss Garden and touch 3,000 year old timbers. Or what about a trip through the watery region of The Fens, or along the crumbling cliffs of the Suffolk Coast. Not forgetting, the home of horseracing, the world's oldest Saxon chapel, a trail of wind and water mills, and a pint or two at a Georgian brewery. You can also visit the places connected to The Queen Mother, Lord Nelson, Katherine of Aragon and the Witchfinder General. Plus don't forget to pay your respect at the tomb of the dragon slayer!

Cycling Discovery Maps

- available at £1.50 each (excl. postage & packing). Printed on waterproof and tear-proof paper, and incorporating Ordnance Survey Landranger mapping.
(SP = starting point)

C1 The Great Ouse - SP: Bedford, Beds. 25m/40km. Explore the beautiful Ouse Valley with its fine river settings, ancient limestone villages and medieval bridges.

C2 The Thatcher's Way - SP: Bedford, Beds. 24m/37km. Discover picturesque thatched villages, a magnificent collection of flying machines and the unique Swiss Garden.

C3 Roisia's Path - SP: Therfield (nr. Royston), Herts. 28m/45km. Well-wooded countryside, panoramic views and pretty timber-framed villages lie at some of the highest points in the region.

C4 Two Rivers' Way - SP: Burnham-on-Crouch, Essex. 25m/40km. Between the Rivers Blackwater and Crouch, discover the weather-boarded villages, pretty sailing hamlets and the tiny chapel of St. Peter.

Discover all this and more in our exciting range of Cycling Discovery Maps, specially created to allow you to explore this picturesque corner of England. Each one uses mainly quiet lanes and well-surfaced tracks, and will take a leisurely day to complete. The mileage ranges from 15 to 30 miles, and you'll find lots of places to visit and welcoming refreshment stops along the way. There are also two longer distance routes in the region, ideal for short breaks. The maps (as listed below) are available from Tourist Information Centres and bookshops within the region, or directly from the East of England Tourist Board (see overleaf for contact details).

C5 The Witchfinder's Way - SP: Harwich, Essex. 27m/43km. Follow in the footsteps of 'The Witchfinder General' through rolling countryside, riverside hamlets and the seafaring town of Harwich.

C6 The Miller's Trail - SP: Ixworth (nr. Bury St. Edmunds), Suffolk. 23m/37km. Watch the turning sails and waterwheels of historic mills. Climb their towers and enjoy great views of the gently rolling landscapes.

C7 The Brecks - SP: Swaffham, Norfolk. 20m/32km. Visit the unique heathland and pine forests of Breckland. Climb a wind turbine and go back in time to an Iron Age village.

C8 The Lost Villages of Breckland - SP: Gressenhall (nr. Dereham), Norfolk. 23m/37km. Discover the abandoned medieval hamlets of Godwick and Little Bittering, amongst the rolling countryside and valley of the River Nar.

C9 The Bishop's Chapel - SP: Dereham, Norfolk. 23m/37km. Follow quiet country lanes through the pretty mid-Wensum Valley, to visit the romantic ruins of an 11th C. Norman chapel.

C10 Nelson's Norfolk - SP: Fakenham, Norfolk. 29m/47km. Pretty flint villages and spectacular views of the North Norfolk coast, on this pilgrimage to the birthplace of one of England's greatest heros.

C11 Katherine's Wheels - SP: Grafham Water (nr. Huntingdon), Cambs. 15m/24km. From Britain's third largest man-made reservoir, visit the final two residences of Queen Katherine of Aragon.

C12 Peterborough Green Wheel (North) - SP: Peterborough, Cambs. 29m/47km. Amongst gentle limestone hills and unique Fenland landscapes, discover cream-coloured villages and prehistoric remains.

C13 Peterborough Green Wheel (South) - available summer 2002.

C14 Apples and Ale. SP: Wisbech, Cambs. 13m/21km. From the medieval port of Wisbech, enjoy a tour through rich fruit orchards, then a real ale or two at a Georgian brewery.

C15-C20, C23, C24 - other routes around the county of Lincolnshire are available, please contact the East of England Tourist Board for further information.

C21 The Jockey's Trail - SP: Newmarket, Suffolk. 28m/45km. From the horse-racing capital of the world, discover chalk grasslands, paddocks, woodland and picturesque villages.

C22 Churches, Copses and Country Lanes - SP: Carlton Colville (nr. Lowestoft), Suffolk. 24m/39km. Head into the gently rolling landscape of attractive villages, old country estates, ancient woodlands, historic churches as well as visiting the unspoilt coastline.

C24 Romans and Royalty - SP: Hatfield (old town), Herts. 16m/26km. From the old town of Hatfield this route passes through woodlands and wildlife habitats, heads to a roman city and visits the birthplace of the 'Mosquito'.

C25 Literary Landscapes - SP: Welwyn, Herts. 25m/40km. Cycle through unspoilt countryside - along a valley, into the foothills of the Chilterns as well as visiting the hidden retreat of George Bernard Shaw.

Longer Distance Routes
Available at £3.50 each (excl. postage & packing). Incorporates Ordnance Survey Landranger and Explorer mapping.

A Suffolk Coastal Cycle Route - SP: various locations. 88m/142km. This pack of information includes the 88 mile circular route through the peaceful countryside of coastal Suffolk. Also includes 2 forest maps for off-road detours.

B The Fens Cycle Way - SP: Wisbech and Ely. Two loops of 40m/64km and 34m/55km. This pack of information includes 2 circular routes with a linear link. Discover the unique panorama of the Fens, criss-crossed by waterways and offering stunning skyscapes and sunsets.

All maps can be ordered directly from the East of England Tourist Board - please call 01473 825624 for further information.

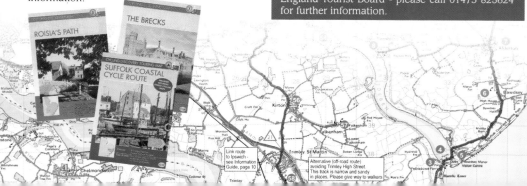

aviation heritage
in the
East of England

On December 17th 1903, the Wright Brothers lifted their aircraft into the skies - and the birth of aviation was forced upon an unbelieving world. Since then the progress of aviation has developed as a result of our challenge to conquer the skies and space. In the East of England, you can discover

Britain's great aviation heritage, from the very beginnings of flight with balloons and airships, to the former/present day airfields of the Royal Air Force (RAF)/ United States Air Force (USAF). Discover exciting museums, spectacular air shows and poignant memorials.

Balloons and airships

In Sept 1784, Britain's first hot air balloon flight was undertaken by Vincenzo Lunardi. He ascended from London, then touched down first at Welham Green (Herts), then twelve miles later in the hamlet of Standon Green End (Herts), where a boulder now marks the spot. The East of England has two major airship connections - an airship factory was constructed at Cardington (Beds) from 1917, later becoming one of the world's best facilities, home of the R101 and R100. They were housed in two gigantic sheds which remain today. To the east of the region, Pulham St. Mary (Norfolk), was another world famous airship station from 1915-1935. The R33 airship is shown on the village sign here.

de Havilland

In 1920, one of the greatest names in aircraft design/construction was born 'The de Havilland Aircraft Company'. Their greatest creations are the Moth and Mosquito - the latter designed in secret at Salisbury Hall, nr. St. Albans (Herts) in 1940. A huge factory complex was also built at Hatfield (Herts). In 1977, de Havilland became part of British Aerospace, who developed the Comet and Trident at Hatfield.

RAF and United States Army Air Force (USAAF)

With its flat landscape and proximity to Europe, the East of England was ideal for the construction of airfields. From the mid 1930's, with war looming, the RAF began a massive programme of expansion. In 1942, the Americans arrived, and many RAF airfields were made available to the USAAF, so by 1943 there were over 100,000 US airmen based in Britain. The largest concentration was in the East of England, where most of the 8th Air Force and some of the 9th were located on near a hundred bases. The 8th Air Force was the largest air striking force ever committed to battle, the first units arriving in May 1942.

With the end of the war, many of the wartime airfields were closed down, whilst others were developed for peacetime duties. Today the East of England is home to some of Britain's most important airbases:-

RAF Coltishall (Norfolk) - opened 1940. During the Second World War many fighter squadrons (and famous pilots) were based here. Home today to entire RAF Jaguar force.

RAF Marham (Norfolk) - developed in 1930's as bomber/fighter station. Became RAF's major reconnaissance base in 1993. Home today to Tornado squadrons.

RAF Lakenheath (Suffolk) - assumed full station status in 1943, with RAF Bomber Command. In 1948, the USAF arrive. Home of the 48th Tactical Fighter Wing (since 1960), flying F-15 Eagles.

RAF Mildenhall (Suffolk) - opened 1934, and used for the start of the world's greatest air race to Australia. Began life with RAF Bomber Command. The USAF arrive in 1950, and in 1959, the airfield becomes the 'Gateway to the UK' for US forces, and later the HQ of the Third Air Force.

RAF Wittering (Cambs) - started life as training airfield from 1916. Once home to Central Flying School. Became fighter station from 1935. Today known as 'the home of the Harrier'.

Alongside these, visitors can also discover many of the old airfields which have found new uses or have been returned to agricultural land. Some are identified by special signs, memorials to past squadrons, or original control towers lovingly restored. One of the most famous memorials is the only Second World War American Military Cemetery in Britain, at Madingley, nr. Cambridge.

Aviation Heritage Map

The East of England Tourist Board has produced a special map providing a comprehensive guide to airfields used by the USAAF during World War II. It provides information about the current use of the airfields, the groups that were stationed here, and memorials erected in memory of the sacrifices made. The map is available from the East of England Tourist Board, priced £4.95 (excl. postage & packing) - please contact: (01473) 825624 for further information.

American Air Museum, Imperial War Museum, Duxford, Cambridgeshire

Museums

There are lots of aviation museums and collections in the area, such as the impressive Imperial War Museum at Duxford (Cambs). For a full listing, please refer to the 'Machinery and Transport' section (for each county) within this guide.

Air shows

The region holds an impressive range of air shows during the year, including the huge Mildenhall Air Fete. Please refer to the 'Diary of Events' for full details (p12-20).

If you are interested in finding out more why not visit our website:

www.eastofenglandtouristboard.com

where you can delve deeper into the aviation heritage of this region and discover a car tour that allows you to explore aviation-related places to visit, and learn more about relevant events and museums that can be found throughout this region.

Celebrate The Queen's Golden Jubilee in the East of England.
2002 will mark the 50th anniversary of Her Majesty The Queen's Accession to the Throne. The focal point of the celebrations will be the National Service of Thanksgiving at St Paul's Cathedral (London) on Tuesday 4 June, part of a whole weekend (1-4 June) of special events. In-fact, the whole summer from May-July will be given over to celebrations in every region, city, town and village across the UK. Visit www.goldenjubilee.gov.uk for the latest details. The East of England Tourist Board will also be compiling information about events in our region over the coming months, so don't forget to give us a call, or visit one of our local Tourist Information Centres.

During 2002, one place not to miss is *Sandringham* (nr. King's Lynn, Norfolk), the country retreat of Her Majesty The Queen. Set in sixty acres of beautiful grounds, visitors can wander through the house, and see the rooms used by The Royal Family. During 2002 you will also be able to visit 2 special exhibitions- 'The Royal Family at Christmas' and view the 'Royal Stamp Collection'.

When you have completed your visit, why not take a tour of our other great 'Golden' connections - take a stroll along the 'Golden Mile', come face-to-face with 'Golden Tamarids' and smell the delicate fragrance of the 'Golden Jubilee' rose. All these and more.....

The Golden Jubilee Trail - Tour 1
Starting point: Sandringham

Day 1
Morning - take the B1440/A148/A1067 to *Fakenham*, and visit the *Pensthorpe Waterfowl Park* (home to 'Barrow's and European Goldeneye' ducks). Continue on the A1067 to *Norwich*, and explore the Norman Castle with its superb treasures of the civic regalia.
Afternoon - take the A47 to *Great Yarmouth*. Enjoy a stroll on the 'Golden Mile', and try your luck at the Casino.

Day 2
Morning - take the A143 to *Bungay*. Just to the south is *St. Peter's Brewery*, where you can enjoy a tasting of the 'Golden Ale'. This part of the route passes through Suffolk's rich golden wheat fields.
Afternoon - two choices. Either head south on the A144/A12 to visit the treasure trove of *Sutton Hoo* (nr. Woodbridge), the burial site of Anglo-Saxon Kings. Or head west on the A143 to the market town of *Bury St. Edmunds*. Explore the lovely Abbey Gardens, home of 'Golden Pheasants'.

Day 3
Take the A12/A14 to *Colchester*, Britain's oldest recorded town. Visit the excellent zoo to see the 'Golden Lion Tamarids'. Then continue south on the A12/A130 to *Rettendon*, and *Hyde Hall Garden*. Enjoy a wander in the 'Gold Garden', with its golden daffodils in spring, and conifers in autumn/winter.

The Golden Jubilee Trail - Tour 2
Starting point: Sandringham

Day 1
Morning - head south on the A148 to *King's Lynn*. Visit the *Tales of the Old Gaol House* to see the civic regalia. Then learn all about poor King John who lost his gold in *The Wash*.
Afternoon - take the A47 to *Wisbech*, set amongst the rich dark soil of *The Fens*. Visit 'pick-your-own' farms and wayside stalls to try delicious fruit, including 'Golden Delicious' apples.

Day 2
Morning - head to *Peterborough* on the A47, and take a ride on the *Nene Valley Railway*. Imagine yourself as James Bond, as scenes from 'GoldenEye' were shot here.
Afternoon - south along the A1/A14 to historic *Cambridge*. Visit the *Fitzwilliam Museum*'s gold coin collection. If you fancy a quick detour east, head to Newmarket - where, during 2002, you can see a special Royal Exhibition.

Day 3
Morning - take the M11 south to *Harlow*, then the A414 to *Hatfield House*, childhood home of Queen Elizabeth I.
Afternoon - follow the A1057 to *St. Albans*, and *The Gardens of the Rose*. Enjoy a wander amongst the sweet smelling roses, whose varieties include 'Golden Years' and 'Golden Jubilee'.

Tourist Information Centres

* Not open all year

Bedfordshire
Bedford, 10 St Pauls Square,. Tel: (01234) 215226
Dunstable, The Library, Vernon Place,
Tel: (01582) 471012
Luton , The Bus Station, Bute Street,
Tel: (01582) 401579
Mid Beds, 5 Shannon Court, High Street, Sandy
Tel: (01767) 682728

Cambridgeshire
Cambridge, The Old Library, Wheeler Street,
Tel: (01223) 322640
Ely, Oliver Cromwell's House, 29 St Mary's Street,
Tel: (01353) 662062
Huntingdon, The Library, Princes Street,
Tel: (01480) 388588
Peterborough, 3-5 Minster Precincts,
Tel: (01733) 452336
St Neots, The Old Court, 8 New Street,
Tel: (01480) 388788
Wisbech and Fens, 2-3 Bridge Street,
Tel: (01945) 583263

Essex
Braintree, Town Hall Centre, Market Square,
Tel: (01376) 550066
Brentwood, Pepperell House,
44 High Street, Tel: (01277) 200300
Chelmsford, County Hall, Market Road,
Tel: (01245) 283400,.
Clacton-on-Sea, 23 Pier Avenue,
Tel: (01255) 423400
Colchester, 1 Queen Street, Tel: (01206) 282920
Harwich, Iconfield Park, Parkeston,
Tel: (01255) 506139
Maldon, Coach Lane, Tel: (01621) 856503
Saffron Walden, 1 Market Place,
Market Square, Tel: (01799) 510444
Southend-on-Sea, 19 High Street,
Tel: (01702) 215120
Thurrock, Granada Motorway Service Area, M25,
Grays, Tel: (01708) 863733
Waltham Abbey, 2-4 Highbridge Street,
Tel: (01992) 652295

Hertfordshire
Birchanger, Welcome Break Service Area,
J8 M11 Motorway, Tel: (01279) 508656
Bishop's Stortford, The Old Monastery, Windhill,
Tel: (01279) 655831

Hemel Hempstead, Dacorum Information Centre,
Marlowes, Tel: (01442) 234222
Hertford, 10 Market Place, Tel: (01992) 584322
Letchworth Garden City, 33-35 Station Road,
Letchworth Garden City, Tel: (01462) 487868
St Albans, Town Hall, Market Place,
Tel: (01727) 864511

Norfolk
Aylsham, Bure Valley Railway Station, Norwich Road,
Tel: (01263) 733903
Cromer, Prince of Wales Road,
Tel: (01263) 512497
Diss, Meres Mouth, Mere Street,
Tel: (01379) 650523
Downham Market, The Priory Centre,
78 Priory Road, Tel: (01366) 387440
* **Great Yarmouth**, Marine Parade,
Tel: (01493) 842195
* **Hoveton**, Station Road, Tel: (01603) 782281
Hunstanton, Town Hall, The Green,
Tel: (01485) 532610
King's Lynn, The Custom House,
Purfleet Quay, Tel: (01553) 763044
* **Mundesley**, 2 Station Road, Tel: (01263) 721070
Norwich, The Forum, Millennium Plain,
Tel: (01603) 727927
* **Sheringham**, Station Approach,
Tel: (01263) 824329
* **Wells-next-the-Sea**, Staithe Street,
Tel: (01328) 710885
Wymondham, Market Cross, Market Place,
Tel: (01953) 604721

Suffolk
Aldeburgh, 152 High Street,
Tel: (01728) 453637
* **Beccles**, The Quay, Fen Lane,
Tel: (01502) 713196
Bury St Edmunds, 6 Angel Hill,
Tel: (01284) 764667
Felixstowe, The Seafront, Tel: (01394) 276770
* **Flatford**, Flatford Lane, East Bergholt,
Tel: (01206) 299460
Ipswich, St Stephens Church, St Stephens Lane,
Tel: (01473) 258070 (I/J10)
* **Lavenham**, Lady Street, Tel: (01787) 248207
Lowestoft, East Point Pavilion, Royal Plain,
Tel: (01502) 533600
Mid Suffolk, Wilkes Way, Stowmarket,
Tel: (01449) 676800
Newmarket, Palace House, Palace Street,
Tel: (01638) 667200
Southwold, 69 High Street, Tel: (01502) 724729
Sudbury, Town Hall, Market Hill,
Tel: (01787) 881320
Woodbridge, Station Buildings,
Tel: (01394) 382240

See each county section for further TIC details.

WorldWideWeb

Useful Web Addresses

Surf the web to discover the East of England on-line. Over the next two pages we have brought together a selection of both informative and fun web sites, giving you lots of useful information about the region.

General information

East of England Tourist Board
www.eastofenglandtouristboard.com

British Tourist Authority
www.visitbritain.com

East of England Government Office
www.go-eastern.gov.uk

East England Arts
www.eab.org.uk

Eastern Screen *(film and television)*
www.eastern-screen.demon.co.uk

English Heritage
www.english-heritage.org.uk

The National Trust
www.nationaltrust.org.uk

Sport England
www.sportengland.org

Tastes of Anglia *(food and drink)*
www.tastesofanglia.com

County information

Bedfordshire County Council
www.bedfordshire.gov.uk

Cambridgeshire County Council
www.camcnty.gov.uk

Essex County Council
www.essexcc.gov.uk

Hertfordshire County Council
www.hertsdirect.org

Norfolk County Council
www.norfolk.gov.uk

Suffolk County Council
www.suffolkcc.gov.uk

Major cities and towns

Bedford, Bedfordshire
www.bedford.gov.uk

Bury St. Edmunds, Suffolk
www.stedmundsbury.gov.uk

Cambridge, Cambridgeshire
www.cmsc.co.uk

Chelmsford, Essex
www.chelmsfordbc.gov.uk

Colchester, Essex
www.colchester.gov.uk

Ely, Cambridgeshire
www.eastcambs.gov.uk

Great Yarmouth, Norfolk
www.great-yarmouth.gov.uk

Hertford, Hertfordshire
www.eastherts.gov.uk

Ipswich, Suffolk
www.ipswich.gov.uk

King's Lynn, Norfolk
www.west-norfolk.gov.uk

Luton, Bedfordshire
www.luton.gov.uk

Lowestoft, Suffolk
www.visit-lowestoft.co.uk

Norwich, Norfolk
www.visitnorwich.co.uk

Peterborough, Cambridgeshire
www.peterborough.gov.uk

St. Albans, Hertfordshire
www.stalbans.gov.uk

Southend-on-Sea, Essex
www.southend.gov.uk

Watford, Hertfordshire
www.watford.gov.uk

Travelling around

Traveline *(public transport information)*
www.traveline.org.uk

UK Public Transport Guide (PTI)
www.pti.org.uk

London Luton Airport
www.london-luton.com

London Stansted Airport
www.baa.co.uk

Norwich International Airport
www.norwichinternational.com

National Express *(coach travel)*
www.gobycoach.com

The Train Line *(on-line booking service)*
www.thetrainline.com

UK Railways on the Net
(links to train operating companies)
www.rail.co.uk

Reference and Maps

Up My Street *(local services in your area)*
www.upmystreet.com
Yellow Pages
www.yell.co.uk
Multimap
www.multimap.com
Street Map
www.streetmap.co.uk

Accommodation

East of England Tourist Board
www.eastofenglandtouristboard.com

British Holiday and Home Parks Association
www.bhhpa.org.uk
The Camping and Caravanning Club
www.campingandcaravanningclub.co.uk
Farm Holiday Bureau
www.farmstayanglia.co.uk
The Landmark Trust
www.landmarktrust.co.uk
Wolsey Lodges
www.wolsey-lodges.co.uk
Youth Hostel Association
www.yha.org.uk

Accessibility

Holiday Care Service *(information on holidays)*
www.holidaycare.org.uk
RADAR *(Royal Association for Disability
and Rehabilitation)*
www.radar.org.uk

Miscellaneous

Bedfordshire,Hertfordshire and Luton Tourism
www.bhl.org.uk
The Brecks *(Norfolk/Suffolk)*
www.brecks.org
The Broads Authority *(Norfolk/Suffolk Broads)*
www.broads-authority.gov.uk
Fens Tourism
www.fenswaterways.com
Heritage Suffolk
www.heritage-suffolk.org.uk
Norfolk
www.visitnorfolk.co.uk
University of Cambridge
www.cam.ac.uk
Blue Badge Guides
www.tourist-guides.net
The British Activity Holiday Association
www.baha.org.uk
British Waterways Association
www.british-waterways.org
Church Search *(find a church)*
www.church-search.com

English Nature
www.english-nature.org.uk
English Wine Producers
www.englishwineproducers.com
Farmers' Markets
www.farmersmarketseast.org.uk
The Forestry Commission
www.forestry.gov.uk
The Good Beach Guide
(Marine Conservation Society)
www.goodbeachguide.co.uk
The Meteorological Society *(weather)*
www.meto.gov.uk
National Cycle Network *(cycle routes in Britain)*
www.sustrans.org.uk
The National Gardens Scheme
(private gardens open days)
www.ngs.org.uk
North Sea Cycle Route
www.northsea-cycle.com
The Racecourse Association
(horseracing in Britain)
www.comeracing.co.uk
The Ramblers Association
www.ramblers.org.uk
RSPB *(Royal Society for the Protection of Birds)*
www.rspb.org.uk
The Tree Register *(notable trees in Britain)*
www.tree-register.org
USAF *(US Air Forces in Europe)*
www.usafe.af.mil/home.html
WI *(Women's Institute)* Country Markets
www.wimarkets.co.uk
The Wildfowl and Wetlands Trust
www.wwt.org.uk
The Wildlife Trust
www.wildlifetrusts.org
The Woodland Trust
www.woodland-trust.org.uk

Fun stuff

The British Royalty
www.royal.gov.uk
Dad's Army locations in the East of England
www.dadsarmy.locations.cwc.net
Earthcam *(web cams around the world)*
www.earthcam.com
Find a Grave *(burial sites of the famous)*
www.findagrave.com
Knowhere Guide to the UK
(residents views of places)
www.knowhere.co.uk

Bedfordshire & Hertfordshire

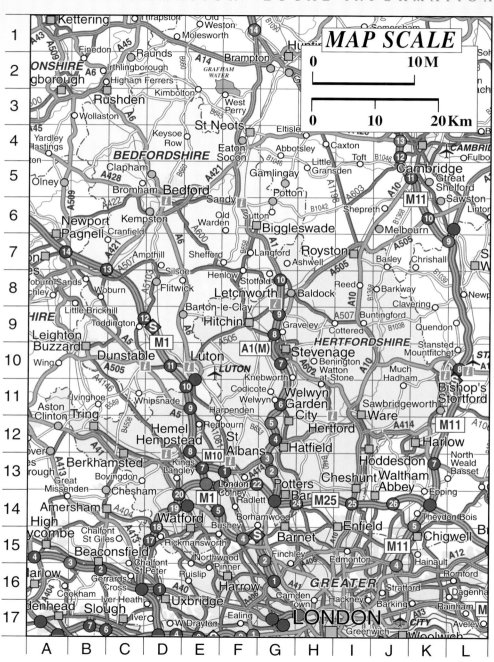

MAP SCALE

0	10M

0	10	20Km

Bedfordshire

County Town: Bedford
Population: 560,000 approx (including Luton).
Highest Point: Dunstable Downs 244m (801 feet)
Rivers: Beane, Flit, Grand Union Canal, Hiz, Ivel, Lea, Ouse, Ouzel.
Landmarks: A1 (Great North Road), Cardington airship hangers,
The Chiltern Hills, Dunstable Downs (chalk lion), London Luton Airport,
M1 Motorway (Britain's first motorway), Watling Street & Icknield Way (ancient roads),
Woburn Abbey.

Industry Past & Present:

Luton has long been recognised as the centre of British hat making. The industry that thrives today has its roots deep in the 17th C. when local straw was plaited, then sewn together to form hats. Visit the 'Plaiter's Lea' conservation area, home of today's hat manufacturers. To the north of the county, Bedford and the villages of the Ouse Valley, saw a thriving *pillow-lace* industry from the late 16-19th C. This was reputedly started by Katherine of Aragon (Henry VIII's first wife), whilst held at Ampthill Castle. Today *arable farming* has taken over much of the county, but *market gardening* flourishes around Biggleswade and Sandy. To the west, *clay, sand* and *chalk* have been quarried in vast quantities around Leighton Buzzard and Marston Moretaine. *Agricultural* and *aeronautical research* also figures prominently at Silsoe and Cranfield. The former airship complex at Cardington is now home of the British Research Establishment. Famous names include - Jordan's (breakfast cereals/crunchy bars), Charles Wells (brewing), Gossard (lingerie) and Vauxhall (vehicle manufacture).

Famous People:

Katherine of Aragon *(Henry VIII's first wife)*, Lady Margaret Beaufort *(mother of Henry VII)*, Dukes of Bedford *(Woburn Abbey)*, Robert Bloomfield *(poet)*, John Bunyan *(author/preacher)*, Henry VIII, John Howard *(prison reformer)*, Glenn Miller *(US bandleader)*, Mary Norton *(author)*, Dorothy Osborne *(17th C. letter writer)*, Sir Joseph Paxton *(English gardener)*, Thomas Tompion *(watch and clock maker)*, Samuel Whitbread *(brewer)*.

Hertfordshire

County Town: Hertford
Population: 1,000,000 approx.
Highest Point: Hastoe 245m (803 feet).
Rivers: Colne, Grand Union Canal, Ivel, Lea, Mimram, Rib, Stort, Ver.
Landmarks: A1 (Great North Road), Ashridge Estate, The Chiltern Hills, Ermine Street (ancient road), Grand Union Canal, Hatfield House, Lee Valley Park, M1 & M25 Motorways, St. Albans Cathedral, Verulamium.

Industry Past & Present:

Hertfordshire has always been an *agricultural* county, long famous for its *market gardening*, *watercress* and *roses*. In the 19th C. the key industries were *straw plaiting* in North Herts, *papermaking/printing* in the Watford area, and *brewing* in East Herts - in 1838, there were some eighty maltings, but the industry declined after 1880. The Lee Valley was a centre for *nursery gardening*, so by 1930, it had the world's largest accumulation of glasshouses - later it would be used for *gravel extraction*. The south east of the county is noted as a focal point for *film* and *television production*, particularly the town of Borehamwood (Elstree), Britain's very own Hollywood since 1914. To the north, the former Rolls Royce factory at Leavesden is now a major film studio, whilst St. Albans saw early experiments in film. The county also has a place in the history of *aviation*, Britain's first hot air balloon flight landed at Standon, the Mosquito Bomber was manufactured at London Colney and British Aerospace were based at Hatfield. St. Albans was once home to Ryder Seeds, remembered in golf's 'Ryder Cup', whilst Letchworth is noted for its former 'Spirella' corset factory. Famous names include - Glaxo SmithKline (pharmaceutical), Kodak (photographic), McMullen's (brewing) and Tesco.

Grand Union Canal

Famous People:

Saint Alban *(first martyr for the Christian faith to die in Britain)*, Francis Bacon *(essayist/statesman)*, Nicholas Breakspear *(only English pope)*, Edward Bulwer-Lytton *(author)*, Dame Barbara Cartland *(author)*, William Cowper *(poet)*, Charles Dickens *(author)*, Elizabeth I, Captain William Earl Jones *(author)*, Lady Katherine 'the wicked lady' Ferrers *(highwaywoman)*, EM Forster *(author)*, Graham Greene *(author)*, Charles Lamb *(essayist)*, Henry Moore *(sculptor)*, George Orwell *(author)*, Beatrix Potter *(author)*, Cecil Rhodes *(British Empire builder)*, George Bernard Shaw *(author)*, Anthony Trollope *(author)*, HG Wells *(author)*.

Roman Theatre, Gorhambury

Cities
towns &
Villages

MD:	Market Day
EC:	Early Closing
i	Tourist Information Centre

Bedfordshire

Ampthill *(D7)*
Ancient market town under the brow of the Greensand Ridge. Picturesque narrow streets are lined with fine Georgian buildings and quaint antique shops. Ampthill Park was once home to a 15th C. castle, where Henry VIII stayed, and his wife, Katherine of Aragon, was kept during their divorce proceedings. A stone cross now marks the spot. **MD**: Thurs, monthly farmers market.

Bedford *(D5/6)*
Ancient county town, dating back to before Saxon times. Fine buildings and mound of Norman castle. The Embankment is one of the country's finest river settings, with tree-lined walkways, gardens, bandstand and elegant suspension bridge. Connections to John Bunyan, preacher/author ('The Pilgrim's Progress'); Glenn Miller, the World War II bandleader; and the former Bedfordshire lace industry. **MD**: Wed to Sat. **EC**: Thurs. **i**

Biggleswade *(F6)*
Set on the River Ivel, this busy town is set in the heart of market gardening country. During the 18th C. it was an important coaching centre on the Great North Road, and many old inns remain today. Dan Albone (1860-1906), racing cyclist and inventor of the tandem bicycle, established the Ivel Cycle Works in the town. **MD**: Sat.

Dunstable *(C/D10)*
Set at the junction of the 4,000 year old Icknield Way and 'Roman' Watling Street, this ancient market town was started in the 12th C. by Henry I. The Augustinian priory, founded in 1131, was chosen by Henry VIII for the divorce proceedings of his first wife Katherine of Aragon. Later the town became a major coaching centre, and was noted for its straw plait and hat making industries. **MD**: Wed and Sat and small market on Fri. **i**

Leighton Buzzard *(B10)*
Situated on the Grand Union Canal, the town has always been famous for its sand. Fine Georgian buildings line the wide High Street, alongside a medieval market cross, 19th C. town hall and charming mews. The 13th C. parish church is noted for its 191 foot high spire. Adjoining Linslade is popular with boaters, anglers and walkers. **MD**: Tues and Sat. **EC**: Thurs.

Luton *(E10)*
Situated on the edge of the Chiltern Hills, Luton is a thriving town with a long history. From the 17th C. it was noted for its straw plait and hat making industries. There is also a long association with the car industry. St. Mary's Church has one of the finest double arch stone screens in Europe. The famous Luton Shopping Centre, excellent entertainment/leisure facilities and several landscaped parks are other key attractions. **MD**: Mon to Sat. **i**

WHERE time PASSES
BEDf⊖RD
WITH imaɕination

INformation
souveNiRs
ɕuided walks
aNd much, much more...

Bedford Tourist Information Centre
10 St Paul's Square,
Bedford MK40 1SL
Tel: 01234 215226

Bedfordshire ● Hertfordshire

Potton *(G6)*

Ancient market town, centred on an enclosed medieval square. Red-brick 18th C. houses and Neo-Georgian clock house. Narrow streets radiate out from the square, lined with Georgian and ironstone buildings. The 13/14th C. church has gravestones adorned with angels and skulls. **EC**: Thurs.

Sandy *(F6)*

Set against a backdrop of greensand hills, with their parklands, woodlands and heath, Sandy is one of the earliest places in the county where market gardening was recorded. Excavations show the town dates back to Roman times. An Elizabethan-style mansion (The Lodge) is now the headquarters of the RSPB. **MD**: Fri. **i**

Woburn *(B8)*

Surrounded by wooded countryside and parkland, this beautifully preserved Georgian town is acknowledged as one of the most historically important in Britain. 18/19th C. houses and period shop-fronts line the High Street. Today it has become an excellent centre for antiques and collectables. The old church is now a Heritage Centre. **EC**: Wed (partial).

Northill

Pick of the villages

1 **Aspley Guise** - former 19th C. health resort, set amid sandy pine woods. *(B8)*
2 **Biddenham** - lies in a loop of the river. Stone and colour-washed houses. *(D5)*
3 **Billington** - hilltop village with thatched cottages and 13th C. church. *(B10)*
4 **Bletsoe** - castle remains, once home of Lady Margaret Beaufort, mother of Henry VII. *(D4)*
5 **Bromham** - 13th C. medieval bridge and restored water mill (17th C.) *(C5)*
6 **Cardington** - well-kept green, with 200 year old cottages. Huge airship sheds. *(E6)*
7 **Clophill** - 17/18th C. buildings, former lockup/pound and ruined hilltop church. *(E7)*
8 **Elstow** - 16th C. timber-framed Moot Hall. John Bunyan was born nearby in 1628. *(D6)*
9 **Felmersham** - hilltop village, with finest early English church in county. *(C4)*
10 **Harlington** - connections to John Bunyan. 17th C. manor house and half-timbered cottages. *(D9)*
11 **Harrold** - tree-lined green with 18th C. butter cross and circular lock-up. *(B4)*
12 **Heath and Reach** - old cottages set beside a green, with pump and clock tower. *(B9)*
13 **Ickwell** - classic English village with cricket pitch and permanent maypole. *(F6)*
14 **Northill** - 18th C. thatched cottages and the church sit beside a little pond. *(F6)*
15 **Old Warden** - picturesque village recreated in Swiss-style by the 3rd Lord Ongley. *(F6)*
16 **Pavenham** - limestone houses and splendid church. Former rush-matting industry. *(C4)*
17 **Shefford** - a former inland port. Home of 19th C. poet Robert Bloomfield. *(F7)*
18 **Shelton** - tiny hamlet with pretty cottages and a Georgian rectory. *(D2)*
19 **Silsoe** - small village with over 130 listed buildings. Close by is Wrest Park. *(D8)*
20 **Southill** - estate village, with Southill Park, home of the Whitbread Family since 1795. *(F7)*
21 **Stevington** - 14th C. medieval market cross where John Bunyan once preached. *(C5)*
22 **Studham** - one of the highest villages in Beds. Once noted for its hat-making. *(C/D11)*
23 **Sutton** - 14th C. packhorse bridge and ford. Church has 19th C. barrel organ. *(G6)*
24 **Swineshead** - pretty main street, including limestone spire of 14th C. church. *(D3)*
25 **Thurleigh** - remains of Norman castle. Timber-framed and thatched buildings. *(D4)*
26 **Toddington** - hilltop village with elegant houses/cottages. Large green with pump. *(C9)*
27 **Totternhoe** - set below a chalkland spur, and once noted for its building stone. *(C10)*
28 **Turvey** - 19th C. estate village, set beside the River Great Ouse. 13th C. bridge. *(B5)*
29 **Whipsnade** - set on famous downs, surrounded by common land. Unusual tree cathedral. *(C11)*
30 **Willington** - 16th C. stables and stone dovecote (once housing 1,500 nesting birds). *(E5)*

Bedfordshire ● *Hertfordshire*

Hertfordshire

Baldock *(G8)*

An important Iron Age/Roman settlement, whose borough was founded in 1250 by the Knights Templar. The town gained importance in the coaching era when it was the first main stop on the Great North Road out of London. It has retained much of its old-world charm, with handsome 16-18th C. buildings. The town's greatest feature is St. Mary's Church. tower. **MD**: Wed. **EC**: Thurs.

Berkhamstead *(C12/13)*

This thriving town is steeped in history, with a large section of the elegant High Street designated a conservation centre. Close by are the romantic ruins of the former 11th C. castle. The town has strong literature links, including Graham Greene, William Cowper and J.M. Barrie. Just to the north is the 4,000 acres of The National Trust's 'Ashridge Estate'. **MD**: Sat. **EC**: Wed.

Bishop's Stortford *(K10/11)*

Set on the River Stort, this ancient market town is the birthplace (1853) of Cecil Rhodes, who went to South Africa and found his fortune in the diamond mines. A former coaching centre, the town prospered from the malting and brewing industry. There are many fine 16/17th C. buildings, alongside the remains of a Norman castle. **MD**: Thurs and Sat. **EC**: Wed. [i]

Borehamwood and Elstree *(F/G14/15)*

Borehamwood is largely a modern town with much postwar housing. It is historically associated with the film industry, although today only two studios remain. The BBC Elstree Studio is home to the set of 'Eastenders'. The much older settlement of Elstree, sits on the 'Roman' Watling Street with old houses and inns of timber-framed and brick construction. **MD**: Tues and Sat.

Buntingford *(I9)*

Once an important coaching town in the 18/19th C. Buntingford lies on the 'Roman' Ermine Street. Many fine listed buildings can be found in the High Street, including St. Peter's Church, the first brick built church in England, and the rare 16th C. turret clock. The River Rib, well known for kingfishers, runs through the town. **MD**: Mon. **EC**: Wed.

Bushey *(E/F15)*

Small town, retaining its village atmosphere. Links with the Monro Circle of early English watercolourists, and the Victorian artist, Sir Hubert von Herkomer, who founded an art/film studio here (a rose garden now stands on the site). Attractive green and 13th C. church with hammerbeam roof.

Cheshunt and Waltham Cross *(I113)*

These adjoining towns are set on the edge of the Lee Valley Park. Cheshunt is a popular shopping centre, with a pond and fountain at its centre. Waltham Cross (to the south) is noted for its beautiful 'Eleanor Cross', a Grade I listed monument, erected by King Edward I in 1290 in memory of his beloved queen. **MD**: Wed and Fri.

Westmill, Hertfordshire

Castle Grounds, Hertford

Harpenden *(E/F11/12)*

From agricultural origins, Harpenden has developed into an attractive small town. Designated a conservation area, the tree-lined High Street has many listed 17/18th C. buildings, interesting shops and a variety of pubs and restaurants. The town boasts many fine open spaces, such as Rothamsted Park and the Common with its ponds, picnic areas and nature trail.

Hatfield *(G12)*

The old town dates back to Saxon times, with Georgian houses and former coaching inns. Charles Dickens visited The Eight Bells, and later featured it in 'Oliver Twist'. During the 1930's, Hatfield's growth was linked to the aviation industry, with both the Mosquito and Trident built here. In 1948, the 'new town' of Hatfield was established. **MD**: Wed and Sat. **EC**: Thurs.

Hemel Hempstead *(D12/13)*

Unlike most New Towns, Hemel Hempstead developed around a charming old settlement, centred on St. Mary's Church (which dates from c.1150). The preserved High Street has 17/18th C. houses, specialist shops and a lively arts centre. The New Town is a vibrant centre with an undercover shopping mall, parkland and water gardens. **MD**: Thurs to Sat (antiques market on Wed). *i*

Hertford *(H11/12)*

Historic county town, at the meeting place of four rivers, and a royal borough for more than 1,000 years. The former castle with its Norman mound, massive walls and 15th C. gatehouse stand in attractive gardens. Impressive 18th C. Shire Hall, and the oldest 'Quaker' Friend's Meeting House (c.1670) in the world. The town has also become famed as an antiques centre, especially along St. Andrew Street. **MD**: Sat. **EC**: Thurs. *i*

Hitchin *(F9)*

Ancient market town dating back to Saxon times. A former Royal Manor, Hitchin prospered from the wool trade, and retains its medieval plan with narrow streets and lanes. The large market square is surrounded by Tudor and Georgian buildings, and overlooked by the largest parish church in the county. Close by is Hitchin Priory, an 18th C. mansion. **MD**: Tues, Fri and Sat. **EC**: Wed.

Hoddesdon *(I/J12)*

Set on the edge of the Lee Valley Park, this bustling market town has several fine listed buildings, including the Swan Inn and the Salisbury Arms, both of which date from the 17th C. The town centre has been designated a conservation area, and the Clock Tower (built in 1835) is an historic focal point. There has been a market here since the 13th C. **MD**: Wed and Fri. **EC**: Thurs.

Letchworth *(G8)*

The world's first Garden City, founded in 1903 - its unique design based on the ideas of Ebenezer Howard. His dream was to combine "the health of the country with the comfort of the town", with carefully planned and well designed housing and industries. Wide tree-lined avenues, parks and gardens add to its unique appeal. Famous black squirrels. **MD**: (indoor market) Mon to Sat (except Wed). **EC**: Wed. *i*

Barkway, Hertfordshire

Bedfordshire ● Hertfordshire

Much Hadham *(J11)*
This is one of Hertfordshire's showpiece villages, and for 800 years the country seat of the Bishops of London. The long High Street has well-preserved timber/brick houses, and grand 18/19th C. residences. Former home of sculptor Henry Moore.

Redbourn *(E12)*
Named after the River Red, this small town sits on the 'Roman' Watling Street. During the 17/18th C. it was a popular coaching stop. Ancient pubs and restored water mill. The Common was the site of the first recorded cricket match in Hertfordshire in 1666.

Rickmansworth *(D15)*
A former market town with a charter dating from 1542. The town boasts a fine conservation area, including St. Mary's Church with its 17th C. tower. Basing House has associations with William Penn, famous Quaker statesmen and founder of the state of Pennsylvania, USA. To the south east of the town is Rickmansworth Aquadrome, offering water-based activities.

Royston *(I7)*
Busy market town, which grew up around a cross erected by Lady Roisia (around 1066). This marked the intersection of the ancient Icknield Way and 'Roman' Ermine Street. In the 17th C. Royston became a hunting base for James I. Several historic buildings, award-winning gardens and an unusual man-made cave, with medieval carvings. **MD**: Wed and Sat. **EC**: Thurs.

St Albans *(F13)*
An historic city shaped by 2,000 years of history. Named after St. Alban, Britain's first Christian martyr, the city is built beside the site of Verulamium, the third largest Roman town in Britain. Today's settlement developed in Saxon times, around the precincts of the 10th C. monastery. Discover Roman remains, the magnificent 11th C. Cathedral/Abbey Church, historic buildings/inns, attractive parkland and bustling shopping areas. **MD**: Wed and Sat. *i*

Sawbridgeworth *(K11)*
Described as 'one of the best small towns in the county', Sawbridgeworth prospered from the malting industry, and is dominated by the spire of its 13th C. church. Today the riverside maltings have been converted into an antiques centre. The town centre is a conservation area with picturesque streets, old inns and Georgian/Victorian buildings. **EC**: Thurs.

Stevenage *(G10)*
Sitting amongst open farmland, Stevenage was a small market town until 1946, when it was designated Britain's first New Town. Divided into neighbourhoods, Stevenage is noted for its parks, leisure facilities and Britain's first pedestrianised shopping centre. The quaint 'old town' offers pubs, restaurants and shops. **MD**: Wed and Sat (outdoor); and Wed to Sat (indoor).

Tring *(B12)*
Lying amidst the wooded Chiltern Hills, on the Grand Union Canal, this small attractive market town has been important since the 17th C. The wealthy Rothschild family had a strong influence on the town, their mansion (now a private school) is set in 300 acres of landscaped parkland. Famous zoological museum, beautiful memorial garden and brick maze. **MD**: Fri. **EC**: Wed.

Ware *(I11/12)*
Once a major centre for brewing, this delightful town is set on the navigable section of the River Lee. The town has many historic buildings, including old coaching inns, 18th C. riverside gazebos and the unique flint and shell decorated Scott's Grotto. Lady Jane Grey was proclaimed Queen in the town in 1553, but only reigned for nine days. **MD**: Tues. **EC**: Thurs.

St. Albans, Hertfordshire

Bedfordshire ● Hertfordshire

Watford *(E14/15)*
Hertfordshire's largest town is a busy and prosperous regional centre for shopping and entertainment. Impressive 'Harlequin Shopping Centre', elegant Edwardian theatre and popular football club, supported by Sir Elton John. To the south is Cassiobury Park with open space, woodland and boat trips on the Grand Union Canal. **MD**: Tues, Fri, Sat.

Welwyn *(G11)*
Set on the River Mimram, this historic town has Georgian houses and former coaching inns. The sister of painter, Vincent Van Gogh, taught at a former school. Just outside the town are the remains of a 3rd C. Roman bathing suite, discovered in 1960.

Welwyn Garden City *(G12)*
The town was developed from 1920, as England's second Garden City (after Letchworth). Based on the ideas of Ebenezer Howard, its design saw separate residential and industrial areas laid out amongst landscaped parkland and tree-lined boulevards. The neo-Georgian town centre has shopping areas set around a fountain and lawns.

Pick of the villages

1 **Aldbury** - classic English village. Green with duck pond, stocks and whipping post. *(C12)*
2 **Aldenham** - mentioned in Domesday book. Reservoir and country park. *(F14)*
3 **Ardeley** - green with horseshoe of thatched cottages, well and church. *(H9)*
4 **Ashwell** - fine houses, 19th C. lock up and elegant church tower. Source of River Cam. *(G7)*
5 **Ayot St. Lawrence** - secluded woodland village. Former home of George Bernard Shaw. *(F11)*
6 **Ayot St. Peter** - set amongst narrow lanes and fine trees. Red-brick church spire. *(G11)*
7 **Barkway** - former coaching centre, with elegant High street and 18th C. milestone. *(J8)*
8 **Barley** - noted for its early Tudor town house, lock-up and rare 'gallows' pub sign. *(J7)*
9 **Benington** - timbered cottages and church set around green/duck pond. *(H10)*
10 **Braughing** - once important Roman centre. 17th C. cottages, ford and green. *(J9/10)*
11 **Brent Pelham** - hilltop village. Stocks/ whipping post and tomb of dragon slayer. *(J9)*
12 **Chipperfield** - wooded common with cricket pitch and Apostles Pond. *(D14)*
13 **Furneux Pelham** - thatched cottages and Elizabethan hall. *(J9)*
14 **Great Amwell** - source of 17th C. (artificial) 'New River'. Pretty islands with monuments. *(I12)*
15 **Great Gaddesden** - set beside River Gade. Restored church and 18th C. mansion. *(D12)*
16 **Hertingfordbury** - former coaching centre with attractive Georgian houses. *(I12)*
17 **Hunsdon** - weather-boarded/timbered cottages set around green. *(J11/12)*
18 **Kings Walden** - hamlet of cottages and farms in parkland. Neo-Georgian mansion. *(F10)*
19 **Little Berkhamstead** - wooded village, overlooking Lea Valley. 18th C. Stratton's Folly. *(H13)*
20 **Little Gaddesden** - set amongst woods/common, on edge of Ashridge estate. *(C12)*
21 **Little Hadham** - fine timber-framed cottages, Elizabethan hall and windmill. *(K10)*
22 **Markyate** - set on 'Roman' Watling Street. Many listed buildings. *(D11)*
23 **Reed** - Hertfordshire's highest village. Winding lanes with traces of medieval moats. *(I8)*
24 **St. Pauls Walden** - well-wooded parish. Childhood home of The Queen Mother. *(F10)*
25 **Standon** - former market town. Detached church tower and puddingstone. *(J10)*
26 **Stanstead Abbotts** - thriving village, once a brewing centre. Listed buildings and marina. *(J12)*
27 **Therfield** - pretty houses, 12th C. castle mound and extensive chalk/grass heathland. *(I8)*
28 **Walkern** - 17/18th C. houses, dovecote, water mill and Hertfordshire's oldest church. *(H9/10)*
29 **Westmill** - neat village with triangular green, tile-roofed pump and thatched cottages. *(I9)*
30 **Wheathampstead** - dates back to pre-Roman times. Devil's Dyke earthwork. *(F12)*

Tourist Information
Centres

With so much to see and do in this area, it's impossible for us to mention all of the places you can visit. You will find Tourist Information Centres (TICs) throughout Bedfordshire and Hertfordshire, with plenty of information on all the things that you can do and the places you can visit. TICs can book accommodation for you, in their own area, or further afield using the 'Book A Bed Ahead Scheme'. They can be the ideal place to purchase locally made crafts or gifts, as well as books covering a wide range of local interests. A list of the TICs in this area can be found below.

* Not open all year

Bedfordshire

Bedford (D5), 10 St Pauls Square,
Tel: (01234) 215226
Email:touristinfo@bedford.gov.uk
Web: www.bedford.gov.uk
Dunstable (C/D10), The Library, Vernon Place,
Tel: (01582) 471012
Email: dunstable-tic@bedfordshire.gov.uk
Luton (E10), The Bus Station, Bute Street,
Tel: (01582) 401579
Email: tourist.information@luton.gov.uk
Web: www.luton.gov.uk
Mid Beds (F6), 5 Shannon Court
High Street, Sandy
Tel: (01767) 682728

Hertfordshire

Birchanger Green (L10), Welcome Break Service Area, J8 M11 Motorway, Tel: (01279) 508656
Bishop's Stortford (K10/11), The Old Monastery, Windhill, Tel: (01279) 655831
Email: tic@bishopsstortford.org
Web: www.bishopsstortford.org
Hemel Hempstead (D12/13),
Dacorum Information Centre, Marlowes,
Tel: (01442) 234222
Email: stephanie.canadas@dacorum.gov.uk
Web: www.dacorum.co.uk
Hertford (H/I12/13),10 Market Place
Tel: (01992) 584322
Web: www.hertford.net

Letchworth Garden City (G8/9), 33-35 Station Road Letchworth Garden City
Tel: (01462) 487 868
Email: info@letchworth.com
St Albans (F13), Town Hall, Market Place,
Tel: (01727) 864511
Web: www.stalbans.gov.uk

Blue Badge Guides:

There are also experts available to help you explore some of our towns and cities. These Registered Blue Badge Guides have all attended a training course sponsored by the East of England Tourist Board. Below are some of the tours offered by these Guides - you can obtain further information by contacting the appropriate Tourist Information Centre, unless otherwise indicated. Some Blue Badge Guides have a further qualification to take individuals or groups around the region for half day, full day or longer tours if required.

Bedfordshire

Pre-booked group tours of Bedfordshire and Hertfordshire including Mid-Beds Scenic Route, North Bedfordshire, Bunyan and Hertfordshire Villages.
Contact: Lynda Smith.
Tel: (01582) 882519 or
email:lynda@rolyntravel.co.uk

Hertfordshire

St Albans
Regular City Walks, from Tourist Information Centre, Wed, Sat: 1500, Sun 1115 and 1500, Easter - end Oct. Ghost walk last Wed in month Easter - end Oct. Verulamium walk departs Verulamium Museum, Easter - end Oct, Sun 1500. Guides also on duty Roman Theatre, Easter - end Oct, Sat, Sun, 1430 - 1700. Themed coach tours in Bedfordshire and Hertfordshire in your own coach.
Tel: Tours Secretary (01727) 833001 or
TIC (01727) 864511. Group bookings welcome.

historic houses

Bedfordshire

⊛ Elstow Moot Hall
Elstow Green, Church End
Tel: (01234) 266889
A medieval market hall containing exhibits of 17thC life including beautiful period furniture. Publications and antique maps for sale. *Open 29 Mar-29 Sep, Tue-Thu, Sun, Bank Hol Mon, 1300-1600. Please contact for details of admission prices. (D6)*

⊛ Woburn Abbey
Tel: (01525) 290666
An 18thC Palladian mansion, altered by Henry Holland, the Prince Regent's architect, containing a collection of English silver, French and English furniture and art. *Please contact for details of opening times. £7.50/£3.50/£6.50. (B8)*

Hertfordshire

Shaw's Corner
Tel: (01438) 820307
The home of George Bernard Shaw from 1906 until his death in 1950 with literary and personal relics in 5 rooms maintained as in his lifetime. *Open 27 Mar-3 Nov, Wed-Sun, Bank Hol Mon, 1300-1700. £3.50/£1.75. (G11)*

Gorhambury
Tel: (01727) 854051
A classical-style mansion built from 1777-1784 by Sir Robert Taylor with 16thC enamelled glass, 17thC carpet and historic portraits of the Bacon and Grimston families. *Open 2 May-26 Sep, Thu, 1400-1700. £6.00/£3.00/£4.00. (E12/13)*

Moot Hall, Elstow, Bedfordshire

Bedfordshire ● Hertfordshire

Hatfield
⍟ Hatfield House and Gardens Ｑ
Tel: (01707) 287010
Winner of
Excellence in England Regional Award 2001
Magnificent Jacobean house, home of the Marquess of Salisbury. Exquisite gardens, model soldiers and park trails. Childhood home of Queen Elizabeth I. *Open 30 Mar-30 Sep, House daily, 1200-1600, guided tours Mon-Fri; Park, West Gardens, Restaurant and Shops, daily, 1100-1730, Fri, (Connoisseurs' Day), East Gardens also open. £7.00/£3.50. (G12)*

Hoddesdon
⍟ Rye House Gatehouse
Rye House Quay, Rye Road
Tel: (01992) 702200
A 15thC moated building, the scene of the 'Rye House Plot' to assassinate King Charles II in 1683. Features include an exhibition and a shop. *Open Good Fri (29 Mar) -29 Sep, Sun, Bank Hols, 1100-1700; Whitsun and summer school hols, Mon-Fri, 1100-1700. £1.30/75p. (I/J12)*

Shaw's Corner, Ayot St Lawrence, Hertfordshire

DID YOU KNOW

John Bunyan (1628-1688) is one of the world's most widely-read Christian writers. He was born, and lived most of his life in and around the town of Bedford.

THE WONDER OF WOBURN
Imagine a thousand deer roaming the largest park in England, providing the moving backcloth to a Magnificent House, much loved home of the same family for 400 years. At Woburn you can wander at your own pace, absorbing the glory of marvellous paintings, exquisite porcelain, fine furniture and beautiful silver, Woburn Abbey - a world away from the pace of modern life.

Special Events
May/June/July Exhibition 'Women in Focus'
May 18/19 Professional Koi Dealers Association
June 14/15/16 Woburn Garden Show
June 22/23 BMW Car Club of GB

Open daily 24 March - 29 September 2002
Weekends only 1 Jan to 23 Mar and
30 Sep - 27 Oct 2002

Woburn Abbey, Woburn, Bedfordshire MK17 9WA
Tel: (01525) 290666

HATFIELD HOUSE
House, Park & Gardens
Open Easter Saturday to 30th September
Telephone 01707 287010
Hatfield, Hertfordshire AL9 5NQ
www.hatfield-house.co.uk

Entrance opposite HATFIELD STATION

Bedfordshire ● Hertfordshire

Knebworth
⊛ Knebworth House, Gardens and Park
Tel: (01438) 812661

Tudor manor-house, re-fashioned in the 19thC, housing a collection of manuscripts, portraits, Jacobean banquet hall. Formal gardens and adventure playground. *Please contact for details of opening times and admission prices. (G10)*

Ware
⊛ The Priory
High Street Tel: (01920) 460316

Grade I Listed, the Priory stands in 7 acres of picturesque riverside grounds. Founded as a Franciscan Friary in 1338. *Open all year, by appointment only - please phone for details. (I11/12)*

Knebworth House, Gardens and Park, Hertfordshire

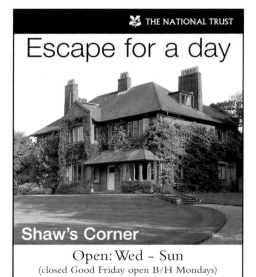

ancient *Monuments*

Bedfordshire

Ampthill
Houghton House
Tel: (01536) 402840
The ruins of a 17thC country house, built in the 'heights' near Ampthill and believed to be the 'House Beautiful' in Bunyan's 'The Pilgrim's Progress'. *Open at any reasonable time. (D7)*

Colmworth
⊛ Bushmead Priory
Tel: (01234) 376614
A small Augustinian priory founded in about 1195 with a magnificent 13thC timber roof of crown-post construction. There are also medieval wall paintings and stained glass. *Open 6 Jul-31 Aug, Sat, Sun, Bank Hol Mon 1000-1300, 1400-1800. (E4)*

Dunstable
Priory Church of St Peter
Church Street
Tel: (01582) 477422
A Grade I Listed building which is an active parish church. Is the surviving part of an Augustinian priory founded in 1131. *Open all year, daily, 0900-1600. (C/D10)*

Flitton
De Grey Mausoleum
Tel: (01760) 755161
A large mortuary chapel of the de Greys of Wrest Park containing fine sculptured tombs of monuments from 16th-19thC and some brass and alabaster. *Open Sat, Sun, please contact key keeper on Tel: (01525) 860094. (D8)*

Hertfordshire

Berkhamsted
Berkhamsted Castle
Tel: (01536) 402840
The extensive remains of an 11thC motte-and-bailey castle which was the work of Robert of Mortain, half brother of William of Normandy, who learnt he was king here. *Open all year, summer, daily, 1000-1800; winter, 1000-1600. (C12/13)*

Bishop's Stortford
⊛ Castle Mound
The Castle Gardens
Tel: (01279) 655261
Remaining mound of a castle built by William I, set in the gardens just minutes from the town. Key to gate available from Bishop's Stortford Tourist Information Centre. *Open all year Mon-Fri, 0930-1600. Closed Bank Hols. (K10)*

Gorhambury
Roman Theatre of Verulamium
Tel: (01727) 854051
The only completely exposed Roman theatre in Britain with the remains of a townhouse and underground shrine. *Open 1 Jan-28 Feb, daily, 1000-1600; 1 Mar-31 Oct, daily, 1000-1700; 1 Nov-31 Dec, daily, 1000-1600; closed 25, 26 Dec. £1.50/50p/£1.00. (E12/13)*

Hertford
⊛ Hertford Castle
The Castle
Tel: (01992) 584322
A 15thC Edward IV gatehouse, Mayor's parlour and robing room with 15thC stone, brick and timber screens. The town's insignia is also on display on special open days. *Please contact for details of opening times. (H11/12)*

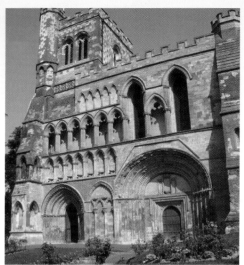

Priory Church of St. Peter, Dunstable, Bedfordshire

Royston
Royston Cave
Melbourn Street
Tel: (01763) 245484

A man-made cave with medieval carvings made by the Knights Templar dated from around the beginning of the 14thC. Possibly a secret meeting place for initiations. *Open 30 Mar-29 Sep, Sat, Sun, Bank Hol Mon, 1430-1700. £2.00/free/£1.00. (I7)*

St Albans
⊚ Cathedral and Abbey Church Q of St Alban
The Chapter House
Tel: (01727) 860780

A Norman abbey church on the site of the martyrdom of St Alban, Britain's first Christian martyr. The 13thC shrine has been restored and is a centre of ecumenical worship. *Open all year, daily, 0900-1745; closed 25 Dec from 1300. (F13)*

St Albans
Clock Tower
Market Cross
Tel: (01727) 866380

A curfew tower, built in approximately 1405 with small exhibitions on aspects of local history. The belfry and 1866 clock mechanism can be viewed. Fine views from the roof. *Open 29 Mar-mid Sep, Sat, Sun, Bank Hol Mon, 1030-1700. 30p/15p. (F13)*

Ware
Scott's Grotto
Scott's Road
Tel: (01920) 464131

Grotto (English Heritage) extending 67ft into the hillside, including passages and 6 chambers decorated with fossils, shells, pebbles and flints. Unlit so torches are necessary. *Open 6 Apr-28 Sep, Sat, Bank Hol Mons, 1400-1630. (I11/12)*

Cathedral and Abbey Church of St. Alban, Hertfordshire

DID YOU KNOW

Buntingford in Hertfordshire, is home to the earliest (purpose-built), brick church in Britain (built 1614-26).

Bedfordshire ● Hertfordshire

Museums, heritage & Craft Centres

Bedfordshire

⊛ Bedford Museum Q

Castle Lane Tel: (01234) 353323
The museum displays cover local human and natural history and there is a changing programme of temporary exhibitions, events and children's activities. *Open all year, Tue-Sat, 1100-1700; Sun, Bank Hol Mon, 1400-1700; closed 29 Mar. Telephone for Christmas opening times. £2.10. (D5/6)*

⊛ Cecil Higgins Art Gallery

Castle Lane
Tel: (01234) 211222
A Victorian mansion, furnished late 19thC style. A large collection of watercolours, prints, drawings, glass, ceramics and porcelain in modern galleries. *Open 29 Jan-31 Dec, Tue-Sat, 1100-1700; Sun, Bank Hol Mon, 1400-1700; closed 29 Mar, 25, 26 Dec. (D5/6)*

John Bunyan Museum and Bunyan Meeting Free Church

Mill Street Tel: (01234) 213722
Museum housing the personal effects of John Bunyan (1628-1688) and copies of The Pilgrim's Progress in over 170 languages, together with other works by Bunyan. *Open 5 Mar-26 Oct, Tue-Sat, 1100-1600. Closed 29 Mar. (D5/6)*

The Gallery

Cardington Workshops, Harrowden Lane
Tel: (01234) 741677
Situated round the courtyard of renovated farm buildings The Gallery houses an exhibition area, workshops and showrooms of 5 local craftsmen. *Open all year, daily, 1000-1700. Closed 24 Dec-7 Jan. (D/E6)*

⊛ Elstow Moot Hall

See entry in Historic Houses section

⊛ John Dony Field Centre

Hancock Drive, Bushmead
Tel: (01582) 486983
A natural history site whose facilities include displays featuring local history, natural history, conservation and archaeology. *Open all year, Mon-Fri, 0930-1630; Sun, 0930-1300; closed 29, 31 Mar, Bank Hol Mon, 25-27 Dec, 1 Jan. (E10)*

⊛ Luton Museum and Art Gallery

Wardown Park Tel: (01582) 546739
A Victorian mansion set in 50 acres of parkland with costume lace and hat-making displays, Victorian street displays, natural history and the archaeology of South Bedfordshire. *Open all year, Tue-Sat, 1000-1700; Sun, 1300-1700; closed 25, 26 Dec, 1 Jan. Guided tours available by appointment. (E10)*

Mossman Collection

Stockwood Country Park, Farley Hill
Tel: (01582) 738714
The Mossman Collection is Britain's largest collection of horse-drawn carriages which are displayed in a new purpose-built building. *Open 5 Jan-31 Mar, Sat, Sun, 1000-1600; 2 Apr-31 Oct, Tue-Sat, 1000-1700, Sun, 1000-1800; 2 Nov-29 Dec, Sat, Sun, 1000-1400. Closed 25, 26 Dec, 1 Jan. (E10)*

Bedfordshire ● *Hertfordshire*

Luton

◈ Stockwood Craft
Museum and Gardens
Stockwood Park, Farley Hill
Tel: (01582) 738714

Housed in an 18thC stable block and featuring Bedfordshire craft displays and workshops including a blacksmith, wheelwright, saddler, shoemaker and thatcher. *Open 5 Jan-31 Mar, Sat, Sun, 1000-1600; 2 Apr-31Oct, Tue-Sat, 1000-1700; Sun, 1000-1800; 2 Nov-29 Dec, Sat, Sun, 1000-1400. Closed 25, 26 Dec, 1 Jan. (E10)*

Hertfordshire

Ashwell

Ashwell Village Museum
Swan Street Tel: (01462) 742956

A collection of village bygones and agricultural implements set in a small but interesting timber building. *Open all year, Sun, Bank Hol Mon, 1430-1700. £1.00/25p. (H7)*

Bushey

◈ Bushey Museum and Art Gallery
Rudolph Road
Tel: (020) 8950 3233

Community museum telling the story of Bushey. Archaeology, social history, local trades and industries. Art galleries show changing exhibitions. *Open 3 Jan-22 Dec, Thu-Sun, 1100-1600. (E/F15)*

Hatfield

Mill Green Museum and Mill
Mill Green Tel: (01707) 271362

An 18thC watermill, restored to working order, with a museum in the adjoining miller's house displaying local and social history and archaeology. *Open all year, Tue-Fri, 1000-1700; Sat, Sun, Bank Hol Mon, 1400-1700. Closed 25, 26 Dec. Donations welcome. (G12)*

Hertford

◈ Hertford Museum
18 Bull Plain Tel: (01992) 582686

A 17thC building with main exhibits on the archaeology, natural and local history of Hertfordshire with a collection of Hertfordshire Regiment regalia and changing exhibitions. *Open all year, Tue-Sat, 1000-1700; closed 29 Mar, 24-26 Dec. (H11/12)*

Hitchin
The Hitchin British Schools
41/42 Queen Street Tel: (01462) 420144
Rare elementary school buildings including 1837 monitorial school room for 330 boys and 1853 galleried classroom demonstrating period lessons. Family trail activities. *Open 5 Feb-2 Apr, Tue, 1000-1600; 7 Apr-27 Oct, Tue, 1000-1600, Sun, 1430-1700; 29 Oct-26 Nov, Tue, 1000-1600. £2.00/£1.00. (F9)*

Hitchin
Hitchin Museum and Art Gallery
Paynes Park Tel: (01462) 434476
A converted 19thC house on 2 floors with displays of costume, local history, a Victorian chemist's shop, a physic garden and temporary art exhibitions. *Open all year, Mon-Sat, except Wed, 1000-1700. (F9)*

Hoddesdon
Lowewood Museum
High Street Tel: (01992) 445596
A Georgian house with a museum on the first floor with local artefacts concerning Broxbourne Borough along with temporary exhibitions. *Open all year, Wed-Sat, 1000-1600; closed 29 Mar, 25 Dec-1 Jan. (I/J12)*

Letchworth
First Garden City Heritage Museum
296 Norton Way South
Tel: (01462) 482710
A museum housing displays relating to the Garden City movement and the social history of Letchworth including a collection of Parker and Unwin architectural drawings. *Open all year, Mon-Sat, 1000-1700; closed 25, 26 Dec. Non-residents £1.00/free/50p, Residents 50p/free/50p. (G8)*

Letchworth
Letchworth Museum
Broadway Tel: (01462) 685647
A museum which features local natural history, archaeological displays and a programme of temporary exhibitions. *Open all year, Mon, Tue, Thu-Sat, 1000-1700. Closed 29 Mar, 1 Apr, 26 Dec. (G8)*

Much Hadham
The Forge Museum and
Victorian Cottage Garden
High Street
Tel: (01279) 843301
Set in a Grade II Listed building. Houses displays on blacksmithing, beekeeping, the parish of Much Hadham and the Page family who were blacksmiths for over 150 years. *Open 1 Mar-22 Dec, Fri-Sun, Bank Hol Mon, 1100-1700. £1.00/50p/50p. (J11)*

Redbourn
Redbourn Village Museum
Silk Mill House, The Common
Tel: (01582) 793397
History of Redbourn and surrounding area from Iron Age to present day. Housed in a Grade II listed building standing in its own grounds. *Open 5 Jan-29 Dec, Sat, 1400-1700, Sun, 1200-1700. Please contact for Bank Hol Mon opening times. £1.00/50p. (E12)*

Rickmansworth
Batchworth Lock Canal Centre
99 Church Street Tel: (01923) 778382
A canal information centre. Canal history, shop and restaurant. *29 Mar-30 Sep, Mon, Wed, Fri, 1000-1600, Sat, Sun, 1300-1700. (D15)*

Batchworth Lock Canal Centre, Rickmansworth, Hertfordshire

Verulamium Museum, St. Albans, Hertfordshire

St Albans
⊛ Museum of St Albans ‖Q‖
Hatfield Road Tel: (01727) 819340
Purpose-built as a museum in 1898, displays include craft tools and local and natural history telling the St Albans story from Roman times to the present day. Wildlife garden. *Open all year, Mon-Sat, 1000-1700; Sun, 1400-1700; closed 25, 26 Dec. (F13)*

St Albans
Saint Albans Organ Museum
320 Camp Road Tel: (01727) 851557
A collection of organs by Mortier, DeCap, Bursens, Weber and Steinway, duo-art reproducing pianos, Mills violano-virtuoso music boxes and Wurlitzer and Rutt theatre pipe organs. *Open all year, Sun, 1400-1630. £3.50/£1.00/£2.50. (F13)*

St Albans
⊛ Verulamium Museum ‖Q‖
St Michaels Tel: (01727) 781810
The museum of everyday life in Roman Britain. Award-winning displays of re-created Roman rooms, 'hands-on' areas and videos of Roman Verulamium. *Open all year, Mon-Sat, 1000-1730; Sun, 1400-1730; closed 25, 26 Dec. £3.20/£1.85/£1.85. (F13)*

Stevenage
Stevenage Museum
St George's Way Tel: (01438) 218881
A lively award-winning museum which tells the story of Stevenage from the Stone Age to the present. Displays include a 1950s living room and a programme of exhibitions. *Open all year, Mon-Sat, 1000-1700; closed 29 Mar, 1 Apr, 25, 26 Dec, 1 Jan. Please contact to confirm Sun opening. (G10)*

Ware
Ware Museum
The Priory Lodge, 89 High Street
Tel: (01920) 487848
An independent museum featuring the Story of Ware from the Roman town through the malting industry of the 18th-20thC and modern times. *Please contact for details of opening times. (I11/12)*

Watford
Watford Museum
194 High Street Tel: (01923) 232297
A museum building, built in 1775 with displays of local history, brewing, printing and archaeology. Regular changing programme of temporary exhibitions. *Open all year, Mon-Fri, 1000-1700; Sat, 1000-1300, Sun 1400-1700. Please contact for Christmas closing. (E14/15)*

Welwyn
Welwyn Roman Baths
Welwyn Bypass Tel: (01707) 271362
The baths are a small part of a villa which was built at the beginning of the 3rdC and occupied for over 150 years. The villa had at least 4 buildings. *Open 5 Jan-24 Nov, Sat, Sun, Bank Hol Mon, 1400-1700 or dusk if earlier; school holidays, daily, 1400-1700 or dusk if earlier. £1.00. (G11)*

Wendy
British Museum of Miniatures
Maple Street
Tel: (01223) 207937
Dolls house and miniatures museum, including the largest dolls house in the world. On site parking for up to 60 cars. Coffee shop, plus a dolls house and miniatures shop. *Open all year, Mon-Sat, 1000-1700, Sun, 1200-1600. Please ring for Bank Hol opening times. Closed 25, 26 Dec, 1 Jan. £2.50/£1.50. (E13)*

Stevenage Museum, Hertfordshire

Bedfordshire ● Hertfordshire

machinery & transport

Bedfordshire

Biggleswade
⚙ Shuttleworth Collection
Old Warden Aerodrome
Tel: (01767) 627288

A unique historical collection of aircraft from a 1909 Bleriot to a 1942 Spitfire in flying condition and cars dating from an 1898 Panhard in running order. *Open 2 Jan-31 Mar, daily 1000-1600; 1 Apr-31 Oct, daily 1000-1700; 1 Nov-19 Dec, daily, 1000-1600; closed 20 Dec-1 Jan, please phone to confirm.* £6.00. (F6)

Leighton Buzzard
⚙ Leighton Buzzard Railway
Page's Park Station, Billington Road
Tel: (01525) 373888

An authentic narrow-gauge light railway, built in 1919, offering a 65-minute return journey into the Bedfordshire countryside. *Please contact for details of opening times.* £5.00/£2.00/£4.00. (B10)

Shuttleworth Collection, Bedfordshire

Stondon Museum, Bedfordshire

Lower Stondon
⚙ Stondon Museum
Station Road Tel: (01462) 850339

A museum with transport exhibits from the early 1900s to the 1980s. The largest private collection in England of bygone vehicles from the beginning of the century. *Open all year, daily, 1000-1700; closed 24 Dec-2 Jan.* £5.00/£2.50/£4.00. (F13)

Hertfordshire

London Colney
De Havilland Aircraft Heritage Centre
PO Box 107, Salisbury Hall
Tel: (01727) 822051

Museum showing the restoration and preservation of a range of De Havilland aircraft including the prototype Mosquito. Also engines, propellers, missiles and memorabilia. *Open 2 Mar-31 Oct, Tue, Thu, Sat, 1400-1730, Sun, Bank Hol Mon, 1030-1730.* £5.00/£3.00/£3.00. (F13)

DID YOU KNOW

The De Havilland Aircraft Heritage Centre is the oldest aircraft museum in Britain. Based at the historic 17th C. Salisbury Hall, in Herts the famous de Havilland 'Mosquito Bomber' was designed here in secret in 1940.

Bedfordshire ● Hertfordshire

Hertfordshire

Much Hadham
Cromer Windmill
c/o The Forge Museum, High Street
Tel: (01279) 843301
Hertfordshire's sole-surviving postmill. Video and audio display, exhibitions on Hertfordshire's windmills, the history of Cromer Mill and the restoration of the mill. *Open 11 May-8 Sep, Sun, Bank Hol Mon, 2nd, 4th Sat in month, 1430-1700. £1.50/25p. (J1)*

St Albans
⊛ **Kingsbury Watermill**
St Michael's Street Tel: (01727) 853502
A 16thC watermill with working machinery, a collection of farm implements, an art gallery and gift shop. There is also the Waffle House tearoom and restaurant. *Open all year, summer, Mon-Sat, 1000-1800, Sun, 1100-1800; winter, Mon-Sat, 1000-1700, Sun, 1100-1700. Closed 25, 26 Dec. £1.10/60p/75p. (F13)*

Bedfordshire

Bromham
⊛ **Bromham Mill**
Stagsden Road (Bridge End)
Tel: (01234) 824330
Restored watermill in working condition. Static displays of machinery and interpretation of waterways and milling. Art gallery, craft sales, picnic site and flour for sale. *Open 1 Mar-31 Oct, Wed-Sat, 1300-1700, Sun, 1030-1700. £2.50/£1.50/£1.50. (C5)*

Stevington
⊛ **Stevington Windmill**
Tel: (01234) 228330
A fully-restored 18thC postmill. Entry is via keys which are available from the pubs in the village for a small returnable deposit. *Open all year, daily, collect keys from the pubs in the village. (C5)*

St Albans
Redbournbury Windmill
Redbournbury Lane
Tel: (01582) 792874
An 18thC working watermill with riverside walks. *Open 1 Jan, 1030-1600; 31 Mar-29 Sep, Sun, 1430-1700; National Mills Day, 11, 12 May. £1.50/80p/80p. (F13)*

Kingsbury Watermill, St. Albans, Hertfordshire

gardens &
Vineyards

Bedfordshire

Old Warden
❀ The Swiss Garden
Tel: (01767) 627666

An attractive garden dating from the 19thC and taking its name from the tiny Swiss thatched cottage at its centre. Contains ponds, bridges, magnificent trees and banks of daffodils and rhododendron in season. Restored by Bedfordshire County Council. *Open 6 Jan-24 Feb, Sun, 1100-1500; 1 Mar-30 Sep, Mon-Sat, 1300-1800; Sun, Bank Hols, 1000-1800; 6-27 Oct, Sun, 1100-1500. £3.00/£2.00. (E6)*

Silsoe
❀ Wrest Park Gardens
Wrest Park   Tel: (01525) 860152

One hundred and fifty years of English gardens laid out in the early 18thC including painted pavilion, Chinese bridge, lakes, classical temple and Louis XV-style French mansion. *Open 1 Apr-27 Oct, Sat, Sun, Bank Hol Mon, 1000-1800/1700 in Oct, last admission 1 hour before closing. £3.80/£1.90/£2.90. (D/E8)*

Woburn
❀ Woburn Abbey
See entry in Historic Houses section.

Hertfordshire

Ayot St Lawrence
Shaw's Corner
See entry in Historic Houses section.

Benington
Benington Lordship Gardens
Tel: (01438) 869228

Edwardian garden and historic site. Ornamental, vegetable, rose/water garden. Herbaceous borders, lakes and contemporary sculptures. *Please contact for details of opening times. Please phone for snowdrop openings in Jan. £3.00. (H10)*

Frithsden
Frithsden Vineyard
Roman Road
Tel: (01442) 864732

A vineyard planted with various grape varieties on a south-facing slope overlooking the village with wine-making equipment. Winery open, tours and tastings available. *Open all year, Wed-Sat, 1000-1700; Sun, 1200-1500; closed 25, 26 Dec. (C12)*

Gorhambury
Gorhambury
See entry in Historic Houses section.

Wrest Park Gardens, Bedfordshire

Gardens of the Rose, St Albans

Hatfield
⊛ **Hatfield House and Gardens** Q
See entry in Historic Houses section.

Hitchin
Saint Pauls Walden Bury Garden
Saint Pauls Walden Bury
Tel: (01438) 871218
A formal woodland garden laid out in about 1730 and covering 40 acres with temples, statues, lake, ponds and flower gardens. The childhood home of the Queen Mother. *Open 21 Apr, 12 May, 9 Jun, Sun, 1400-1700. £2.50/50p/£2.50. (F9)*

Knebworth
⊛ **Knebworth House,
Gardens and Park**
See entry in Historic Houses section.

St Albans
⊛ **The Gardens of the Rose**
The Royal National Rose Society, Chiswell Green
Tel: (01727) 850461
The Royal National Rose Society's Garden with 27 acres of garden and trial grounds for new varieties of rose. Roses of all types displayed with 1,700 different varieties. *Open 1 Jun-29 Sep, Mon-Sat, 0900-1700; Sun, Bank Hol Mon, 1000-1800. £4.00/£1.50/£3.50. (F13)*

Ware
⊛ **The Priory**
See entry in Historic Houses section.

DID YOU KNOW

The Royal National Rose Society at Chiswell Green (Herts) is Britain's oldest and largest specialist plant society. Visit their gardens of over 30,000 roses.

The Gardens of the Rose

The Royal National Rose Society's Gardens are a wonderful display of one of the best and most important collections of roses in the world. There are over 30,000 roses in 1800 different varieties. The Society has introduced many companion plants which harmonise with the roses including over 100 varieties of clematis.
The Queen Mother Garden, named for the Society's patron, contains a fascinating collection of old garden roses. Various cultivation trials show just how easy roses are to grow and new roses can be viewed in its International Trials Ground.

**CHISWELL GREEN, ST ALBANS AL2 3NR
Tel: 01727 850461**

*Open Summer Season:
1 June - 29 September, Mondays - Saturdays: 9am - 5pm.
Sundays and Bank Holidays: 10am - 6pm.*

nurseries
& garden centres

Chenies, Nr. Rickmansworth
⊛ The Van Hage Garden Company
Chenies, Nr. Rickmansworth WD3 6EN

Tel: (01494) 764545

Fax: (01494) 762216

Junction 18, M25 on A404

towards Amersham

Established over 23 years ago this delightful garden centre, nestling in the Hertfordshire/ Buckinghamshire countryside, offers customers a fantastic selection of both indoor and outdoor plants. Staff are always on hand to offer comprehensive information and the centre is full of inspirational ideas for the garden. Coffee Shop, Aquatics, BBQ's, Garden Buildings, Garden Furniture, Hard Landscape, Statues, Christmas Grotto. *(C/D14)*

Hertfordshire

Bragbury End
⊛ The Van Hage Garden Company
Bragbury Lane,

Bragbury End, Stevenage

Tel: (01438) 811777

Fax: (01438) 815485

Junction 7, off A1(M) at Stevenage South, follow signs A602 to Ware.

A series of listed farm buildings linked together each retaining many original features and individuality. The emphasis is on top-quality plants and inspirational displays in the award winning Plant Nursery and Houseplant Department. The courtyard Café serves a fine selection of homemade food. Other attractions include display garden, children's play area, Aquatics Centre and Christmas Grotto. Information, Free Parking, Coaches (limited at weekends) WC, Disabled facilities, Wheelchairs, Baby Changing. *(G/H10)*

Baldock Market, Hertfordshire

Great Amwell
⊛ The Van Hage Garden Company
Great Amwell, Ware SG12 9RP
Tel: (01920) 870811
Fax: (01920) 871861
On A1170 (Junction 25 off M25).

One of Europe's top gardening retailers offering an outstanding selection of products and inspirational displays to meet all gardening requirements. Van Hage is a leisure destination for the whole family. Visit the Maize Maze from July to September. It only lasts for one season, so visit every year and try out a completely new theme and designed maze. It is a mystical adventure for all who dare enter! Don't miss our Christmas Wonderland, the ultimate festive shopping experience. *Entrance to Garden Centre FREE. Disabled, Information, Parking (Ample - FREE), Coaches, WC, Shops, Catering - Hot Meals, Snacks, Beverages, Self-service, Groups welcome. (J12)*

Potters Bar
⊛ The Dutch Nursery
see entry under Coggeshall, Essex

Smallford
⊛ Notcutts Nurseries
Hatfield Road, Smallford, St. Albans
Tel: 01727 853224

Discover a world of ideas and inspiration around every corner for you, your home and your garden. From fabulous plants to gifts and treats galore, there's so much to see. Gift ideas from around the world, houseplants, books, fresh cut & silk flowers, 3,000 varieties of hardy plants (with a 2 year replacement guarantee), pet centre, restaurant, expert friendly advice about seasonal and bedding plants, garden furniture and barbecues. Keep an eye open for regular offers on key garden products. *Notcutts open 7 days a week, free car-parking. (F13)*

Bushey, Hertfordshire

Bedfordshire ● Hertfordshire

St. Albans
Aylett Nurseries Limited
North Orbital Road, St. Albans AL2 1DH
Tel: (01727) 822255

Undoubtedly one of the best Garden Centres in the southeast. Famous for our Dahlias having been awarded Gold medals by the Royal Horticultural Society for 36 consecutive years. In spring our greenhouses are well worth a visit to see our geraniums, fuchsias, hanging baskets and other summer bedding plants. Our plant area is a gardener's paradise, with all year round displays. Houseplants are another speciality. Light lunches and snacks are available at our Coffee House. Visit our Gift and florist shop before you leave. *Christmas Wonderland opens mid-October. Open daily including Sunday except Easter Sunday, Christmas and Boxing Day. (F13)*

Braughing, Hertfordshire

DID YOU KNOW

Letchworth (Herts), is the world's first 'Garden City'. Developed by Ebenezer Howard in 1903, its unique design combined the benefits of both the city and countryside.

Ware, Hertfordshire

Bedfordshire ● *Hertfordshire*

Bedfordshire

Aspley Guise
⊛ HULA Animal Rescue: South Midlands Animal Sanctuary
Glebe Farm, Salford Road Tel: (01908) 584000
A 17-acre registered agricultural holding, headquarters of the registered charity founded in 1972. Visitors can see round the animal house and veterinary unit. *Open 31 Mar-2 Nov, Sat, Sun, 1300-1500. Please contact to confirm Bank Hol opening and admission prices. (B8)*

Dunstable
Toddler World
Dunstable Leisure Centre, Court Drive
Tel: (01582) 604307
An indoor adventure play area. *Open all year, daily, 0930-1700; closed 25 Dec. Child £2.75. (C/D10)*

Dunstable
Whipsnade Wild Animal Park
Tel: (01582) 872171
Whipsnade Wild Animal Park has over 2,500 animals set in 600 acres of beautiful parkland, the Great Whipsnade Railway and free animal demonstrations. *Please contact for details of opening times and admission prices. (C/D10)*

Leighton Buzzard
Mead Open Farm and Rare Breeds Q
Stanbridge Road, Billington
Tel: (01525) 852954
A working farm with a wide range of traditional farm animals and rare breeds, a pet's corner, children's play area and a tearoom. *Please contact for details of opening times. £4.25/£3.25/£3.75. (B10)*

Slip End
Woodside Farm and Wildfowl Park
Woodside Road Tel: (01582) 841044
A 6-acre park with farm shop, rare breeds, wildlife, farm animals, arts and crafts centre, a children's play area and coffee shop. Indoor hands-on sessions. *Open all year, daily, summer 0800-1800, winter 0800-1700; closed 25, 26 Dec, 1 Jan. £3.50/£2.50/£2.50. (D11)*

Wilden
⊛ Bedford Butterfly Park Q
Rennold Road Tel: (01234) 772770
In landscaped haymeadows, park features tropical glasshouse where visitors walk through lush foliage with butterflies flying. Tearoom, gift shop, trails and playground. *Open 18 Feb-31 Oct, daily, 1000-1700. £4.00/£2.00/£3.00. (D/E5)*

Woburn
⊛ Woburn Safari Park Q
Woburn Park Tel: (01525) 290407
Winner of
England for Excellence National Award 2000.
Drive through the safari park with 30 species of animals in natural groups just a windscreen's width away plus the action-packed Wild World Leisure Area with shows for all. *Please contact for details of opening times and admission prices. (B8)*

Hertfordshire

Broxbourne
⊛ Paradise Wildlife Park
White Stubbs Lane
Tel: (01992) 470490
A marvellous day out for the family with many daily activities, adventure playgrounds, shows, woodland railway, paddling pool, catering facilities and picnic areas. *Open 1 Jan-28 Feb, daily, 1000-dusk; 1 Mar-31 Oct, daily, 0930-1800; 1 Nov-31 Dec, daily, 1000-dusk. £8.50/£6.50/£6.50. (I/J13)*

Hatfield
Activity World
Longmead, Birchwood
Tel: (01707) 270789
A large children's indoor adventure play centre with 6,000 sq ft of giant slides, ball pools and mazes. Birthday parties are catered for and special schemes for playgroups. *Open all year, daily, 0930-1830; closed 25, 26 Dec. Child from £2.75. (G12)*

"Come up and see me some time."

Come and see Amba at
Shepreth Wildlife Park,
She's waiting!

Free guide
book with
this advert

Open 7 days 10am - 6pm
01763 26 22 26
www.SheprethWildlifePark.co.uk

 Just 6 miles south of Cambridge on the A10

Hatfield
Toddler World
The Galleria, Comet Way
Tel: (01707) 257480
An indoor adventure play area. *Open all year, Mon-Sat, 1000-1800; Sun, 1100-1700; closed 25 Dec. Child £2.75. (G12)*

Letchworth
Standalone Farm
Wilbury Road   Tel: (01462) 686775
An open farm with cattle, sheep, pigs, poultry, shire horses a wildfowl area, natural history museum, farm walk and daily milking demonstration. *Open 1 Mar-30 Sep, daily, autumn half term, 1100-1700. £3.50/£2.50/£2.50. (G8)*

London Colney
⊛ **Bowmans Open Farm**
Coursers Road Tel: (01727) 822106
A working farm with a variety of farm animals in their natural environment with displays and demonstrations. Hertfordshire's largest open farm set in over 1,500 acres. *Please contact for details of opening times and admission prices. (F13)*

Sawbridgeworth
Adventure Island Playbarn
Parsonage Lane   Tel: (01279) 600907
A £200,000 high-quality barn conversion into an indoor children's play centre incorporating a toddler area for the under 5's, soft play, slides and much more. *Open all year, daily, 1000-1800; closed 24-26 Dec, 1 Jan. Child from £1.00. (K11)*

Shepreth
Shepreth Wildlife Park Willersmill
Station Road Tel: (01763) 262226
Wildlife Park started in 1979 for unwanted pets or road accident casualties. Fish farm also open to public. Fully fledged wildlife park with wolves, monkeys and otters. *Open all year, summer, 1000-1800; winter, 1000-dusk; closed 25 Dec. £4.50/£3.20/£3.50. (G13)*

Whitwell
Waterhall Farm and Craft Centre
Tel: (01438) 871256
An open farm featuring rare breeds and offering a 'hands-on' experience for visitors with a craft centre and tea-room. *Open all year, Sat, Sun, daily during school holidays, summer 1000-1700, winter 1000-1600. Closed 25, 26 Dec. £2.75/£1.75/£1.75. (F10)*

Countryside

Leighton Buzzard

Country Parks and Nature Reserves

Bedfordshire

Dunstable Downs
Tel: (01582) 608489
Scenic views over the vale of Aylesbury. Countryside Centre where kites, souvenirs and publications can be purchased. Site of Specific Scientific Interest. *Open at any reasonable time; countryside centre, 5 Jan-30 Mar, Sat, Sun, Bank Hols, 1000-1600; 31 Mar 1000-1800; 1 Apr-31 Oct, Tue-Sat, 1000-1700; Sun and Bank Hols, 1000-1800; 2 Nov-29 Dec, Sat, Sun, 1000-1600. (C/D10)*

◉ Lodge Nature Reserve
Sandy Tel: (01767) 680551
A reserve with mixed woodland and heathland supporting a wide variety of birds and wildlife. There are also formal gardens which are run by organic methods open to the public. (RSPB) *Nature Reserve open daily, dawn-dusk. Visitor Centre open all year, Mon-Fri, 0900-1700; Sat, Sun, 1000-1700; closed 25-26 Dec. £3.50/50p/£1.50. (F5/6)*

The Marston Vale Millennium Country Park
Marston Moretaine Tel: (01234) 767037
Country park with visitor centre. Bike hire, exhibition, café and bar, bistro, art gallery and shop. *Open summer, daily, 1000-1800, winter, daily, 1000-1600. £2.00/£1.25/£1.25. (C7)*

Priory Country Park
Bedford Tel: (01234) 211182
Over 300 acres of open space with 2 lakes and riverside. Fishing facilities, water sports, bird-watching hides, guided walks and talks. *Open at any reasonable time; visitor centre all year, daily, except Sat, opening times may vary. (D5/6)*

Sundon Hills Country Park
Sundon
Chalk downland within the Chilterns Area of Outstanding Natural Beauty, a Site of Specific Scientific Interest, adjoining the Icknield Way long distance footpath. (NT) *Open at any reasonable time. (D9)*

Hertfordshire

Aldenham Country Park
Elstree Tel: (020) 89539602
Meadow and woodland consisting of 175 acres with rare breeds farm, playgrounds, angling, nature trail and toilets. Refreshments. Site of 'Winnie the Pooh's' 100 acre wood. *Open 1 Jan-28 Feb, daily, 0900-1600; 1 Mar-30 Apr, daily, 0900-1700; 1 May-31 Aug, daily, 0900-1800; 1 Sep-31 Oct, daily, 0900-1700; 1 Nov-31 Dec, daily, 0900-1600. Closed 25 Dec. (F14)*

Ashridge Estate
Ringshall Tel: (01442) 851227
About 4500 acres of wood, heath and downs including the 700ft Ivinghoe Beacon and the Bridgewater Monument. (NT) *Estate: open at any reasonable time, Visitor Centre: 29 Mar-27 Oct, Mon-Thu, Good Fri, 1400-1700, Sat, Sun, Bank Hol Mon, 1200-1700. £1.00/50p. (C12)*

Fairlands Valley Park
Stevenage Tel: (01438) 353241
A 120-acre park with an 11-acre lake for windsurfing and sailing. The Park has a boating lake, play area, paddling pools and a wildfowl sanctuary. *Open at any reasonable time. Closed 25 Dec, 1 Jan. (G/H10)*

Bedfordshire ● *Hertfordshire*

⊛ Fowlmere
Nature Reserve RSPB
Fowlmere Tel: (01763) 208978

An 100-acre nature reserve incorporating a nature trail and 4 bird-watching hides. Attractions include unspoilt wetland scenery and birdlife including the kingfisher. (RSPB) *Open at any reasonable time. Admission £2.00/£1.00/£1.00. (J6)*

Rye Meads Nature Reserve
Site Office, Rye Meads Sewage Treatment Works, Stansted Abbotts
Tel: (01279) 793720

A nature reserve offering good views of wild birds and different marshland habitats with good paths and observation hides throughout. A common tern colony and kingfisher bank. (RSPB) *Open all year, daily, 1000-1700, or dusk, if earlier. Closed 25, 26 Dec. £2.50/£1.00/£1.00. (J12)*

Naturalists' Organisations & Other Abbreviations used in this section

⊛ RSPB: Royal Society for the Protection of Birds, HQ: The Lodge, Sandy, Beds, SG19 2DL. Tel: (01767) 680551.
East Anglia Regional Office, Stalham House, 65 Thorpe Road, Norwich NR1 1UD. Tel: (01603) 660066.

SSSI: Site of Special Scientific Interest

Fairlands Valley Park, Stevenage, Hertfordshire

Dunstable Downs, Bedfordshire

Activities & Sport

Boat Hire and Regular Excursions

Bedfordshire

⊛ Leighton Lady Cruises
Brantoms Wharf, Leighton Buzzard
Tel: (01525) 384563
www.leightonlady.freeuk.com
70 foot narrow boat. Heated passenger saloon with cushioned seats, seating up to 54. Cream teas and buffet available on request. *Phone for public trips list. (B9/10)*

Hertfordshire

⊛ Adelaide Marine
Lee Valley Boat Centre, Broxbourne
Self-Drive Hire Tel: (01992) 462085
Motorboats, day boats, rowing boats and traditional narrow boats for hire by the week or short breaks. Also three chalets; 2 for up to 6 people, 1 specifically for disabled people for up to 5. *(I/J13)*

⊛ Adventuress River Cruises
Lee Valley Boat Centre,
Old Nazeing Road, Broxbourne
Passenger Boat Hire: Tel: (01992) 466111
Passenger boats, Adventuress and Lady of Lee Valley. Self-drive hire boat, day, motor, narrow boats and rowing boats. Passenger boat public trips. *Open 1 Mar-31 Oct, daily, please contact for details of opening times and admission prices. (K11)*

Golf Courses

Hertfordshire

⊛ Whitehill Golf Centre
Dane End, Ware   Tel: (01920) 438495
Email: whitehillgolfcentre@btinternet.com
18 hole golf course plus range, shop and lounge/bar. Course open every day except 25 Dec, 0700-dusk. Open to members and non-members. *Please contact for full details of opening times for the range. (I11/12)*

Leisure Centres and Indoor Activities

Bedfordshire

⊛ Bedford Oasis Beach Pool
Cardington Road, Bedford
Tel: (01234) 272100
Fun pool with 2 giant waterslides, spa baths, toddlers' paddling area, lazy river ride, outside water lagoon, water cannon, wave machine and water mushroom. *(C/D5/6)*

Hertfordshire

⊛ Gosling Sports Park
Stanborough Road,
Welwyn Garden City
Tel: (01707) 331056
Gosling Sports Park offers a wealth of sporting facilities, housed in a 52 acre complex in the heart of Welwyn Garden City. *Please contact for details or call the brochure request line on 01707 384325. (G12)*

⊛ Lee Valley Leisure Pool
New Nazeing Road, Broxbourne
Tel: Freephone (0800) 3287758
A great family centre with a wave machine pool, learner pool, toddlers' soft play area, sports café and fitness suite, all close to public transport. It's an excellent family day out. *(I/J13)*

Specialist Holidays and Activities

Bedfordshire

⊛ Shirescapes
Walk and Discover the Shires
Tel: (01234) 326010
Escorted and self-guided walking and cycling holidays, many based on a local theme in unspoilt corners of Bedfordshire, Cambridgeshire and Hertfordshire. Leisurely short breaks offering a package of quality accommodation, meals, transport and luggage transfer. Escorted walking and cycling days available throughout the year. Brochure available. Shirescapes Holidays Ltd, P O Box 197, Bedford MK40 4ZE. *(D5/6)*

restaurants

Hertfordshire

Great Munden
The Plough
Great Munden, Near Ware, Herts
Tel: (01920) 438335
Web: www.angelfire.com/on2/theplough
Unique inn set in beautiful countryside. Home of the mighty Compton cinema organ. Free house. Good food. Organists every Friday and Saturday evenings and Sunday lunchtime. Garden at rear. Pool. Darts. Sky TV. Parties and groups welcome. Disabled facilities. Large car park and camping/caravan club site. *(111/12)*

St. Albans
Sopwell House Hotel, Country Club & Spa
Cottonmill Lane, Sopwell, St Albans AL1 2HQ
Tel: (01727) 864477 Fax: (01727) 844741
Email: enquiries@sopwellhouse.co.uk
http://www.sopwellhouse.co.uk
Sopwell House Hotel is an elegant Georgian country house set in 12 acres of countryside, yet just a short drive from London, minutes off the M1 and M25, and close to Luton Airport. With 112 en-suite bedrooms and 16 Mews Apartments, the hotel accommodates your every need. Enjoy the excellent leisure facilities which include an indoor pool, spa bath, sauna, steam rooms, health spa and fitness studios. Places to visit include: Gardens of the Rose, Hatfield House and the Cathedral City of St. Albans – all within close proximity. Come and savour our award winning 2 AA Rosette Magnolia Restaurant or informal Bejerano's Brasserie. *(F13)*

St. Albans
◉ Waffle House
Kingsbury Watermill Museum Limited
St Michaels Street, St Albans AL3 4SJ
Tel: (01727) 853502 Fax: (01727) 832662
Freshly baked, Belgian-style waffles are the star attraction in this delightfully informal venue on the outskirts of town. The menu ranges from best-seller ham and mushroom to pecan with butterscotch sauce. The kitchen cares about quality, making use of organically farmed beef, stoneground flour and free-range eggs. Situated next to a historic watermill, museum and gift shop. Eat in the rustic dining room (once the Miller's Parlour), or outside in the shade of huge parasols. *Open: Mon-Sat 10am – 6pm. Sun & Bank Holidays 11am – 6pm (5pm winter). Waffles from £1.80 to £5.75, £12.00 per head for three courses, without drinks (unlicensed). (F13)*

afternoon teas

Near Buntingford
The Old Swan Teashop
Hare Street Village (on the B1368)
Near Buntingford SG9 0DZ
Tel: (01763) 289265
A picturesque hall house dating back to 1475. Set in two acres of beautiful east Hertfordshire countryside, the teashop specialises in traditional home baking, licenced, serving breakfast, lunch, afternoon tea and early evening meals. Sunday roasts but please book. *Open 10.00am-6.00pm Thursday-Sunday and all bank holidays except Christmas. (19)*

Bedfordshire ● Hertfordshire

discovery
tours

Bloomin' Beautiful

Enjoy the spectacular colours and delicate fragrances of some of England's finest gardens.

Tour 1

Starting point: St. Albans, Herts *(F13)*
Mileage: 10m/16km
Morning - enjoy a stroll amongst the parkland and lakes of Verulamium, the site of Britain's third largest Roman city. Then take the B4630 to Chiswell Green, and the sweet-smelling *Gardens of the Rose*.
Afternoon - return to St. Albans and take the A1057 to Hatfield. Visit the 17th C. gardens of *Hatfield House*.

Tour 2

Starting point: Luton, Beds *(E10)*
Mileage: 21m/34km
Morning - explore nine centuries of gardening history at the *Stockwood Craft Museum and Gardens*.
Afternoon - take the A6 north for 10m, to visit the unusual follies at *Wrest Park Gardens*. Then return to the A6, and at the roundabout with the A507, turn right. 4m later, turn left onto the A600, then at the next roundabout, turn right onto the B658. After 4m, turn left to Old Warden and the eccentric *Swiss Garden*.

*Swiss Garden,
Old Warden, Bedfordshire*

Wings and Wheels

Transport yourself to the world of planes, trains and automobiles.

Tour 1

Starting point: Bedford, Beds *(D6)*
Mileage: 18m/29km
Morning - follow the A603 to the roundabout with the A421. Join the road to *Cardington*, and its giant airship hangers. At the T-junction, turn right to Old Warden, and the vintage planes of *The Shuttleworth Collection*.
Afternoon - turn right from the exit gate, then at the roundabout with the B658 turn right again. After 4 miles, turn left at the first roundabout on the A600, then left again at the second one. 1 1/2 miles later (at the third roundabout), turn right remaining onto the A600. 1 1/2 miles later, turn right to visit the private transport collection of the *Stondon Museum*.

Tour 2

Starting point: Luton, Beds *(E10)*
Mileage: 15m/24km
Morning - start at *The Mossman Collection*, Britain's largest collection of horse-drawn carriages. Then take the A505 to Dunstable. Follow the B489 onto the *Dunstable Downs*, to enjoy the gliders soaring overhead.
Afternoon - leave the Downs on the B489 towards Tring. At the roundabout with the A4146, turn right to Leighton Buzzard. Enjoy a ride on the *Leighton Buzzard Railway*, then end the day with a cruise along the Grand Union Canal, aboard *Leighton Lady Cruises*.

Hollywood Hertfordshire

Starting point: Borehamwood, Herts *(F/G14/15)*
Mileage: 17m/27km
Morning - explore the Borehamwood Film Walk, home to historic and present-day film/television studios. Watch out, you might spot a famous face or two!
Afternoon - take the A1 north to junction 7, passing the airfield at Hatfield, used for the vast sets of the wartime epic 'Saving Private Ryan'. End the day at Knebworth House, used as Wayne Manor in 'Batman'.

Bedfordshire ● Hertfordshire

Walk on the Wildside

Enjoy a wild adventure, on our animal safari into deepest Beds and Herts.

Starting point: Tring, Herts *(B12)*
Mileage: Walter Rothschild Zoological Museum and Whipsnade Wild Animal Park 8m/13km.
Walter Rothschild Zoological Museum and Woburn Safari Park 20m/32km.
Morning - visit the unique *Walter Rothschild Zoological Museum*, with its 4,000 species of animals and birds.
Afternoon - take the B488/B489 to the roundabout with the A4146. Two choices, either go straight ahead, remaining on the B489, then at the next roundabout, turn right onto the B4540 to *Whipsnade Wild Animal Park*. Or turn left onto the A4146 to Leighton Buzzard, then take the A4012 to *Woburn*, and its famous *Safari Park*.

Antiques, Auctions, Bids and Bargains

Explore priceless antique towns and stately homes filled with heirlooms.

Tour 1

Starting point: Bishop's Stortford, Herts *(K10)*
Mileage: 32m/51km
Morning - take the A1184 south to *Sawbridgeworth*, and lose yourself in the large antique centres. Continue on the A1184 to Harlow, where you join the A414 west to historic *Hertford*, noted for its antique shops.
Afternoon - remain on the A414/A1057 to *St. Albans*. Explore the narrow streets and lanes of this historic city, including the interesting antique and curio shops of George Street.

Tour 2

Starting point: Hitchin, Herts *(F9)*
Mileage: 22m/35km
Morning - begin in *Hitchin*, with its speciality shopping and regular antiques fairs. Then take the B655 to Barton-le-Clay, where you join the A6 north to Clophill. Turn left at the roundabout on the A507. After a short distance, visit *Ampthill*, with its quaint antique shops.
Afternoon - rejoin the A507/A4012 to *Woburn* with its antique shops, and the famous *Woburn Abbey*.

The Pilgrim Trail

In the pursuit of heavenly inspiration, follow our trail of the area's spiritual heritage.

Starting point: Bedford, Beds *(D6)*
Mileage: 30m/48km
Morning - discover Bedford's connections to the preacher/author John Bunyan (1628-88). Visit the *Bunyan Museum*, then head to nearby *Elstow* (where he grew up), and the timber-framed Moot Hall.
Afternoon - take the B530 south to Ampthill, then the A5120 to *Dunstable*. Visit the 12th C. Augustinian Priory, where Henry VIII got his divorce. End the day by taking the A5/A5183 to *St. Albans*, and the Cathedral and Abbey Church, built on the execution site of St. Alban, Britain's first Christian martyr.

Birds and Bees

Wander amongst the rich countryside and wildlife of Bedfordshire.

Starting point: Sandy, Beds *(F6)*
Mileage: 18m/29km
Morning - start the day amongst the birds at *The Lodge Reserve* (RSPB headquarters). Then take the A603 towards Bedford. In the village of Willington, turn right to Great Barford. Then at the traffic lights, turn left (over the bridge) to reach the crossroads with the A421. Go straight ahead to Wilden, and the tropical *Bedford Butterfly Park*.
Afternoon - head to the B660, and take this south to Bedford. Then take the A428 to the village of *Bromham*. Explore the working 17th C. *Bromham Mill*, set in meadows rich in bird and plant life.

RSPB Nature Reserve, Sandy, Bedfordshire

Bedfordshire ● Hertfordshire

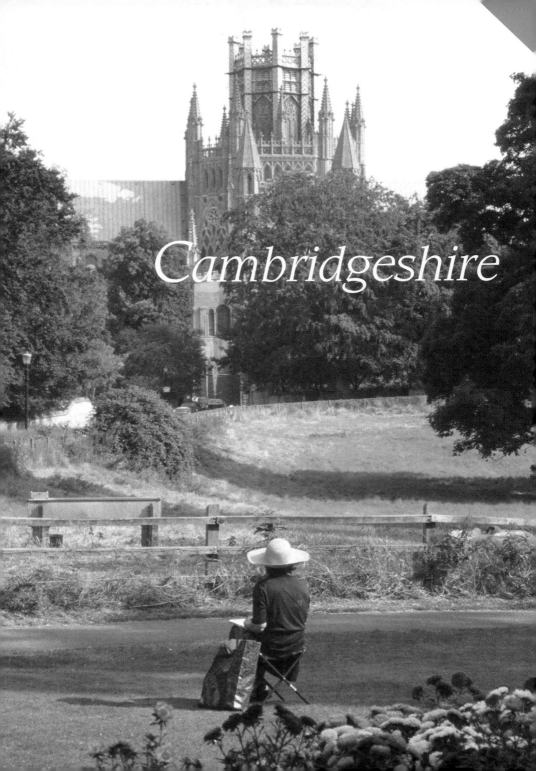

Cambridgeshire

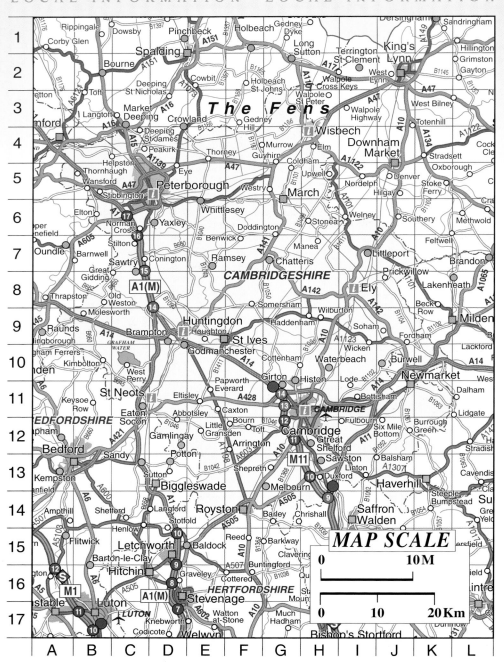

MAP SCALE

0   10M

0   10   20Km

Cambridgeshire

County Town: Cambridge
Population: 703,300 approx. (including Peterborough).
Highest Point: Great Chishill 146m (480 feet).
Rivers: Cam, Granta, Nene, New Bedford, Old Bedford, Ouse.
Landmarks: Cambridge American Cemetary, Cambridge Science Park, Ely Cathedral, The Fens, Gog Magog Hills, King's College Chapel, Peterborough Cathedral.

Industry Past and Present:

Before technology, the county flourished with the *wool* trade, and through the production of its *worsted cloth*. In the 18th C. *pillow lace, straw plaiting* and *lime-burning* were also common. To the north of the county, the village of Barnack became famous for its stone, worked from Roman times until the 18th C. *Agriculture* remains the key industry, and the 17th C. Fen drainage gave the county some of the richest soil in Britain, used to grow *cereals, root crops, fruit* and *flowers*. Associated businesses include *food processing, packaging* and *haulage*. Other traditional Fen industries include *wildfowling, peat-cutting, willow basket making* and *reed-cutting* (for thatch). Cambridge also started life as agricultural market town, but later, *academic studies* (the University), *tourism* and *scientific/hi-tech research* (Cambridge Science Park) would became the key industries. To the north, March was once home to Britain's largest *railway marshalling* yard. While Peterborough (a famous *brick making/railway centre*) has become the headquarters for many well-known companies, such as Thomas Cook (travel), Pearl Assurance and Freemans (shopping). Other famous names include - Elgood's and Son (brewing), Huntingdon Life Sciences (research), London Brick Company and Marshall's (aviation/motoring).

Famous People:

Sixty-two Nobel prize-winners, thirteen British prime ministers and nine archbishops of Canterbury are linked with Cambridge and its University. Those who attended/taught at colleges include - Rupert Brooke *(poet)*, Lord Byron *(poet)*, Prince Charles, Charles Darwin, Professor Stephen Hawking, AA Milne *(author)*, Sir Issac Newton and Samuel Pepys. Other famous names of the county include - Katherine of Aragon *(Henry VIII's first wife)*, Capability Brown *(landscape gardener)*, Thomas Clarkson *(slavery abolisher)*, St. Etheldreda *(founder of Ely)*, Oliver Cromwell *(statesman)*, Octavia Hill *(National Trust founder)*, Thomas Hobson *(carrier of 'Hobson's Choice' fame)*, John Major *(former prime minister)*, Hereward the Wake *(Saxon rebel)*.

Cambridgeshire ———————————————

Cities
towns &
Villages

MD: Market Day	
EC: Early Closing	
i	Tourist Information Centre

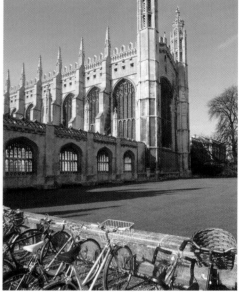

Cambridge

Cambridge *(G/H11/12)*
Famous university city, noted for its historic colleges (the first founded in 1284), complete with their courtyards and bridges across the River Cam. The crowning glory is King's College Chapel, noted for its fan-vaulted ceiling. Enjoy a walking tour of the city, or take a river trip through the watermeadows and gardens of 'The Backs', aboard the famous punts. Explore medieval churches, parks, bookshops and specialist museums. **MD**: Mon to Sat. *i*

Chatteris *(G7)*
This small town has a long main street lined with Georgian/Victorian buildings. The 14th C. church tower overlooks a square of lawns and trees. A fire in the 14th C. destroyed most of the abbey founded in 980AD. Chatteris is thought to have been the last refuge of Queen Boudicca. **MD**: Fri. **EC**: Wed.

Ely *(I8)*
One of England's most beautiful cities, dominated by its spectacular cathedral. Ely was once an island surrounded by marshes. Narrow streets and lanes are lined with historic buildings, such as the former home of Oliver Cromwell, now a visitor centre. Sweeping parkland leads to the attractive riverside area with its marina and antiques shops. **MD**: Thurs and Sat. **EC**: Tues.

Cambridgeshire

Godmanchester

Godmanchester *(D/E9/10)*
Delightful little town, separated from Huntingdon by attractive water meadows and a 13th C. bridge. Originally an important Roman settlement, it became one of England's first boroughs in 1212. Elegant 17/18th C. town houses and timber-framed cottages. The charming Island Hall and Chinese Bridge were originally built in 1827 by the architect Gallier.

Huntingdon *(D/E9)*
Historic market town, the birthplace (1599) of Oliver Cromwell. The town grew up around an important crossing of the River Great Ouse, then from the 16-18th C. prospered as a coaching stop on the Great North Road. The old stone river bridge is one of England's finest medieval bridges. Close by is the Hinchingbrooke Country Park and the National Hunt Racecourse. **MD**: Wed and Sat. 🛈

Kimbolton *(B10)*
This attractive village was once an important medieval town, with both a market and fair. Interesting alleyways and lanes. Handsome 17/18th C. buildings, displaying pan-tiled roofs and Georgian facades. The 13th C. church has a 'Tiffany' window and painted medieval screen.

Linton *(I13)*
A large village with a long, narrow High Street. Adjacent lanes contain thatched cottages and timber-framed buildings. 13/14th C. church, and early half-timbered Guildhall (16th C.). From the Middle Ages until the 1860's, this was a thriving market town. A Saxon burial ground has been found nearby.

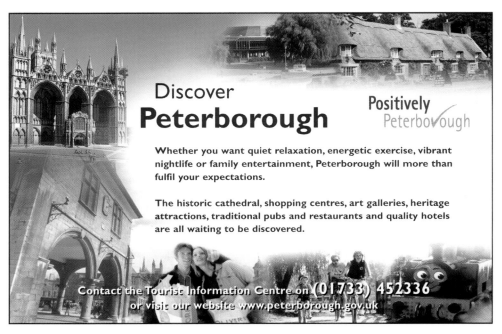
Cambridgeshire

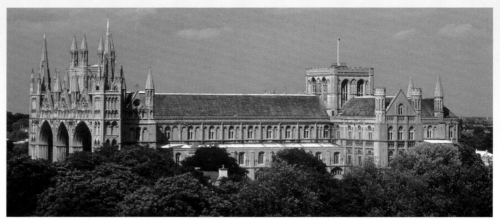

Peterborough Cathedral

Littleport *(I7)*

Before the Fens drainage, this ancient small town was an island, joined to Ely by a causeway. It has been both a coaching centre, and a busy port for barges. In 1816, the Littleport riots, saw local men violently demonstrating their anger at their low wages, and the high price of bread. **MD**: Tues. **EC**: Wed.

March *(G5/6)*

Busy market town, which originally prospered as a minor port, trading and religious centre. The 'West End' riverside area, has been likened to a Thames-style village in miniature, with its old cottages and attractive gardens. St. Wendreda's Church is noted for its outstanding timber roof, a double hammer-beam with 120 carved angels. **MD**: Wed and Sat. **EC**: Tues.

Peterborough *(C/D5/6)*

Steeped in history, Peterborough was originally founded around a Saxon monastery. It has developed into a modern city, that tastefully combines the old with the new. The historic centre is dominated by the magnificent Norman cathedral, and the excellent undercover Queensgate Shopping Centre. To the west of the city centre is the Nene Park, with its landscaped parkland and lakes, nature reserves, sporting activities and steam train rides. **MD**: Tues to Sat. *i*

Ramsey *(E7)*

This quiet market town grew up around its 10th C. abbey, founded on the edge of the Fens. In the 12/13th C. it became one of the most important in England. Ramsey later prospered from the rich agricultural land created after the Fen drainage. Remnant of 15th C. Abbey Gatehouse, and 12th C. church containing oak lectern. **MD**: Sat. **EC**: Thurs.

St Ives *(E/F9/10)*

Attractive, riverside market town. The Chapel of St. Leger is one of only four surviving bridge chapels in the country, set midstream on the 15th C. stone bridge spanning the river. On the Market Hill is the statue of Oliver Cromwell, who lived here from 1631-1636. In between here and the Riverside are 'The Lanes' a maze of little alleys.
MD: Mon (main) and Fri. **EC**: Thurs.

St Neots *(C/D11)*

Set beside the River Great Ouse, this is the largest town in the county. It grew up around a priory founded in 974AD, and takes its name from the Cornish saint whose remains were interred here. The large market square is overlooked by the 15th C. church, the 'Cathedral of Huntingdonshire'. Riverside Park offers boat trips and band concerts. **MD**: Thurs. **EC**: Tues. *i*

Soham *(J9)*

Small Fenland town, which grew up in the 7th C. beside the former 'Soham Mere'. The 12th C. church has a splendid beamed roof and tower. The Fountain Inn is noted for its 17th C. steelyard, once used for weighing wagons. 18th C. restored windmill and annual Pumpkin Fair.
MD: Fri. **EC**: Wed.

Cambridgeshire

Whittlesey *(E5/6)*
Small Fenland town, with fine examples of 17/18th C. houses and a butter cross. St. Mary's Church is noted for its beautiful mid 15th C. spire. The local hero, Sir Harry Smith, one of Wellington's generals, is commemorated by the South Chapel in the church. The town is famous for its annual 'Straw Bear Festival' (held each January).
MD: Fri. **EC**: Thurs.

Wisbech *(H3/4)*
Prosperous market town, which grew up around its port, trading from medieval times. After the Fen drainage, it became a busy agricultural centre, evident today in some of the finest Georgian street architecture in Britain (such as North Brink, The Crescent and Museum Square). The town remains at the heart of a fruit and flower growing area.
MD: Thurs and Sat. **EC**: Wed. *i*

Pick of the villages

1 **Alwalton** - conservation village with fine Norman church and pretty cottages. *(C6)*
2 **Ashley** - thatched and colour-washed houses set around a green and duck pond. *(K11)*
3 **Barnack** - once noted for its limestone quarries. Stone-built houses and 18th C. windmill. *(B4)*
4 **Barrington** - attractive village set beside one of the largest green's in England. *(G13)*
5 **Buckden** - old coaching inns, brick houses and former palace of the Bishops of Lincoln. *(D10)*
6 **Burwell** - large Fen-edge village. Splendid church with 'Flaming Heart' gravestone. *(J10)*
7 **Chippenham** - attractive estate village, set beside Lord Orford's 17th C. park. *(K10)*
8 **Elm** - tree-canopied street, with 17/18th C. houses and pastel-washed cottages. *(H4)*
9 **Elton** - fine 17th C. houses, set beside parkland of hall. River Nene with old mill. *(B6)*
10 **Emneth** - surrounded by fruit orchards. Connections to Thomas the Tank Engine. *(H4)*
11 **Eltisley** - beautifully kept green (cricket pitch) bordered by attractive houses. *(E11)*
12 **Gamlingay** - former market town, with many fine buildings, including 17th C. almshouses. *(D12)*
13 **Grantchester** - idyllic setting beside River Cam. Former home of poet Rupert Brooke. *(G12)*
14 **Helpston** - grey-stone village with 12th C. butter-cross. Memorial to 18th C. poet John Clare. *(B4)*
15 **Hemingford Abbots** - brick, timber and thatched houses cluster around a 12th C. church. *(E9)*
16 **Hemingford Grey** - beautiful riverside setting. Old cottages and 12th C. manor house. *(E9)*
17 **Houghton** - riverside village. Thatched/white-washed cottages and water mill. *(E9)*
18 **Leverington** - outstanding church, 17/18th C. houses and Elizabethan hall. *(G3)*
19 **Little Downham** - remains of former 15th C. country palace of the Bishops of Ely. *(I/J8)*
20 **Madingley** - Elizabethan mansion, post-mill and American Military Cemetery. *(G11)*
21 **Marholm** - cream-coloured and thatched houses set around a green. *(C5)*
22 **Meldreth** - 18th C. whipping post and stocks. Base of medieval cross. *(F13)*
23 **Northborough** - many fine stone and thatched cottages. 14th C. manor house. *(C4)*
24 **Prickwillow** - typical Fens village, with houses overlooked by steep river banks. *(J8)*
25 **Reach** - once the medieval port for Cambridge. Pretty green, a venue for annual fairs. *(I10)*
26 **Stilton** - named after the cheese, which was once distributed from the 17th C. Bell Inn. *(C7)*
27 **Swaffham Prior** - noted for its two churches in the same churchyard. *(I10/11)*
28 **Thorney** - remains of Norman abbey (now part of church). 19th C. houses by Duke of Bedford. *(E4)*
29 **Thriplow** - ancient settlement, with an old smithy. Annual daffodil festival. *(G13)*
30 **Wicken** - thatched houses, pond and four separate greens. Britain's oldest nature reserve. *(I9)*

Cambridgeshire

Tourist Information Centres

You will find Tourist Information Centres (TICs) throughout Cambridgeshire with plenty of information on all the things that you can do and the places you can visit. TICs can book accommodation for you in their own area, or further afield using the 'Book A Bed Ahead Scheme'. They can be the ideal place to purchase locally made crafts or gifts, as well as books covering a wide range of local interests. A list of the TICs in this area, together with a map reference can be found below.

Cambridge *(G/H11/12)*, The Old Library, Wheeler Street,
Tel: (01223) 322640
Email: tourism@cambridge.gov.uk
Web: tourismcambridge.com
Ely *(I8)*, Oliver Cromwell's House, 29 St Mary's Street,
Tel: (01353) 662062
Email: tic@eastcambs.gov.uk
Web: www.elyeastcambs.co.uk
Huntingdon *(D9)*, The Library, Princes Street,
Tel: (01480) 388588
Email: huntstic@huntsdc.gov.uk
Web: www.huntsdc.gov.uk
Peterborough *(C/D5/6)*, 3-5 Minster Precincts,
Tel: (01733) 452336
Email: tic@peterborough.gov.uk
Web: www.peterborough.gov.uk
St Neots *(C/D11)*, The Old Court, 8 New Street,
Tel: (01480) 388788
Email: stneots.tic@huntsdc.gov.uk
Web: www.huntsdc.gov.uk
Wisbech and the Fens *(H4)*, 2-3 Bridge Street,
Tel: (01945) 583263
Web: www.fenland.gov.uk

Blue Badge Guides:

There are also experts available to help you explore some of our towns and cities. These Registered Blue Badge Guides have all attended a training course sponsored by the East of England Tourist Board. To the right are some of the tours offered by

EAST OF ENGLAND TOURIST BOARD
EETB
Registered
GUIDE

these Guides - you can obtain further information by contacting the appropriate Tourist Information Centre, unless otherwise indicated. Some Blue Badge Guides have a further qualification to take individuals or groups around the region for half day, full day or longer tours if required.

Cambridge

● **Regular Walking Tours:** Individual visitors may join tours which leave the Tourist Information Centre daily except Christmas Day and up to 4 times a day in summer. Colleges are included as available.
● **City Centre Tours:** These tours do not go into the colleges, but explore the street scenes and the historic past of the city. Evening drama tours take place during mid-summer.
● **Group Tours:** Guides can be booked at any time for private groups, except Christmas Day. Tours last one or two hours, extensions are possible. One guide can escort up to 20 people. Some guides are trained to accompany groups throughout East Anglia, many speak languages other than English. For bookings and enquiries contact us: Tel: (01223) 457574 or fax (01223) 457588. E-mail: Tours@Cambridge.gov.uk Web: www.TourismCambridge.com
● **College Tours for Groups:** All parties of 10 or more who intend to tour the colleges, should be accompanied by a Cambridge registered Blue Badge Guide. Colleges which charge admission are only included on request (cost added to tour price). Most colleges are closed to the public during University examination time, mid Apr-end Jun.

Ely

● **Cathedral & City Tours and City only Tours:** Guides available for pre-booked groups by appointment. Tours can include the cathedral and city or Oliver Cromwell's House. For Cathedral tours, please contact The Chapter Office; Tel: (01353) 667735.
● **Oliver Cromwell's House: Tours and Visits:** Available for pre-booked groups. Evening tours can be arranged. Special rate for school parties and costumed guides are popular.
● **Ghost Tours and Alternative Ely Tours:** With costumed guides can be arranged direct with the guides. Please telephone (01353) 662062 for more information.

Peterborough

● **Group Tours:** Guides are available for city and cathedral tours at any time for private groups, each tour lasts approximately one and a half hours. Contact the Tourist Information Centre. Tel: (01733) 452336.

Cambridgeshire

historic houses

Arrington
⊛ **Wimpole Hall and Home Farm**
The National Trust Tel: (01223) 207257
An 18thC house in a landscaped park with a folly, Chinese bridge, plunge bath and yellow drawing room in the house, the work of John Soane. Home Farm has a rare breeds centre. *Please contact for details of opening times and admission prices. (JF12/13)*

Elton
⊛ **Elton Hall**
Tel: (01832) 280468
An historic house and gardens open to the public with a fine collection of paintings, furniture, books and Henry VIII's prayer book. There is also a restored rose garden. *Open 3, 4 Jun, Bank Hols, 1400-1700; 5-26 Jun, Wed, 1400-1700; 3 Jul-29 Aug, Wed, Thu, Sun, Bank Hol Mon, 1400-1700. 26 Aug, Bank Hol Mon, 1400-1700. House and garden £5.00. Garden £3.00 (B6)*

Ely
⊛ **Oliver Cromwell's House** Ⓠ
29 St Marys Street Tel: (01353) 662062
The family home of Oliver Cromwell with a 17thC kitchen, parlour, a haunted bedroom, a Tourist Information Centre, souvenirs and a craft shop. *Please contact for details of opening times and admission prices. (I8)*

Godmanchester
⊛ **Island Hall**
Tel: (020) 7491 3724
A mid-18thC mansion of architectural importance on the Great Ouse river. A family home with interesting ancestral possessions. *Please contact for details of opening times. £3.50. (D/E9/10)*

Peckover House, Wisbech

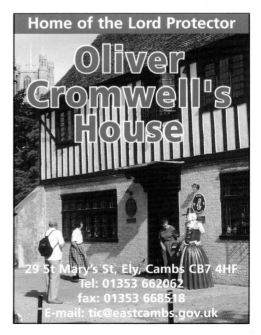
Cambridgeshire

Hemingford Grey
The Manor
Tel: (01480) 463134

The 'Green Knowe' children's book were based on this ancient house. Also see the Lucy Boston patchworks. Garden is 4.5 acres with topiary. Appointment only. *Garden open all year, daily, 1000-1800, dusk in winter. House open by appointment only. House and Garden £4.00/£1.50/£3.50. Garden £2.00/50p. (E9/10)*

Kimbolton
Kimbolton Castle
Tel: (01480) 860505

A Tudor house, remodelled by Vanburgh with Pelligrini mural paintings, an Adam gatehouse and fine parklands. The castle is now occupied by an independent school. *Open 31 Mar, 1 Apr, Sun, Bank Hol Mon, 25, 26 Aug, Sun, Bank Hol Mon, 1400-1700. £3.00/£2.00. (B10)*

Lode
⊛ Anglesey Abbey
Gardens and Lode Mill
Tel: (01223) 811200

A 13thC abbey with a later Tudor house and the famous Fairhaven collection of paintings and furniture. There is also an outstanding 100-acre garden and arboretum. *Please contact for details of opening times and admission prices. (I11)*

Wisbech
⊛ Peckover House and Gardens
North Brink Tel: (01945) 583463

A merchant's house on the north brink of the River Nene, built in 1722 with a plaster and wood rococo interior and a notable and rare Victorian garden with unusual trees. *Please contact for details of opening times and admission prices. (H3/4)*

Wimpole Hall, Arrington

Take time out to visit our website
www.eastofenglandtouristboard.com

... and discover some great deals on short breaks and holidays, as well as information on places to visit and events taking place throughout this picturesque corner of England.

Cambridgeshire

Ancient *Monuments*

Fengate
⊛ Flag Fen Bronze Age Excavations
Fourth Drove Tel: (01733) 313414
Visitor Centre with landscaped park, ongoing archaeological excavation, rare breed animals, roundhouses and museum of the bronze age. *Open all year, daily, 1000-1700; guided tours 10 Apr-31 Oct; closed 25 Dec-2 Jan. Please contact for details of admission prices. (C/D5/6)*

Isleham
⊛ Isleham Priory Church
A rare example of an early Norman church with much herringbone masonry. It has been little altered despite later conversion to a barn. *Open at any reasonable time.*

Longthorpe
⊛ Longthorpe Tower
Thorpe Road Tel: (01733) 268482
The 14thC tower of a fortified manor-house with wall paintings which form the most complete set of domestic paintings of the period in northern Europe. *Open 6 Apr-27 Oct, Sat, Sun, Bank Hols, 1200-1700. £1.60/80p/£1.20. (C5)*

Cambridge
Kings College Chapel
Kings College
Tel: (01223) 331212
The chapel, founded by Henry VI includes the breathtaking fan-vault ceiling, stained glass windows, a carved oak screen and Ruben's masterpiece 'The Adoration of the Magi'. *Please contact for details of opening times. £3.60/£2.50/£2.50. (G/H11/12)*

Chittering
⊛ Denny Abbey
Ely Road
Tel: (01223) 860489
The remains of a 12thC Benedictine abbey and a 14thC dining hall of a religious house. It was run as a hospital by the Knights Templar and became a Franciscan Convent in 1342. *Open 1 Apr-31 Oct, daily, 1200-1700. £3.50/£1.30/£2.50. (H9)*

Coton
Cambridge American Cemetary
Tel: (01954) 210350
A cemetary with a visitor reception for information, the graves area and a memorial chapel, operated and maintained by the American Battle Monuments Commission. *Open 1 Jan-15 Apr, daily, 0800-1700; 16 Apr-30 Sep, daily, 0800-1800; 1 Oct-31 Dec, daily, 0800-1700. (G11)*

Ely
⊛ Ely Cathedral
Chapter House, The College
Tel: (01353) 667735
One of England's finest cathedrals with guided tours and tours of the Octagon and West Tower, monastic precincts and also a brass rubbing centre and stained glass museum. *Open 1 Jan-31 Mar, Mon-Sat, 0730-1800, Sun, 0730-1700; 1 Apr-31 Oct, daily, 0700-1900; 1 Nov-31 Dec, Mon-Sat, 0730-1800, Sun, 0730-1700. £4.00/free/£3.50. (I8)*

Ely Cathedral, Ely

Thorney
Thorney Abbey Church
Tel: (01733) 270388
Abbey church with a Norman nave (c1100), a fine church organ originally built in 1787-1790 and a stained glass east window depicting the miracles of St Thomas Becket. *Open all year, daily, 1000-dusk. (E4/5)*

Walpole St Peter
Walpole Saint Peters Church
Church Road, Wisbech
Tel: (01945) 780252
A masterpiece of 14thC architecture. *Open all year, daily, 0930-1700. (H3/4)*

Whittlesford
 Duxford Chapel
A 14thC chapel which was once part of the Hospital of St John. *Open daily till dusk. (L25)*

DID YOU KNOW

The Imperial War Museum at Duxford is home to the largest collection of military and civil aircraft in Britain.

March
Saint Wendreda's Church
Church Street Tel: (01354) 654783
This church is noted for its exceptional double hammerbeam timber roof which contains 120 carved angels. *Open all year, daily, 1000-1600; key obtainable at nearby Stars public house which is signed on the church notice board. (G5/6)*

Peterborough
⊛ **Peterborough Cathedral**
Minster Precincts Tel: (01733) 343342
A Norman cathedral with an early English west front, a 13thC painted nave ceiling and the tomb of Catherine of Aragon. It was also the former burial place of Mary Queen of Scots. *Open all year, Mon-Sat, 0830-1715; Sun, 1200-1745, closed 26 Dec. (C/D5/6)*

Ramsey
Ramsey Abbey Gatehouse
Abbey School
Tel: (01263) 738000
The ruins of a 15thC gatehouse. *Open 1 Apr-31 Oct, daily, 1000-1700. (E7)*

museums, heritage & Craft Centres

Decanter from Fitzwilliam Museum, Cambridge

Bourn
Wysing Arts
Fox Road
Tel: (01954) 718881
Art centre and gallery exhibiting contemporary art. Continuous programme of courses for adults and children. Eleven acre site open all year round. *Open daily, 0930-1730. Please contact for opening times for Easter and Christmas. (F12)*

Burwell
Burwell Museum Trust
Mill Close Tel: (01638) 605544
A rural village museum housed in a re-erected 18thC timber-framed barn. Also war memorablia, forge, wagons and carts. Displays of village shop and old school room. *Please contact for details of opening times and admission prices. (J10)*

Cambridge
Broughton House Gallery
98 King Street Tel: (01223) 314960
Monthly art exhibitions, paintings, drawings, prints and sculpture by living artists. In an 18thC house with garden. *Open 12 Mar-21 Dec, Tue-Sat, 1030-1730. Closed 29 Mar-1 Apr. (G/H11/12)*

Burwell Museum, Burwell

Cambridge
Cambridge and County Folk Museum
2-3 Castle Street Tel: (01223) 355159
A part timber-framed 17thC inn, retaining many original fittings. Established as a museum of Cambridgeshire life in 1936. Strong collections. *Open 2 Jan-31 Mar, Tue-Sat, 1030-1700; Sun, 1400-1700; 1 Apr-30 Sep, Mon-Sat, 1030-1700; Sun, 1400-1700; 2 Oct-22 Dec, Tue-Sat, 1030-1700; Sun, 1400-1700; closed 29 Mar, 23 Dec-2 Jan. £2.50/75p/£1.50. (G/H11/12)*

Cambridge
Cambridge Contemporary Art
6 Trinity Street Tel: (01223) 324222
Changing exhibitions highlight paintings, sculpture, hand-made prints, textiles, crafts and furniture. With work by acknowledged masters and established artists. *Open all year, Mon-Sat, 0900-1730. Closed 29 Mar, 1, 31 Apr, 24-26 Dec, 1 Jan. (G/H11/12)*

Cambridge
⊛ **Fitzwilliam Museum**
Trumpington Street Tel: (01223) 332900
A large, internationally-renowned collection of antiquities, applied and fine arts. The original buildings are mid-19thC with later additions. *Open all year, Tue, 1000-1700, Wed, 1000-1900, Thu, Fri, 1000-1700, Sat, Sun, 1200-1700. Closed 16 Dec-4 Jan. (G/H11/12)*

Cambridgeshire

Flag Fen Bronze Age Excavations, Fengate

Cambridge
Kettle's Yard

Castle Street Tel: (01223) 352124
A major collection of 20thC paintings and sculpture exhibited in a house of unique character. Also changing contemporary art exhibitions in the gallery. *Please contact for details of opening times. (G/H11/12)*

Cambridge
Sedgwick Museum

Department of Earth Sciences,
Downing Street
Tel: (01223) 333456
A large collection of fossils from all over the world, both invertebrate and vertebrate with some mounted skeletons of dinosaurs, reptiles and mammals. *Open all year, Mon-Fri, 0900-1300, 1400-1700, Sat, 1000-1300. Closed Easter (29 Mar-1 Apr). Please phone to confirm Christmas closure. (G/H 11/12)*

Cambridge
University Museum of Archaeology and Anthropology

Downing Street Tel: (01223) 333516
Displays relating to world prehistory and local archaeology with anthropology displays, opened in July 1990. *Open 2 Jan-28 Mar, Tue-Sat, 1400-1630; 2 Apr-8 Jun, Tue-Sat, 1400-1630; 11 Jun-10 Sep, Tue-Sat, 1030-1630. (G/H11/12)*

Cambridge
Whipple Museum of the History of Science

Free School Lane Tel: (01223) 334545
Recently designated as a museum with a pre-eminent collection. The Whipple Museum houses an extensive collection of scientific instruments and related ephemera. *Open all year, Mon-Fri, 1330-1630, closed Bank Hols; please telephone to confirm during university vacations. (G/H11/12)*

Ely
Babylon Gallery

Waterside
Tel: (01353) 669022
The Babylon Gallery offers a mixture of national touring exhibitions and high quality curated exhibitions of work by local and regional artists. *Open 11 Jan-23 Dec, Tue-Sat, 1000-1600; Sun, Bank Hol Mon, 1100-1700. (I8)*

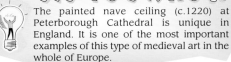

The painted nave ceiling (c.1220) at Peterborough Cathedral is unique in England. It is one of the most important examples of this type of medieval art in the whole of Europe.

Cambridgeshire

Ely
Ely Museum
The Old Gaol, Market Street
Tel: (01353) 666655
A chronological account of the history of Ely and the Isle from prehistory to the present day. The collections consist of archaeology, social and military history. *Please contact for details of opening times and admission prices. (18)*

Ely
Stained Glass Museum
The Cathedral   Tel: (01353) 660347
A museum housing examples of stained glass from the 13thC to the present day in specially lighted display boxes with models of a modern workshop. *Please contact for details of opening times. £3.50/£2.50. (18)*

Eynesbury St Neots
◉ St Neots Picture Gallery
23 St Marys Street
Tel: (01480) 215291
Watercolours, pastels and photographs of St Neots and surrounding area. Comprehensive range of artists materials, hand-made studio pottery and greeting cards. *Open all year, Tue-Sat, 0900-1730. (C/D11)*

Oliver Cromwell, Cromwell Museum, Huntingdon

Fengate
◉ Flag Fen Bronze Age Excavations
See Ancient Monuments Section.

Huntingdon
Blacked-Out Britain War Museum
1 St Marys Street   Tel: (01480) 450998
Blacked-Out Britain War Museum has everyday items of life from 1939-45. From evacuation to rationing, bus tickets to bombs. Capture the feel of what life was like. *Open all year, Mon-Sat, 0900-1700; Sun, 1000-1400. Please contact to confirm Bank Hol opening. (D/E9)*

Huntingdon
Cromwell Museum
Grammar School Walk   Tel: (01480) 375830
A museum with portraits, signed documents and other articles belonging to Cromwell and his family. *Please contact for details of opening times. (D/E9)*

March
March and District Museum
High Street   Tel: (01354) 655300
A general collection of artefacts relating to social history, agricultural tools, many local photographs and 19thC record material and a restored blacksmith's forge. *Open all year, Wed, 1000-1200; Sat, 1030-1530; 2 Jun, 7 Jul, 4 Aug, 1 Sep, Sun, 1430-1700; closed 21 Dec-5 Jan. (G5/6)*

Peterborough
**◉ Peterborough Museum
and Art Gallery**
Priestgate Tel: (01733) 343329
Museum of local history, geology, archaeology, natural and social history, a world-famous collection of Napoleonic POW work, a period shop and many temporary exhibitions. *Open all year, Tue-Sat, 1000-1700; Sun, 1200-1600, closed 25, 26, Dec, 1 Jan. (D/E9)*

Ramsey
Ramsey Rural Museum
The Wood Yard, Cemetary Road
Tel: (01487) 815715
Rebuilt farm buildings housing a collection of old farm implements of the Fens and Victorian life in the home and now including a chemist's and a cobbler's shop. *Open 4 Apr-29 Sep, Thu, Sun, 1400-1700. £1.00/50p/50p. (E7)*

Cambridgeshire

St Ives
Norris Museum
The Broadway Tel: (01480) 497314
Museum displaying the history of Huntingdon from earliest times to the present day with fossils, archaeology, history, an art gallery and library. *Please contact for details of opening times. (E/F9/10)*

St Neots
Saint Neots Museum
The Old Court, 8 New Street
Tel: (01480) 388788
A former police station and Magistrates' Court, now housing the local history museum. *Open all year, Tue-Sat, 1030-1630. Please phone to confirm. Closed 24-26 Dec. £1.50/75p/75p. (C/D11)*

Thorney
Thorney Heritage Museum
Station Road Tel: (01733) 270780
Showing the development from monastic days, Walloon and Flemish influence after Vermuydens drainage; also 19thC model housing by the Duke of Bedford. *Open 30 Mar-29 Sep, Sat, Sun, 1400-1700. (E4/5)*

Walpole St Peter
⊛ Walpole Water Garden
See entry in Gardens section.

Waterbeach
Farmland Museum
Denny Abbey, Ely Road
Tel: (01223) 860988
An agricultural estate since medieval times with an abbey and an interactive museum. Lots of fun for families with animal, medieval and craft events throughout the year. *Open 1 Apr-31 Oct, daily, 1200-1700. £3.50/£1.30/£2.50. (H10)*

Whittlesey
Whittlesey Museum
Town Hall, Market Street
Tel: (01733) 840986
Museum of archaeology, agriculture, hand tools, brickmaking, local photographs, a Sir Harry Smith exhibition, costume display and temporary exhibitions. *Open all year, Fri, Sun, 1430-1630; Sat, 1000-1200. 50p/20p. (E5/6)*

Wisbech
⊛ Elgood's Brewery and Garden
North Brink Brewery Tel: (01945) 583160
Independent family brewery established in 1795. Visitors can watch traditional methods of brewing and sample a range of real ales. A 4-acre garden contains many features and maze. *Open 1 May-29 Sep, Wed, Fri, Sun, Bank Hol Mons, 1300-1700; Brewery Tours, Wed-Fri, 1400. Please contact for details of admission and tour prices. (H3/4)*

Wisbech
Octavia Hill Birthplace Museum
1 South Brink Place Tel: (01945) 476358
A museum in the Grade II Georgian building in which Octavia Hill, social reformer and co-founder of the National Trust, was born, commemorating her life, work and legacy. *Open 20 Mar-30 Oct, Wed, Sat, Sun, Bank Hol Mon, 1400-1730; last admission 1700, closed 25, 26 Dec. £2.00. (H3/4)*

Wisbech
Skylark Studios
Hannath Road, Tydd Gote
Tel: (01945) 420403
An art gallery showing monthly exhibitions by local and national artists along with a permanent display of art and crafts. *Open 5 Jan-21 Dec; Tue-Fri, 1000-1700; Sat, 1100-1700. (H3/4)*

Wisbech
Wisbech and Fenland Museum
Museum Square Tel: (01945) 583817
One of the oldest purpose-built museums in the country, situated next to Wisbech's fine Georgian crescent. Displays on Fen landscape, local history, geology and archaeology. *Open 8 Jan-30 Mar, Tue-Sat, 1000-1600; 2 Apr-28 Sep, Tue-Sat, 1000-1700; 1 Oct-21 Dec, Tue-Sat, 1000-1600. Please telephone for Easter openings. (H3/4)*

Fitzwilliam Museum, Cambridge

Cambridgeshire

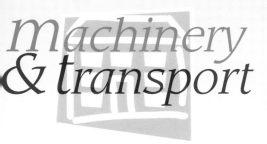

Imperial War Museum, Duxford

Burwell
Burwell Museum Trust
See entry in Museums section.

Cambridge
Museum of Technology
The Old Pumping Station,
Cheddars Lane
Tel: (01223) 368650

A Victorian pumping station housing unique Hawthorn Davey steam pumping engines, electrical equipment and a working letterpress print shop. Hands-on pumps. *Please contact for details of opening times. £2.00/£1.00/£1.50. (G/H11/12)*

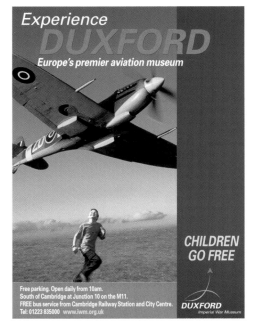

Duxford
◎ **Imperial War Museum** Q
Tel: (01223) 835000

Over 180 aircraft on display with tanks, vehicles and guns, an adventure playground, shops and a restaurant. *Please contact for details of opening times and admission prices. (H13)*

Peterborough
◎ **Railworld**
Oundle Road Tel: (01733) 344240

Railworld highlights modern trains and transport environmental connections. Model railway, steam age exhibits and flowerbeds. *Open 3 Jan-28 Feb, Mon-Fri, 1100-1600; 1 Mar-31 Oct, daily, 1100-1600; 1 Nov-20 Dec, Mon-Fri, 1100-1600. Closed 29 Mar. £2.50/£1.50/£2.00. (C/D5/6)*

Prickwillow
Prickwillow Engine Museum
Main Street
Tel: (01353) 688360

A museum housing a Mirrlees Bickerton and Day diesel engine, a 5-cylinder, blast injection, 250 bhp working unit and a Vicker-Petter, 2-cylinder, 2-stroke diesel and others. *Please contact for details of opening times. £2.00/£1.00/£1.50. (J8)*

Stibbington
◎ **Nene Valley Railway**
Wansford Station Tel: (01780) 784444

A 7.5-mile track between Wansford and Peterborough via Yarwell Mill and Nene Park with over 28 steam and diesel locomotives. Regular steam trains operate over the line. *Open all year, daily, 0930-1630; closed 25 Dec; please phone for train services. £2.00/£1.00. (B5)*

Cambridgeshire

mills

Bourn
Bourn Windmill
Caxton Road
A pre-civil war postmill, restored in the 1980s and receiving a Civic Trust commendation and Europa Nostra diploma. _Open 24 Mar, 28 Apr, 26 May, 23 Jun, 28 Jul, 25 Aug, 29 Sep, Sun, National Mills Day, 1400-1700. £1.00/25p/£1.00. (F12)_

DID YOU KNOW

Wicken Fen is Britain's oldest nature reserve (started in 1899), and is the last remaining un-drained portion of the great Fen levels of East Anglia.

Houghton Mill

Houghton
® **Houghton Mill**
Tel: (01480) 301494
A large timber-built watermill on an island in the River Ouse with much of the 19thC mill machinery intact and some restored to working order. _Open 30 Mar-25 May, Sat, Sun, Bank Hol Mon, 1400-1730; 26 May-25 Sep, Sat-Wed, 1400-1730; 28 Sep-27 Oct, Sat, Sun, 1400-1730; 29-31 Oct, Tues-Thur, 1400-1730. £3.00/£1.50. (E9)_

Soham
Downfield Windmill
Fordham Road Tel: (01353) 720333
A working windmill, dating back to 1726. Flour is produced for sale to visitors and local shops. _Open all year, Sun, Bank Hol Mon, 1100-1700. Closed 25 Dec. 70p/30p. (J9)_

Downfield Windmill, Soham

Cambridgeshire

gardens & Vineyards

Elton Hall

Arrington
❀ Wimpole Hall and Home Farm
See entry in Historic Houses section.

Elton
❀ Elton Hall
See entry in Historic Houses section.

Linton
❀ Chilford Hall Vineyard
Chilford Hundred Limited,
Balsham Road Tel: (01223) 895600
A winery housed in interesting old buildings with a collection of sculptures on view. There is a vineyard, cafe and shop. *Open 1 Mar-30 Oct, daily, 1100-1730, 1 Nov-24 Dec, daily, 1100-1630. £4.50. (I13)*

Lode
❀ Anglesey Abbey
Gardens and Lode Mill
See entry in Historic Houses section.

Shepreth
Docwra's Manor Garden
2 Meldreth Road Tel: (01763) 261473
Walled gardens round an 18thC red-brick house approached by 18thC wrought iron gates. There are barns, a 20thC folly, unusual plants. *Open all year, Wed, Fri, 1000-1600; 7 Apr, 5 May, 2 Jun, 7 Jul, 4 Aug, 1 Sep, 6 Oct, Sun 1400-1700. Closed 25 Dec. £3.00/free/£3.00. (G13)*

Walpole St Peter
❀ Walpole Water Gardens
Chalk Road Tel: 07718 745935
Gallery, tearoom, water gardens, koi carp, black swans, ducks, peacocks and small feature garden. Garden is wheelchair friendly and features eucalyptus, rockeries and palms. *Please contact for details of opening times and prices. (H3)*

Wilburton
Herb Garden
Nigel House, High Street
Tel: (01353) 740824
A herb garden laid out in collections: culinary, aromatic, medical, biblical, Shakespearean, dye bed and astrological. *Open 1 May-30 Sep, daily. Please phone to confirm (H9)*

Wisbech
❀ Peckover House and Gardens
See entry in Historic Houses section.

Anglesey Abbey, Lode

nurseries
& garden Centres

Orton Waterville
Notcutts Garden Centres
Oundle Road, Orton Waterville, Peterborough
Tel: (01733) 234600

Discover a world of ideas and inspiration around every corner for you, your home and your garden. From fabulous plants to gifts and treats galore, there's so much to see. Gift ideas from around the world, houseplants, books, fresh cut & silk flowers, 3,000 varieties of hardy plants (with a 2 year replacement guarantee), pet centre, restaurant, expert friendly advice about seasonal and bedding plants, garden furniture and barbecues. Keep an eye open for regular offers on key garden products. *Notcutts open 7 days a week, free car-parking plus children's play area. (C6)*

DID YOU KNOW

The Fens is an area that has been drained over the centuries to provide probably the best growing soil in Britain. Its rich dark peak/silt soils are excellent for growing crops, fruit, vegetables and flowers.

Benwick

Cambridgeshire

Godmanchester
⊛ Wood Green Animal Shelters
King's Bush Farm, London Road
Tel: (01480) 830014

Europe's most progressive shelter for unwanted animals, including farm animals, cats, dogs and small animals. Some permanent residents, others awaiting caring new homes. *Open all year, daily, 0900-1500. Closed 25, 26 Dec. (D/E9/10)*

Linton
Linton Zoo
Hadstock Road   Tel: (01223) 891308

The zoo has big cats, lynx, wallabies, llamas, toucans, parrots and reptiles, a wonderful combination of beautiful gardens and wildlife. *Open all year, daily, 1000-1800/dusk; closed 25 Dec. £5.50/£4.50/£5.00. (I13)*

River Cam, Cambridge

Peakirk
Peakirk Waterfowl Gardens Trust
Deeping Road Tel: (01733) 252271

Some 137 species of duck, geese and swans in 20 acres of water gardens with a refreshment room, a shop and a children's play area. *Open all year, daily, summer 0930-1730, last admission 1630; winter 0930-dusk, last admission 1400. Closed 24, 25 Dec. £3.50/£1.75/£2.50. (C4)*

Peterborough
Activity World
Padholme Road Tel: (01733) 314446

An indoor and outdoor adventure playground plus, The Laser Maze. *Open all year, daily, 0930-1830; closed 25, 26 Dec. Please contact for details of admission prices. (C/D5/6)*

Sawtry
Hamerton Zoo Park
Tel: (01832) 293362

A wildlife park with tigers, lemurs, marmosets, meerkats, wallabies and a unique bird collection with rare and exotic species from around the world. *Open 1 Jan-26 Mar, daily, 1030-1600; 27 Mar-25 Oct, daily, 1030-1800; 26 Oct-31 Dec, daily, 1030-1600; last admission 1 hour before closing. Closed 25 Dec. Please contact for details of admission prices. (B/C8)*

Cambridgeshire ——————————————————————

Linton Zoo, Linton

Thornhaugh
❧ **Sacrewell Farm and Country Centre**
Sacrewell Tel: (01780) 782254

A 500-acre farm with a working watermill, farmhouse gardens, shrubberies, farm, nature and general interest trails, 18thC buildings, displays of the farm and bygones. *Open all year, daily, 0930-1700; closed 25 Dec-4 Jan. £3.00/£1.50. (B5)*

Woodhurst
❧ **The Raptor Foundation**
The Heath, St Ives Road
Tel: (01487) 741140

A collection of injured birds of prey and wild birds. Hand-reared owls used for fund raising for the hospital. Tearoom, gift shop, craft village and falconry flying area. *Open all year, daily, 1030-1700. £2.50/£1.50. (E9)*

Woodston
Big Sky Adventure Play
24 Wainman Road, Shrewsbury Avenue
Tel: (01733) 390810

An indoor children's soft play activities centre with electric mini go-karts and a monorail rocket ship ride. *Open all year, daily, Mon-Fri, 0930-1800; Sat, Sun and school hols, 1030-1800; closed 25, 26 Dec, 1 Jan. Please contact for details of admission prices. (C/D5/6)*

DID YOU KNOW

Etton was the former home of Mary and Tom Bean, the longest living twins in Britain (101 years).

Countryside

Grafham Water

Country Parks and Nature Reserves

⊛ Fowlmere Nature Reserve RSPB
Manor Farm, High Street, Fowlmere
Tel: (01763) 208978

An 100-acre nature reserve incorporating a nature trail and 4 bird-watching hides. Attractions include unspoilt wetland scenery and birdlife including the kingfisher. (RSPB) *Open at any reasonable time. £2.00/£1.00/£1.00. (G13)*

⊛ Grafham Water
Tel: (01480) 812154

Water park with extensive views, sailing, trout fishing, nature reserve, trails and walks, picnic areas, play areas and refreshments and gift shop. *Open 5 Jan-24 Mar, Sat, Sun, 1100-1600; 25 Mar-1 Nov, Mon-Fri, 1100-1600; Sat, Sun, 1100-1600; Bank Hol Mon, 1100-1700, 2 Nov-15 Dec, Sat, Sun, 1100-1600. Car park charges. (C10)*

Ferry Meadows, Peterborough

Cambridgeshire

Wandlebury Country Park and Nature Reserve
Tel: (01223) 243830

An Iron Age ring ditch, woodlands, footpaths, walks, wildlife and public footpaths to a Roman road and picnic areas. *Open all year, daily, dawn-dusk. Donations requested. (H12)*

⊛ Wicken Fen
National Nature Reserve
Tel: (01353) 720274

The last remaining undrained portion of the great Fen levels of East Anglia, rich in plant and invertebrate life and good for birds. Also a working windpump and restored Fen cottage. (NT) *Open all year, daily except Mon unless Bank Hol Mon, 1000-1700. Closed 25 Dec. £3.80/£1.20/£3.80. (19/10)*

⊛ Wildfowl and Wetlands Trust
Hundred Foot Bank, Welney
Tel: (01353) 860711

A wetland nature reserve of 1000 acres attracting large numbers of ducks and swans in winter, waders in spring and summer plus a range of wild plants and butterflies. *Open all year, daily 1000-1700; closed 25 Dec. Admission £3.50/£2.00/£2.75. (I6)*

Naturalists' Organisations & Other Abbreviations used in this section

CWT: The Wildlife Trust for Cambridgeshire, 3b Langford Arch, London Road, Sawston, Cambridge CB4 4EE. Tel: (01223) 712400.

⊛ NT: The National Trust, Blickling, Norwich, Norfolk NR11 6NF. Tel: (01263) 738030.

⊛ RSPB: Royal Society for the Protection of Birds, HQ: The Lodge, Sandy, Beds, SG19 2DL. Tel: (01767) 680551. East Anglia Regional Office, Stalham House, 65 Thorpe Road, Norwich NR1 1UD. Tel: (01603) 660066.

SSSI: Site of Special Scientific Interest

DID YOU KNOW

Grafham Water is the third largest man-made reservoir in Britain. Constructed in the 1960's, it covers 2 1/2 square miles, and holds 59,000 million litres of water.

Wicken Fen

Cambridgeshire

Activities & Sport

Boat Hire and Regular Excursions

⊛ Fox Boats
10 Marina Drive, March
Tel: (01354) 652770
7 narrow boats, short break/weekly hire. 28.5 miles of Fenland Waterway, stretching from the River Nene, to the River Ouse, which offers possible cruises to nearby Ely, Bedford, Cambridge, Peterborough, Oundle and Northampton. *(G5/6)*

Golf Courses

⊛ Old Nene Golf and Country Club Ltd
Muchwood Lane, Bodsey, Ramsey
Tel: (01487) 815622/813519
Quality Golf Course, 9 holes, 18 tees, floodlit driving range, fishing and fully licensed bar. *(E7)*

⊛ On Par Golf Driving Range
'On Par' Golf Driving Range, Downham Road, Ely
Tel: (01353) 669192 or 07801 293949
9 Hole 'Par 30' golf course and putting green (open Autumn 2002). Pay and display £5pp. Families and children welcome. Full pro shop and hire facilities on site. 16 bay floodlit driving range. Café. *Open seven days a week Mon-Fri & Sunday from 10.30-21.00 and Saturday 10.30-19.00. (I8)*

⊛ Orton Meadows Golf Course
Ham Lane, Orton Waterville,
Peterborough. PE2 5UU
Tel (01733) 237478
www.ortonmeadowsgolfcourse.co.uk
18 Holes. 5613 Yards Par 67. Top pay as you play course with lakes and streams in picturesque setting surrounded by trees and a popular 12-hole pitch and putt course. *Booking necessary. Club/Trolley hire available. (C6)*

⊛ St. Neots Golf Club
Crosshall Road, St Neots PE19 7GE
Tel: (01480) 472363/476513
Oldest Cambridgeshire club boasting attractive parkland course. Visitors welcome mid-week - booking required. Bar, restaurant and Pro Shop. 18 holes, 6033 yards, Par 69. Two for one. Handicap certificate required. *(C/D11)*

⊛ Thorpe Wood Golf Course
Thorpe Wood, Peterborough PE3 6SE
Tel: (01733) 267701   Fax: (01733) 332774
E-mail: enquiries@thorpewoodgolfcourse.co.uk
www.thorpewoodgolfcourse.co.uk
Top UK pay as you play course (Fore! Magazine) in undulating parkland maintained in superb condition. Always open whatever the weather. *Booking necessary. Club/Trolley hire available. (C/D5/6)*

Outdoor Activities

⊛ Grafham Water Centre
Perry, Huntingdon
Tel: (01480) 810521
Sailing, windsurfing, mountain biking, canoeing, kayaking, archery, ropes courses and orienteering. *Brochures available for a range of courses and holidays for adults and young people. (C10)*

Cambridgeshire —————————————

restaurants

Cambridge
Cambridge Garden House Moat House
Granta Place, Mill Lane,
Cambridge CB2 1RT
Tel: (01223) 259988

Nestled on the Banks of the River Cam in the heart of this historic and beautiful city, the Cambridge Garden House Riverside Brasserie offers both lunch and dinner with a stunning menu to complement the stunning surroundings. For a lighter option the Terrace Bar is open all day for snacks or a relaxing drink. For those staying longer in our beautiful city we offer 121en suite bedrooms, many with views of the floodlit garden and river beyond. Membership to Club Moativation leisure centre with indoor pool, sauna, jacuzzi and much more is included in your overnight stay. *(G/H11/12)*

Cambridge
⊛ Arundel House Hotel
Chesterton Road, Cambridge CB4 3AN
Tel: (01223) 367701 Fax: (01223) 367721
Website: www.arundelhousehotels.co.uk
Email: info@arundelhousehotels.co.uk

Elegant, privately owned, 105 bedroom 19th century Victorian terrace hotel beautifully located overlooking the River Cam and open parkland, only a few minutes walk from the historic city centre and famous University colleges. The hotel is well known for its friendly relaxed atmosphere and has a reputation for providing some of the best food in the area, at very modest prices, in its award winning restaurant. The hotel's magnificent Victorian style conservatory, which overlooks an attractive walled garden adjacent to the bar, offers an alternative menu throughout the day, including cream teas with additional seating outside. The hotel facilities also include a large car park. *(G/H11/12)*

Cambridge

DID YOU KNOW
King's College Chapel in Cambridge has the largest fan vaulted ceiling in the world, weighing about 1,875 tons, whilst the Old Cavendish Laboratory on Free School Lane is where the atom was spilt for the first time in 1932, and DNA discovered in the 1950's.

Cambridge
Midsummer House Restaurant
Midsummer Common, Cambridge
Tel: (01223) 369299 Fax: (01223) 302672
Email: reservations@midsummerhouse.co.uk
Website: wwwmidsummerhouse.co.uk
Midsummer House is set in an idyllic location on the banks of the River Cam. This Victorian house, with enchanting conservatory boasts the finest dining in Cambridge. Outstanding French Mediterranean Cuisine produced by Chef/Patron Daniel Clifford incorporates the freshest, finest local produce, wherever possible. This accompanied by arguably the Best Wine List outside London adds to an unforgettable meal in 'picture-postcard' surrounds. *Open for lunch/ dinner. (Closed Sundays and Mondays. Prices from 2-course lunch @ £15.00 to 3-course A La Carte Meal @ £42.00. (G/H11/12)*

Hemingford Abbots

Cambridge
⊛ Panos
Hills Road
Tel: (01223) 212958
Elegant professional standards, close to Botanic Gardens with easy access to the railway station and historic centre. The cuisine has its own special interest and originality, offering a variety of Greek and French dishes - even a traditional 'Mezze' as a first course. Desserts, all home-made, include Crêpe Suzette and Baklava. Turkish coffee and Cappuccino are offered. The expertly chosen range of wines is very reasonably priced. Daily "special" always available. *Restaurant open Mon-Sat dinner and Mon-Fri lunch Sun closed. 3 course dinner £19.50. (G/H11/12)*

Clayhythe, nr Waterbeach
⊛ The Bridge Hotel
Clayhythe, Nr Waterbeach CB5 9NZ
Tel: (01223) 860252 Fax: (01223) 440448
An internationally famous riverside hotel with ensuite rooms and fully licensed restaurant. Conference and weddings catered for. The Bridge Hotel's location is ideal for visiting Newmarket Races, Cambridge, Wimpole Hall and Anglesey Abbey. *Single rooms from £45 and Double £70 including full English breakfast. (H10)*

Cambridgeshire

Duxford
◉ Duxford Lodge Hotel
Ickleton Road, Duxford CB2 4RU
Tel: (01223) 836444 Fax: (01223) 832271
Email: duxford@btclick.com

Beautiful gardens, village setting just south of Cambridge and close to Duxford Air Museum, the pretty villages of Essex and Suffolk and Newmarket Races. The attractive hotel has much going for it. Beautifully maintained public rooms and delightful bedrooms provide a relaxed informal atmosphere. Modern French cooking is the theme for 'Le Paradis' Restaurant, one of only a few 2 Rosette Restaurants in the Cambridgeshire area. Tourist Board Gold award for Quality. Cheerful enthusiastic service and an excellent wine list. *Lunch from £9.99 (2 courses) Dinner from £25.00 (3 courses) Sunday lunch £17.95 children under 10 half price. Private dining our speciality. (H13)*

Ely
◉ The Old Fire Engine House
25 Saint Mary's Street, Ely CB7 4ER
Tel: (01353) 662582 Fax: (01353) 668364

The Old Fire Engine House is a restaurant and Gallery, which has been owned and run by the same family since 1968. An 18th century brick building close to Ely Cathedral, it has a large walled garden, friendly staff and an informal atmosphere. The cooking is based on local ingredients and classic English dishes form the mainstay of the menus. There is an extensive wine list and afternoon teas are also served. Art Gallery features monthly exhibitions of work by local and national artists. *Open for coffee, lunch, tea and dinner - telephone for details. (18)*

Huntingdon
◉ The Old Bridge Hotel
Tel: (01480) 424300

The ultimate 'country hotel in a town'. The lounges extend into a really splendid conservatory with attractive and comfortable cane chairs and tables. Here one can enjoy exceptional brasserie style food. There is also a top-class, panelled restaurant with a wine list regularly named as one of the finest in the UK, including a selection of 20 wines served by the glass. Enjoy tea, coffee and drinks (including a fine selection of real ales) any time of day in the comfortable lounge and bar or outside on the patio. *Open: daily. Average prices: 3 course restaurant meal £24.00. Brasserie meals from £4.50. (D/E9)*

Cambridgeshire

Kimbolton
◉ **The New Sun Inn**
20-22 High Street
Tel: (01480) 860052

16th Century beamed Inn and Restaurant. Real Ales and home made food using local produce. Bar meals £2.25-£7.25. Three-course à la carte meal at an average of £18.75. Traditional Sunday lunch £6.25. *Open 365 days of the year. House Specials include Home-made Steak and Kidney Pudding, Chocolate Fudge and Walnut Pudding. (B10)*

DID YOU KNOW

The lowest place (below sea level) in Britain is Holme Fen, at -10'. The nearby pub, 'The Admiral Arms' is the lowest pub in Britain. Whilst at Holywell the Ferry Boat Inn is the oldest pub in Britain, dating back to the 6th C. when it was a monastic ferry station.

Green Man Pub, Marholm

home

Gardens

Cycling

Aviation

Accommodation

Events

Places to Visit

Take time out to visit our website
www.eastofenglandtouristboard.com
... and discover some great deals on short breaks and holidays, as well as information on places to visit and events taking place throughout this picturesque corner of England.

Cambridgeshire

afternoon teas

Ely
⚜ Steeplegate
16/18 High Street
Tel: (01353) 664731

Proprietor: Mr J S Ambrose Seats: 40. Home-made cakes, scones and fresh cream teas, served in an historic building backing onto the cathedral. Medieval vault on view. Craft goods also sold. Small groups welcome. *Open: Daily except Sun. (18)*

St Ives
⚜ Connies Traditional Tea Rooms and Riverbank Restaurant
4 The Quay, St Ives PE27 5AR
Tel: (01480) 498199

Proprietor: Connie Stevens. Seats: 86 inside, 16 in courtyard. Overlooking the river and 15th century bridge chapel. Connie's exudes an old world charm where lovingly prepared home-made food is served courteously. With emphasis on presentation and quality, we aim to make your visit pleasurable. Home-baking. Full meals. Cream teas. Licensed. Four rooms, three with open fires in winter Courtyard. *Open: All year, 7 days a week. (E/F9/10)*

Houghton

DID YOU KNOW

The Manor at Hemingford Grey is the oldest continually inhabited house in England (circa. 1130)

regional produce

Linton
⚜ Chilford Hall Vineyard
Chilford Hundred Ltd., Balsham Road Linton, Cambridge CB1 6LE
Tel: (01223) 895625

Taste and buy award winning wines from the largest vineyard in Cambridgeshire. See the grapes growing in the eighteen acre vineyard, learn how English wine is made and appreciate the subtle difference between each of the Chilford quality wines. Also on sale, a range of local specialities - browse and buy! *Open from 1 Mar-23 Dec. Group visits by arrangement throughout the year. Vineyard tours £4.50 per person or £3.75 for groups of over 15. Free tastings. Take the A11/1307 then just follow - 'Chilford Hall Vineyard' signs. Telephone for group bookings. (113)*

Cambridgeshire

steeplegate

Ely
⊛ **Steeplegate**
16-18 High Street, Ely
Tel: (01353) 664731
Unusual gifts of good taste in Craft Gallery beside the cathedral. Tearoom. We sell woodwork, books, ceramics, jewellery, lace and toys. *Open all year, daily except Sunday, 0900-1730. (18)*

Want to order more ???

As a special offer you can purchase additional copies of **'East of England - the Official Guide'** for only **£3.00 per copy** *(that's a 35% saving!!).*

Simply complete and return the order form below, ensuring you complete the relevant payment section. *(Unfortunately we can only accept credit card payments – PLEASE DO NOT SEND CASH OR CHEQUES).*

Please send me ☐ copies of the East of England Guide 2002 at the special price of £3.00 per copy *(please note this is exclusive of postage and packing which is charged at £1.00 per copy)*

Name:

Address:

Country:

Credit card details: Visa ☐   Mastercard ☐   Switch ☐   (issue no...................)

Credit card number: ☐☐☐☐☐☐☐☐☐☐☐☐☐☐☐☐   Expiry date:...............................

Name on the card: ....   Signature:............................   Date:...............................

Return to: Publications Department, East of England Tourist Board, Toppesfield Hall, Hadleigh, Suffolk IP7 5DN ENGLAND
Tel: (01473) 825624 Fax: (01473) 823063

EAST OF ENGLAND TOURIST BOARD

Cambridgeshire

WHILE IN THE EAST OF ENGLAND VISIT OUR FAMOUS BEAUTY SPOTS.

All stock subject to availability.

DEBENHAMS
BRITAIN'S FAVOURITE DEPARTMENT STORE
www.debenhams.com

**Bedford, Cambridge, Chelmsford, Colchester, Ipswich,
Kings Lynn, Lakeside, Luton, Norwich, Romford.**

Nene Valley Railway

Cromwell Country

Follow in the footsteps of Oliver Cromwell (1599-1658), the great Lord Protector.

Starting point: Huntingdon, Cambs *(D9)*
Mileage: 21m/34km
Morning - Cromwell was born in *Huntington*. Start at the *Cromwell Museum* with its artefacts and portraits, then take the A1123 to *St. Ives* with its unusual *Bridge Chapel* and statue of Cromwell.
Afternoon - remain on the A1123 to Stretham (about 12 miles), where at the roundabout you turn left onto the A10 to *Ely*. Visit the magnificent *Cathedral* and *Oliver Cromwell's House* - but watch out for his ghost!

Oliver Cromwell's House, Ely

Time Travel East

Jump aboard our time machine, for a journey through the centuries.

Starting point: Peterborough, Cambs *(C/D5)*
Mileage: 7m/11km
Morning - start the day in the Bronze Age with the prehistoric excavations at *Flag Fen*, then it's into Norman times at the beautiful *Peterborough Cathedral*, where the tomb of Katherine of Aragon can be seen.
Afternoon - enjoy a Victorian-style steam train ride aboard the *Nene Valley Railway*, then take the A605 to *Elton Hall*, a romantic 18th C. house.

The Friendly Invasion

Discover the special bond developed between the UK and the US during the Second World War.

Starting point: Cambridge, Cambs *(G/H11/12)*
Mileage: 11m/18km
Morning - enjoy a walking tour of the city, then have a pint in the *Eagle pub*, noted for its Air Force bar.
Afternoon - follow the A1303 to *Madingley*, and the *Cambridge American Cemetery and Memorial*. Then retrace your steps to the M11, and follow this south to junction 10. End the day at Europe's top aviation attraction, the *Imperial War Museum* at Duxford, with its impressive American Air Museum.

Cambridgeshire

Birds and Bees

Wander amongst the rich countryside and wildlife of the Fens.

Starting point: Wisbech, Cambs *(H4)*
Mileage: 30m/48km
Morning - take the A1101 to the *Welney Wildfowl and Wetlands Trust*, home to ducks and swans. Then retrace your steps to *Wisbech* for a wander around the pretty Georgian streets and squares.
Afternoon - visit *Peckover House* with its Victorian garden, complete with an orangery and fernery. Then end the day with a tour of the *Elgood's Brewery*, and enjoy a pint in the adjacent garden with its rare trees.

Bloomin' Beautiful

Enjoy the spectacular colours and delicate fragrances of some of England's finest gardens.

Starting point: Cambridge, Cambs *(G/H11/12)*
Mileage: Cambridge and Anglesey Abbey 5m/8km
Cambridge and Wimpole Hall 9m/14km
Morning - visit the famous *University Botanic Garden*. Then try your hand at punting through 'The Backs'.
Afternoon - two choices: either leave the city on the A1303 towards Newmarket. Then at the roundabout with the A14, take the B1102 to Lode and visit 17th C. *Anglesey Abbey*, renowned for its outstanding 100 acre garden. Alternatively take the A603 to visit *Wimpole Hall*, with its Dutch and vegetable gardens.

Welney Wildfowl and Wetlands Trust

Tales of the Fenland

Discover the story of the Fens, its history, drainage and people.

Starting point: Ely, Cambs *(I8)*
Mileage: 25m/40km
Morning - start at *Oliver Cromwell's House*, and watch the 'drainage of the Fens' video. Then take the B1382 to *Prickwillow*, and visit the *Drainage Engine Museum*.
Afternoon - return to *Ely*, and take the A10 south to *Stretham*. At the roundabout, turn left onto the A1123 to *Wicken*. Visit the last remaining undrained Fen, and a 1930's 'Fen' cottage. End the day by returning to the A10, and heading south to the 12th C. *Denny Abbey and Farmland Museum*.

Writers and Wine

Hunt out great English writers and wine on this vintage tour.

Starting point: Cambridge, Cambs *(G/H11/12)*
Mileage: 29m/47km
Morning - enjoy a literary tour of the city (including Grantchester), and learn of A.A. Milne, Rupert Brooke and Lord Byron. Then take the A603 to New Wimpole, and visit the 18th C. *Wimpole Hall*, former home of Rudyard Kipling's daughter.
Afternoon - retrace your steps to Cambridge, and take the A1307 south east to Linton. Turn left here onto the B1052 towards Balsham. End the day with a tour and tasting at *Chilford Hall Vineyard*.

Katherine's Haunt

Visit the last homes of Katherine of Aragon, the first queen of Henry VIII. But watch out for her ghost!

Starting point: St. Neots, Cambs *(C/D11)*
Mileage: 12m/19km
Morning - start in the riverside town of *St. Neots*. Then take the A1 north to the pretty village of *Buckden*, where Katherine was held (by Henry VIII) in 1533, at the former palace of the Bishops of Lincoln.
Afternoon - take the B661 to *Grafham Water*, where you can enjoy a stroll around Britain's third largest reservoir. Remain on the B661 to Great Staughton, where you turn right onto the B660 to *Kimbolton*. Visit the castle where Katherine spent her last years, dying as a prisoner in 1536.

Cambridgeshire

Discover England's Cycling Country

What better way to relax and unwind than a gentle cycle ride through open countryside with only the birds for company. Whether you regularly cycle and take your bike on holiday, or simply like the idea of spending a leisurely day or two exploring on two wheels, the rolling countryside of the East of England offers perfect cycling country.

The opportunities are endless - from purpose designed cycle tracks along former railway lines, around reservoirs and through forests, to all the specially tailored tours along the numerous quiet country lanes, taking in the beautiful countryside and picturesque villages with plenty of places to stop at for refreshments.

And you don't even need to bring your own bike. There are numerous cycle hire centres where you can hire a range of bikes for anything from just a few hours to a few days. You'll also find companies who will happily organise a cycling holiday for you, providing you with cycles, arranging your accommodation and even transferring your luggage.

The best way to explore England's Cycling Country is with our extensive range of Cycling Discovery Maps. Each map details a route of between 14 and 30 miles, with places of interest and refreshment stops.

ENGLAND'S
Cycling Country

See page 31 to find out more about these routes.

East of England Tourist Board, Toppesfield Hall, Hadleigh, Suffolk IP7 5DN ENGLAND

Tel: (01473) 822922
Fax: (01473) 823063

EAST OF ENGLAND
TOURIST BOARD

Essex

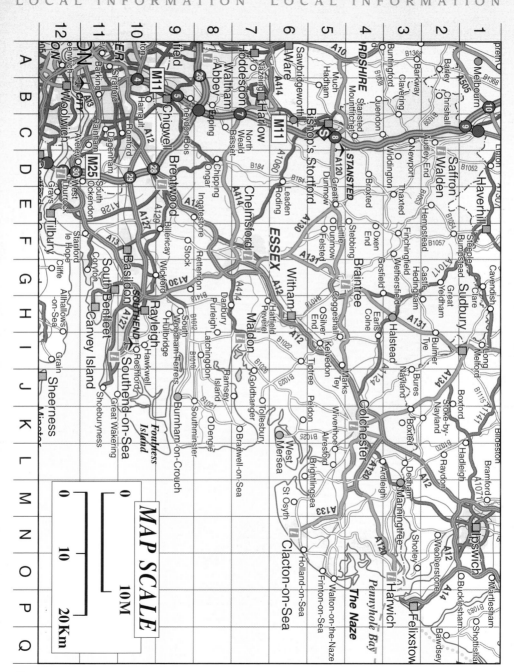

MAP SCALE

| 0 | | 10 | | 20Km |

| 0 | 10M |

Essex

Essex

County Town:	Chelmsford
Population:	1,610,600 approx (including Southend/Thurrock).
Highest Point:	High Wood, nr Langley 146 (480 feet).
Rivers:	Brook, Blackwater, Brain, Can, Chelmer, Colne, Crouch, Lea, Roach, Roding, Rom, Stour, Ter, Wid.
Landmarks:	Colchester Castle, 'Constable Country', Dartford Tunnel and Queen Elizabeth II Bridge, Epping Forest (over 6,000 acres), M25 Motorway, The Naze, Southend Pier (the longest in the world), Stansted Airport, Tilbury Port.

Industry Past & Present:

Essex has always been an *agricultural* county, with superb *corn-growing* countryside - the subsequent grain giving rise to associated *milling, malting* and *brewing* industries. The rich soil was also used to grow the much-need *gardener's seeds*, remembered in such names as the 'Kelvedon Wonder' pea. Essex is also the *jam* (soft fruit) capital of Britain, with both 'Wilkin and Son' and 'Elsenham' producing their preserves here. Saffron Walden gets part of its name from the 'Saffron Crocus' which was once grown in the area, and used for dyeing, medicine and flavouring. The coastline has also brought great wealth, with important *trading, fishing* and *shipbuilding* centres. Many goods were carried on the famous Thames Sailing Barges. Today you can try *sea salt* from Maldon, *oysters* from Colchester and *cockles* at Leigh-on-Sea. To the north of the county came the prosperous medieval *wool*, and later lace and *silk weaving* industries. While to the south there was *cement works* and *brick-making* at Grays, and *gravel extraction* in the Lee Valley. Today Essex is home to Tilbury Docks, the Port of Harwich and Bradwell Power Station. Famous names include - Britvic (beverages), Ford (car manufacturing), GEC Marconi (engineering/research) and Ridleys (brewing).

Famous People:

Thomas Audley *(Lord Chancellor)*, Queen Boadicea, Anne Boleyn *(Henry VIII's second wife)*, John Constable *(painter)*, Daniel Defoe *(author)*, Queen Elizabeth I, King Harold, William Harvey *(discovered circulation of blood)*, Gustav Holst *(composer)*, Matthew Hopkins *(Witchfinder General)*, Christopher Jones *(Master of the Mayflower)*, Guglielmo Marconi *(father of wireless)*, Frances Evelyn Maynard *('Darling Daisy')*, Alfred Munnings *(artist)*, Captain Oates *(explorer)*, John Ray *(botany)*, Dorothy L. Sayers *(author)*, Samuel Pepys,

Dick Turpin *(highwayman)*, Lawrence Washington *(great, great grandfather of George Washington)*.

Cities towns & Villages

Brightlingsea

Basildon *(F10)*
Until the railway arrived in the 19th C. Basildon was a small rural village, whose cottages clustered around the 14th C. Holy Cross Church. In 1949 it become a New Town, and now has a population of around 160,000. The Eastgate Centre is one of the county's major shopping centres.
MD: Tues, Thurs, Fri and Sat.

Billericay *(F9/10)*
Small town, set in well-wooded countryside. Numerous Georgian and period houses. The impressive church tower was built around 1500. Chantry House was the 17th C. home of Christopher Martin, treasurer to the Pilgrim Fathers. Nearby is Norsey Wood Nature Reserve, where 500 men were massacred by King Richard's soldiers in the Peasant's Revolt of 1381.

Braintree *(G4/5)*
Bustling market town standing on the old Roman road. King John gave Braintree its market charter in 1199. The textile industry has brought prosperity here for more than 400 years, firstly with wool, then from the 19th C. silk-weaving. Bradford Street has fine houses once occupied by those in the industry. Close by is the Freeport Designer outlet village. **MD**: Wed and Sat. **EC**: Thurs. **i**

Brentwood *(D/E9)*
The town grew up in the late 12th C. (around a forest clearing), as a convenient stopping place for pilgrims travelling from East Anglia and the Midlands to Canterbury. It later developed as an 18th C. coaching centre with some good inns. Surrounding the town are rural areas of countryside and parkland, offering an excellent centre for walking. **i**

Brightlingsea *(L6)*
A maritime heritage town, Brightlingsea is the only cinque port outside Kent and Sussex. Sitting at the mouth of the River Colne, it is a major yachting centre with one of the best stretches of sailing on the East Coast. The town is also home to one of England's oldest timber-framed buildings, the 13th C. Jacobes Hall. Superb walks alongside the creek and river. **EC**: Thurs.

Burnham-on-Crouch *(J9)*
Quiet, unspoilt riverside town, one of England's leading yachting centres. Known as the 'Cowes of the East Coast', the attractive quayside is lined with colour-washed houses, boat-building yards and sailing clubs. The famous clock tower dates from 1877. The town is also noted for its annual regatta, oysters, smuggling tales and long walks along the sea walls. **EC**: Wed.

Come to Chelmsford for a great day out

▼ **Shop 'til you drop**

▼ **Explore our heritage**

▼ **Treat the children**

▼ **Relax and unwind**

▼ **Go sport mad**

▼ **Enjoy our special events**

▼ **Be entertained**

Chelmsford waits for you in the heart of Essex. With something for everyone, you won't be disappointed.

For further information about visiting Chelmsford call **01245 606520** or visit our website:

www.enjoychelmsford.co.uk

Chelmsford - the Birthplace of Radio

Chelmsford BOROUGH COUNCIL

Chelmsford Cathedral

Canvey Island *(H11)*
This silt island was created by the currents of the Thames estuary. In the 17th C. the land was reclaimed by a group of Dutchmen, under the guidance of Cornelius Vermuyden. From an agricultural area, with a few villages, the island has developed into a large residential area. 16th C. inn, old Dutch cottages and watersports.

Castle Hedingham *(H2/3)*
A former market town, granted a charter by King John in the 13th C. Today the winding lanes of this medieval village are lined with timber-framed buildings and elegant Georgian houses. Dominating the village is the magnificent 12th C. castle keep of the De Vere family, Earls of Oxford.

Chelmsford *(F7)*
Founded in 1199, Chelmsford has been the county town of Essex for more than 700 years. Imposing 18th C. Shire Hall, and 15th C. parish church, designated a cathedral in 1914. Pedestrianised shopping areas and excellent entertainment/leisure facilities, including the Essex County Cricket Ground. In 1899, the world's first radio factory was opened here by Guglielmo Marconi. **MD**: Tues, Wed, Fri and Sat (second hand/collectable market on Thurs). *i*

Chipping Ongar *(D8)*
Surrounded by open farmland, this pleasant little country town owes its existence to the Normans. In 1162, Richard de Lucy, Chief Justice of England, built a great castle here. It was demolished in the 16th C. and today only the impressive mound remains. The wide High Street has houses dating from 1642, and within its parish church are Roman bricks. **EC**: Wed.

Clacton-on-Sea *(N6)*
The capital of the 'Essex Sunshine Coast', Clacton is a popular seaside town with tree-lined streets, long sandy beaches and beautiful seafront gardens. The 19th C. pier offers a range of entertainment and attractions. Water sports, two theatres and good shopping area. Close by is the Clacton Factory Shopping Village. **MD**: Tues and Sat (covered market Mon to Sat). *i*

Coggeshall *(I5)*
Once an important place in the trade of wool and lace-making, Coggeshall is now a major antiques centre. There are many fine timber-framed buildings, including 16th C. Paycockes once home to a wealthy wool merchant. Grange Barn, erected by Cistercian monks in 1140, is all that remains of the former abbey. The clock tower was built in 1887. **MD**: Thurs. **EC**: Wed.

Colchester *(K4)*
Britain's oldest recorded town, with over 2,000 years of history to explore. Discover the largest Norman castle keep in Europe (now an award-winning museum), and Britain's best preserved Roman gateway. Close by are the quaint narrow streets of the Dutch Quarter, where the cloth industry once flourished. Excellent shopping and leisure facilities. Lovely parkland and gardens. **MD**: Fri and Sat (cattle market on Thurs and Sat). *i*

Castle Park, Colchester

Danbury (H7/8)

Hilltop town, built on the site of an Iron Age fort. There are views of the Blackwater Estuary with its barges and yachts. The church is 600 years old and contains notable wooden effigies of knights. Set within a country park is the 19th C. Danbury Palace, a former bishop's residence.

Dedham (L3)

Set by the River Stour, Dedham is in the heart of Constable Country. It was here that the 18th C. landscape painter went to school. The attractive main street is lined with Georgian-fronted houses, old inns and a large arts/crafts centre. The magnificent 15th C. church is noted for its heraldic symbols. East of the village is the former home of the artist Sir Alfred Munnings. **EC**: Wed.

Epping (B9)

Founded in the 13th C. by the canons of Waltham Abbey, Epping is set on the old coaching route from London. Its long, wide High Street is full of attractive buildings and old inns. To the north is the famous Epping Forest, covering some 6,000 acres. This former royal hunting ground was the haunt of legendary highwayman Dick Turpin.
MD: Mon. **EC**: Wed.

Frinton-on-Sea (O5)

With a reputation as an exclusive resort, Frinton retains an atmosphere of the 1920s and 30s. Tree-lined residential avenues sweep down to the elegant Esplanade and cliff-top greensward. The long stretch of sandy beach is quiet and secluded. The main tree-lined shopping street (Connaught Avenue) has been dubbed the "Bond Street" of East Anglia. **EC**: Wed.

Grays/Thurrock (E12/D11)

The manor of Thurrock was granted to Richard de Grays and his family. In those early days, fishing was the local industry, but later Grays became renowned as a brick-making centre. To the west is the popular Lakeside Shopping Centre, and Europe's longest cabled-stayed bridge. **MD**: Fri, Sat. **EC**: Wed.

Great Dunmow (E5)

Historic market town, which prospered from the medieval wool trade. It is home of the Flitch Trials, which date from 1104. This custom takes place every four years, and awards a flitch of bacon to a newly married couple who can prove that they have lived in harmony for a year and a day. The Doctor's Pond is the scene of the first lifeboat experiments in 1784. **MD**: Tues. **EC**: Wed.

Maldon

Halstead (H3)

Lively and picturesque town with a 600 year old church and interesting country-style shops. With the decline of the wool industry, Halstead turned to silk manufacture, started by the Courtauld family in the 1800s. Their weather-boarded mill, which straddles the River Colne, is now a large antiques centre. **MD**: Tues, Fri and Sat. **EC**: Wed.

Harlow (B7)

Designed to relieve the congestion of London in 1947, this New Town has set residential and industrial areas. Its long history still survives though, in the rural parishes that surround 'The High', its modern centre. 'The Lawn' is the first tower block built in Britain in 1951, now listed for preservation. Wide range of sculpture **MD**: Mon to Tues and Thurs to Sat (bric-a-brac on Mon). **EC**: Wed.

Harwich and Dovercourt (O3)

Harwich is famous for its sea-faring history and heritage. It was once the headquarters of the King's Navy, and home of Christopher Jones 'Master of the Mayflower'. Narrow streets, historic buildings and museums, including the Redoubt Fort. Adjacent is the Edwardian style resort of Dovercourt with its sandy beaches, boating lake and park.
MD: Fri. **EC**: Wed. *i*

Dovercourt

Saffron Walden

Ingatestone (E8/9)

Lying beside the busy A12, this little country town has Georgian brick houses and a 16th C. inn. The church is noted for its 15th C. red-brick tower. Inside is a chapel housing the tombs of the Petre family. Sir William Petre moved here in 1539, building Ingatestone Hall.

Maldon (I7)

Ancient hilltop town, port and sailing centre, at the head of the Blackwater estuary. Famed for its unique crystal salt and majestic Thames Sailing Barges. Attractive lanes and 'chases', with many historic buildings, including the 15th C. Moot Hall and 17th C. Dr Plume's Library. All Saints' Church has a unique triangular shaped tower. Edwardian Promenade Park. **MD**: Thurs and Sat. **EC**: Wed. *i*

Manningtree and Mistley (L/M3)

At the head of the Stour Estuary, these two small towns are joined by a waterfront area, noted for its swans. Manningtree is a sailing town with fine Georgian buildings, while Mistley with its swan fountain, was all set to become a spa town in the 18th C. Both places are connected with Matthew Hopkins, the infamous 17th C. 'Witchfinder General'. **MD**: Wed and Sat. **EC**: Wed.

Rayleigh and Rochford (H+I10)

Rayleigh is noted for its handsome 14th C. church, and the mound of its former royal castle built by the Saxons. Adjacent Rochford has a square surrounded by attractive buildings, the oldest dating from 1270. The red-brick tower of the church was once used by smugglers. Nearby is 15th C. Rochford Hall, reputedly the birthplace of Anne Boleyn. Rayleigh **MD**: Wed; Rochford **MD**: Tues. **EC**: Wed.

Essex —————————————

Treat yourself to

Colche$ter

BRITAIN'S
Oldest
RECORDED
TOWN

Over 2000 years *of fascinating history has taken place here in Colchester. It is a history involving the Romans, the Saxons and the Normans who have endowed the town with a rich heritage which you can discover today.*

A flourishing, modern town boasting a distinctive variety of galleries and museums, Colchester today offers a unique choice of places to visit, things to see and an excellent range of shops.

Poised at the gateway to East Anglia with its picturesque villages yet only minutes away from the coast, Colchester is the perfect destination for a well deserved short break or day trip.

Why not treat yourself to Colchester?

To obtain an information pack, simply complete the enquiry slip and send it to us today or call our 24 hour telephone hotline:

01206 282828

Please complete and send to:

**Colchester Visitor Information Centre
1 Queen Street, Colchester, Essex CO1 2PG**

COLCHESTER

Name:

Address:

Postcode:

EAG02

Daytime Tel No:

Writtle

Saffron Walden *(C/D2)*

This ancient town takes its name from the saffron crocus, which grew here in the 16th C. Once a centre for wool production, the wealth generated has left many lovely timber framed buildings, some decorated with pargetting. The parish church, with its elegant spire, is one of the largest in Essex. Also remains of Norman castle and rare turf maze. **MD**: Tues and Sat. **EC**: Thurs. *i*

Southend-on-Sea *(I10/11)*

Traditional family seaside resort with seven miles of seafront, award-winning beaches, and magnificent parks and gardens. The famous 100 year old pier is the longest in the world - take a ride to the end aboard the little trains. Also excellent shopping centre, Kursaal entertainment complex, bandstand concerts, theatre and full calendar of special events. **MD**: Thurs (main), Sat (small market). *i*

Stansted Mountfitchet *(C4)*

Best known for its airport, this small town owes its earlier importance to a castle built here by the Mountfitchet family. The extensive earthworks are now home to the only reconstructed motte and bailey castle in the world. The main part of the town is grouped along a hill. Close by is a 18th C. windmill.

Thaxted *(E3)*

Developed from a Saxon settlement, Thaxted prospered from the cutlery industry in the 14th C. Quaint streets are lined with fine medieval buildings, including the 15th C. Guildhall and thatched almshouses. Beautiful church with 181 foot high tower, and John Webb's 19th C. windmill. Home of the British composer, Gustav Holst and highwayman Dick Turpin. **MD**: Fri. **EC**: Wed.

Tilbury *(E12)*

Modern town, now one of Europe's largest container ports. Henry VIII built riverside block houses at East and West Tilbury, these later becoming Coalhouse and Tilbury Forts. In 1588, Queen Elizabeth I gave her morale boosting speech at Tilbury Fort, as her troops prepared to meet the Spanish Armada. **MD**: Fri.

Tiptree *(I6)*

Best-known for its production of jam, this little town is surrounded by orchards. Fruit farming began here in 1864, and today the family firm of Wilkin and Son's is world-famous for their jams and preserves. The brick windmill was reputed used to hide contraband smuggled up the River Blackwater.

Waltham Abbey *(A8)*

Well preserved town, home to one of the county's most outstanding Norman buildings, 'Waltham Abbey'. It was endowed by King Harold, who was reputedly buried here. Beside the abbey is a lovely area of parkland and gardens. Sitting on the Meridian Line, the town has former coaching inns, and a fine 'Art Nouveau' Town Hall. **MD**: Tues and Sat. **EC**: Thurs. *i*

Essex ————————————————————

Walton-on-the-Naze *(O5)*

Family seaside resort with clean sandy beaches, seafront gardens and quaint narrow streets. The pier is the second longest in Britain. The Naze is a headland jutting into the sea, where the heathland nature reserve is a haven for birdwatchers. Behind the town are 'The Backwaters', a series of saltings and little creeks leading into Harwich harbour. **MD**: Thurs.

Witham *(M6)*

Standing on the River Brain, the manor of Witham was given to the Knights Templar in 1148. It has been a cloth-making centre, spa and coaching town. Newland Street has many fine Georgian buildings, including the council offices with its period garden. Statue of crime-writer Dorothy L. Sayers who lived in the town for 27 years from 1929. **MD**: Sat. **EC**: Wed.

Wivenhoe *(L5)*

Set on the wooded slopes of the River Colne, Wivenhoe has attractive old inns and a pretty quayside. The earliest record of boat-building was in 1575, then in the 18th C. it developed as a port and shipyard. An earthquake in 1884 damaged the church. On the outskirts of the town is Wivenhoe Park, home of the University of Essex.

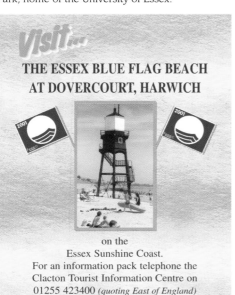
Pick of the villages

1 **Arkesden** - pretty hamlet set around a green. Buildings of wood, plaster and thatch. *(C3)*
2 **Battlesbridge** - attractive riverside village, famed today as a major antiques centre. *(H9)*
3 **Bradwell on Sea** - unusual lock-up, marina and England's oldest Saxon church. *(K7)*
4 **Canewdon** - tales of witchcraft. Massive church tower, village cage and stocks. *(J9)*
5 **Clavering** - remains of former castle, 14th C. church and thatched 'Dolls House'. *(B/C3)*
6 **Felsted** - delightful village with a well-known public school. Victorian brewery. *(F5)*
7 **Finchingfield** - picture postcard village clustered around its green and duck pond. *(F3)*
8 **Goldhanger** - farming/fishing hamlet. Village pump, oyster beds and sea-wall walks. *(J7)*
9 **Great Bardfield** - former market town with pargetted cottages and 19th C. lock-up. *(F3)*
10 **Great Bentley** - reputedly the largest village green in England at 42 acres. *(M5)*
11 **Great Waltham** - restored Guildhall with Tudor chimneys. *(F6)*
12 **Greensted** - home to the oldest wooden church in the world, dating from 945AD. *(D8)*
13 **Hempstead** - quiet village. Birthplace of highwayman Dick Turpin in 1705. *(E2)*
14 **Kelvedon** - attractive village set beside the A12, now an antiques centre. *(I5)*
15 **Leigh on Sea** - quaint 'cockle' fishing centre. Cobbled street and weather-boarded cottages. *(H/I11)*
16 **Little Easton** - pargetted cottages, Tudor chimneys and superb 12th C. church. *(E4)*
17 **Matching** - idyllic setting with church, pond, moated hall and 15th C. 'Wedding Feast House'. *(C6)*
18 **Manuden** - plastered and white-washed houses, some with pargetting. *(C4)*
19 **Newport** - former market town, its main street lined with handsome houses. 15th C. barn. *(C3)*
20 **Pleshey** - impressive remains of 12th C. castle, including huge mound and 15th C. bridge. *(E6)*
21 **Purleigh** - the great grandfather of George Washington was rector here in the 17th C. *(H/I8)*
22 **The Rodings** - eight pretty villages/hamlets set along the valley of the River Roding. *(D6/7)*
23 **St. Osyth** - ancient village, with a 12th C. priory, complete with magnificent gatehouse. *(M6)*
24 **Stock** - pretty village with weather-boarded houses. *(F9)*
25 **Terling** - estate village, with pretty cottages, 15th C. manor house and church. *(G6)*
26 **Tillingham** - property of St. Paul's Cathedral since c.610AD. Weather-boarded cottages. *(K8)*
27 **Tollesbury** - former fishing centre. 19th C. sail lofts. Little square with lock-up. *(J7)*
28 **Wendens Ambo** - colour-washed cottages, thatched and tiled. Large timber-framed barn. *(C3)*
29 **West Mersea** - small resort and sailing centre, with attractive old fishing cottages. *(K6)*
30 **Writtle** - village green and pond, with period buildings. Famous agricultural college. *(F7)*

Essex

Tourist Information Centres

With so much to see and do in this area, it's impossible for us to mention all of the places you can visit. You will find Tourist Information Centres (TICs) throughout Essex, with plenty of information on all the things that you can do and the places you can visit. TICs can book accommodation for you, in their own area, or further afield using the 'Book A Bed Ahead Scheme'. They can be the ideal place to purchase locally made crafts or gifts, as well as books covering a wide range of local interests. A list of the TICs in this area can be found below.

* Not open all year

Braintree *(G4/5)*, Town Hall Centre,
Market Square,
Tel: (01376) 550066
Email: tic@bdctourism.demon.co.uk
Web: www.braintree.gov.uk
Brentwood *(D/E9)*, Pepperell House,
44 High Street, Tel: (01277) 200300
Web: www.brentwood-council.gov.uk
Chelmsford *(F7)*, County Hall, Market Road,
Tel: (01245) 283400
Email: chelmtic@essexcc.gov.uk
Web: www.welcometoessex.co.uk
Clacton-on-Sea *(N6)*, 23 Pier Avenue,
Tel: (01255) 423400
Email: emorgan@tendringdc.gov.uk
Web: www.essex-sunshine-coast.org.uk
Colchester *(K4)*, 1 Queen Street,
Tel: (01206) 282920
Web: www.colchester.gov.uk
Harwich *(O3)*, Iconfield Park, Parkeston
Tel: (01255) 506139
Email: harwich@touristinformation.fsnet.co.uk
Web: www.essex-sunshine-coast.org.uk
Maldon *(I7)*, Coach Lane, Tel: (01621) 856503
Email: tic@maldon.gov.uk
Web: www.maldon.gov.uk
Saffron Walden *(C/D2)*, 1 Market Place,
Market Square, Tel: (01799) 510444
Email: tourism@uttlesford.gov.uk
Web: www.uttlesford.gov.uk
Southend-on-Sea *(J11)*, 19 High Street,
Tel: (01702) 215120
Email: office@sbctic.fsnet.co.uk
Web: www.southend.gov.uk

Thurrock *(D12)*, Granada Motorway Service Area,
M25, Grays, Tel: (01708) 863733
Email: kwillson.tc@gtnet.gov.uk
Web: www.thurrock.gov.uk
Waltham Abbey *(A8)*, 2-4 Highbridge Street,
Tel: (01992) 652295
Email: townclerk@walthamabbey.org.uk
Web: walthamabbey.org.uk

Blue Badge Guides:

There are also experts available to help you explore some of our towns and cities. These Registered Blue Badge Guides have all attended a training course sponsored by the East of England Tourist Board. Below are some of the tours offered by these Guides - you can obtain further information by contacting the appropriate Tourist Information Centre, unless otherwise indicated. Some Blue Badge Guides have a further qualification to take individuals or groups around the region for half day, full day or longer tours if required.

Colchester
● **Regular Town Tours:** 1.75 hours from Visitor Information Centre. 1 Jun-30 Sep, daily 1100. For cost and additional details contact: (01206) 282920.
● **Group Tours:** May be booked at any time of year.

Saffron Walden and Surrounding Areas:
● **Group Tours:** Guides available at any time to conduct tours for private groups. Variety of tours in a number of small rural towns, some tours themed. Can design tours to meet specific needs of groups - no charge at present. Tours last for about 2 hours - can be scaled down to fit into existing itinerary. Prices on application.
● **Day or Half Day Coach Tours:** Uttlesford and Essex guides available to guide tours in a large area of North West Essex and its borderlands. Wide range of standard tours. Can also assist with the design of special and themed tours for particular interests and occasions. Tours organiser: (01799) 526109 for more information.

historic houses

Ingatestone Hall

Coggeshall
❀ Grange Barn
The National Trust, Grange Hill
Tel: (01376) 562226

A restored 12thC barn, the earliest surviving timber-framed barn in Europe with a small collection of early 20thC farm carts and wagons. *Open 2 Apr-13 Oct, Tue, Thu, Sun, Bank Hol Mon, 1400-1700. Please contact for details of admission prices. (I5)*

Coggeshall
❀ Paycockes
West Street Tel: (01376) 561305

A half-timbered merchant's house, built in the 16thC with a richly-carved interior and a small display of Coggeshall lace. Very attractive garden. *Open 31 Mar-31 Oct, Tue, Thu, Sun, Bank Hol Mon, 1400-1730. Please contact for details of admission prices. (I5)*

Gosfield
Gosfield Hall
Tel: (01787) 472914

A Tudor house built around a courtyard with later alterations, an old well and pump house with a 100ft Elizabethan gallery with oak panelling. *House and Grounds open 9 May-19 Sep, Wed, Thu, 1400-1700; Tours, 1430, 1515. £3.00/£1.50. (G/H3/4)*

Hartford End
Leez Priory
Tel: (01245) 362555

An ancient monument, 13thC priory ruins, 16thC redbrick Tudor mansion and tower with 15 acres of parkland, lakes, walled gardens, Tudor tunnels and oak-panelled Great Hall. *Open by appointment only, please phone for details. (F5)*

Ingatestone
❀ Ingatestone Hall
Hall Lane Tel: (01277) 353010

Tudor house and gardens, the home of the Petre family since 1540 with a family portrait collection, furniture and other heirlooms on display. *Open 30 Mar-14 Jul, Sat, Sun, Bank Hol Mon, 1300-1800; 17 Jul-8 Sep, Wed-Sun, Bank Hol Mon, 1300-1800; 14-29 Sep, Sat, Sun, 1300-1800. £4.00/£2.00/£3.50. (E8/9)*

Layer Marney Tower

Layer Marney
◉ Layer Marney Tower
Tel: (01206) 330784

A 1520 Tudor-brick gatehouse, 8 storeys high with Italianate terracotta cresting and windows. Gardens, deer and rare breeds farm, animals and also the nearby church. *Open 29 Mar-6 Oct, daily except Sat, 1200-1700. £3.50/£2.00. (J6)*

Rayleigh
Dutch Cottage
Tel: (01702) 318150

An 8-sided cottage based on the design of 17thC Dutch settlers. *Open all year by appointment, Wed, 1330-1630. (H10)*

Rochford
The Old House
Rochford District Council,
South Street

History is revealed in the rooms of this elegant house, originally built in 1270, lovingly restored and now housing District Council offices. *Open all year by appointment only, Wed, 1400-1630. (I10)*

Saffron Walden
◉ Audley End House and Park Q
Audley End Tel: (01799) 522399

A palatial Jacobean house remodelled in the 18th-19thC with a magnificent Great Hall with 17thC plaster ceilings. Rooms and furniture by Robert Adam and park by 'Capability' Brown. *Grounds open 3 Apr-29 Sep, Wed-Sun, Bank Hols, 1100-1800; House open 1200-1600; House and Grounds open 3-31 Oct, daily, 1100-1500. £6.95/£3.50/£5.20. (C/D2)*

Widdington
◉ Priors Hall Barn
Tel: (01799) 522842

One of the finest surviving medieval barns in south east England, representative of the type of aisled barn in north west Essex, 124 x 30 x 33 ft high. *Open 6 Apr-29 Sep, Sat, Sun, 1000-1800. (D3)*

Writtle
◉ Hylands House
Hylands Park
Tel: (01245) 355455

An historic house, originally built in 1730. After recent restoration work, there are now 6 restored rooms to visit and an exhibition on the history of the house. *Open 6 Jan-31 Mar, Sun, 1100-1800, Mon, 1100-1500; 1 Apr-30 Sep, Sun, Mon, 1100-1800; 6 Oct-30 Dec, Sun, 1100-1800, Mon, 1100-1500. £3.00/£2.00/£2.00. (F7)*

DID YOU KNOW

Layer Marney Tower is the tallest Tudor gatehouse in Britain, built in 1520.

Audley End House and Park

Ancient Monuments

St. Botolph's Priory, Colchester

Billericay
St Mary Magdalene Church
Church Street, Great Burstead

Saxon church with 14thC medieval wall paintings. Christopher Martin, the church warden, led the Pilgrim Fathers' journey to Billericay near Boston in the USA. *Open 5 May-29 Sep, Sun, 1400-1700. (F9/10)*

Bradwell-on-Sea
Saint Peters-on-the-Wall
East End Road
Tel: (01621) 776203

A 7thC Saxon chapel which is always open and offers a small exhibition about its history and a bookstall. *Evening services every Sunday at 1830 during July and August. Open at any reasonable time. (K7)*

St. Andrews Minster Church, Ashingdon

DID YOU KNOW

Colchester is Britain's oldest recorded town (first mentioned in AD77), and the first capital of Roman Britain. Its Norman castle keep (built 1076-1125) is the largest one in Europe, whilst the Balkerne Gate is the largest surviving Roman gateway in Britain.

Brentwood
Cathedral Church of St Mary and St Helen
Ingrave Road
Tel: (01277) 210107

Roman Catholic Cathedral designed by Mr Quinlan Terry. *Open all year, daily, dawn-dusk. (D/E9/10)*

Castle Hedingham
⊛ Hedingham Castle
Tel: (01787) 460261

The finest Norman keep in England, built in 1140 by the deVeres, Earls of Oxford. Visited by Kings Henry VII and VIII and Queen Elizabeth I and besieged by King John. *Open 7 Apr-31 Oct, daily, 1000-1700; please contact for opening times to view the snowdrops. £4.00/£3.00/£3.50. (H2/3)*

Essex

Chelmsford
◉ Chelmsford Cathedral
Cathedral Office, 53 New Street
Tel: (01245) 294480
A late-medieval church, reordered in 1983 and blending old with new. Became a cathedral in 1914 when the Diocese of Chelmsford was created. Modern sculpture and tapestry. *Open all year, Mon-Sat, 0815-1800; Sun, 0730-1230; 1400-1900. (F/G7)*

Colchester
◉ Saint Botolphs Priory Q
Tel: (01728) 621330
The remains of a 12thC priory near the town centre with a nave which has an impressive arcaded west end. One of the first Augustinian priories in England. *Open at any reasonable time. (K4)*

Colchester
Saint Michael and All Angels Church
Church Road, Copford Green
Tel: (01621) 815434
A 12thC church with 12thC wall paintings. *Open all year, daily, 0915-dusk; Sun service, 1100-1200. (K4)*

Cressing
◉ Cressing Temple Barns
Witham Road
Tel: (01376) 584903
The site of a Knights Templar settlement dating from 1137. Two magnificent timber-framed barns survive. The Barley Barn (c1200) and the Wheat Barn (c1250). *Open 3 Mar-28 Apr, Sun, 1030-1730; 1 May-29 Sep, Wed-Fri, 1030-1630, Sun, 1030-1730; 6-27 Oct, Sun, 1030-1730. £3.00/£2.00/£2.00. (H5)*

East Tilbury
Coalhouse Fort
Princess Margaret Road
Tel: (01375) 844203
A Victorian Thames defence fortress housing the Thameside Aviation Museum. The building is set in a riverside park. *Please contact for details of opening times. £2.50/free/£2.00. (F12)*

Greensted
Greensted Church
Greensted Road
Tel: (01277) 364694
The oldest wooden church in the world. The oldest wooden building standing in Europe. *Open all year, daily, dawn-dusk. (C8)*

Hadleigh
◉ Hadleigh Castle
Tel: (01760) 755161
Familiar from Constable's painting, the castle stands on a bluff overlooking the Leigh Marshes with a single, large 50-ft tower and 13thC and 14thC remains. *Open at any reasonable time. (H11)*

Harwich
Harwich Redoubt Fort
Behind 29 Main Road
Tel: (01255) 503429
An anti-Napoleonic circular fort commanding the harbour. Eleven guns on battlements. *Open 6 Jan-28 Apr, Sun, 1000-1200, 1400-1600; 1 May-31 Aug, daily, 1000-1700; 1 Sep-22 Dec, Sun, 1000-1200, 1400-1600. £1.00/free/£1.00. (O3)*

Little Tey
St James the Less Church
Church Lane
A 12thC church with 13thC and 14thC wall paintings which have been uncovered and conserved without any restoration. They are virtually untouched since their original painting. *Open all year, Thu-Sun, Bank Hol Mon, 0930-dusk. (I/J4/5)*

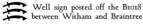

Mistley
⊛ Mistley Towers
Tel: (01223) 582700

Two towers designed by Robert Adam in 1776 as part of the parish church. A rare example of Robert Adam's ecclesiastical work. Key available from Mistley quay workshops. *Open at any reasonable time, key keeper (01206) 393884. (M3)*

Rayleigh
Rayleigh Mount
Tel: (01263) 738030

The former site of the Domesday castle erected by Swein of Essex. *Open 1 Apr-31 Oct, daily, 1000-1700. (H10)*

Rivenhall
Saint Mary and All Saints Church
Church Road
Tel: (01376) 511161

A Saxon church on the earthworks of a Roman villa, restored by early Victorians with 12thC glass and interesting monuments. *Open 28 Apr-6 Oct, Sun, 1430-1630. Key available to casual callers. Easter services. Christmas services 24 Dec, 2330, 25 Dec, 1100. Closed 29-31 Mar. (H/15/6)*

Southend-on-Sea
St Andrew's (Minster) Church
Church Road, Ashingdon

Small, pretty hilltop church, with wonderful views over the River Crouch valley. *Open 1 Apr-30 Sep, Mon-Sat, 1400-1600. (I10/11)*

Mistley Towers

Southminster
Rural Discovery Church
Saint Lawrence
Tel: (01621) 779319

An active church, sited on hill overlooking River Blackwater. Exhibitions of local interest. *Open 25 May-29 Sep, Sat, Sun, Bank Hol Mon, 1430-1630. (J8/9)*

Stansted Mountfitchet
⊛ Mountfitchet Castle
Tel: (01279) 813237

A re-constructed Norman motte-and-bailey castle and village of the Domesday period with a Grand Hall, church, prison, siege tower and weapons. Domestic animals roam the site. *Open 11 Mar-11 Nov, daily, 1000-1700. £4.80/£3.80/£4.00. (C4)*

Tilbury
⊛ Tilbury Fort
No 2 Office Block, The Fort
Tel: (01375) 858489

One of Henry VIII's coastal forts, re-modelled and extended in the 17thC in continental style. *Open 2 Jan-31 Mar, Wed-Sun, 1000-1600; 1 Apr-30 Sep, daily, 1000-1800; 1-31 Oct, daily, 1000-1700; 1 Nov-29 Dec, Wed-Sun, 1000-1600. Closed 25, 26 Dec. £2.75/£1.40/£2.10. (E12)*

Waltham Abbey
Waltham Abbey Church
Highbridge Street
Tel: (01992) 767897

A Norman church, the reputed site of King Harold's tomb. There is a lady chapel with a crypt which houses an exhibition of the history of Waltham Abbey and a shop. *Open all year, Mon, Tue, Thu-Sat, 1000-1600; Wed, 1100-1600; Sun, 1200-1600; (1800 during British Summer time); closed 29 Mar. (A8)*

Willingale
Willingale Churches
The Street

Two ancient churches in one churchyard, side by side. On site since Norman times. A village setting on the Essex Way. *Open all year, daily, dawn-dusk. (D/E7)*

DID YOU KNOW

The 13th C. Church of All Saints at Maldon has the only triangular shaped tower in Britain, whilst The Church of St. Andrew at Greensted is the oldest wooden church in the world dating from 1013).

Essex

museums, heritage & Craft Centres

Battlesbridge
Battlesbridge Antiques Centre
The Old Granary, Hawk Hill
Tel: (01268) 575000
Antiques and collectibles of all descriptions. Visit the motorcycle museum on Sun or by appointment. Tearooms and 2 17thC pubs. *Open all year, daily, 1000-1730. Closed 25, 26 Dec. (G/H9/10)*

Billericay
Barleylands Farm
Barleylands Road
Tel: (01268) 290229
Visitor's centre with a rural museum, animal centre, craft studios, blacksmith's shop, a glass-blowing studio with a viewing gallery, miniature steam railway and a restaurant. *Open 1 Mar-31 Oct, daily, 1000-1700. £3.50/£2.00/£2.00. (F9)*

Billericay
Cater Museum
74 High Street Tel: (01277) 622023
A folk museum of bygones with a Victorian sitting room and bedroom. *Open all year, Mon-Sat, 1400-1700; closed Bank Hol Mon, 21-30 Dec. (F9)*

Bradwell-on-Sea
⦾ **Bradwell Power Station and Visitor Centre**
Tel: (01621) 873395
Exhibits in the centre on energy production, the environment and nuclear power. Visits are arranged to the reactors and the generating station. *Open 24 Mar-31 Oct, Sun-Fri, 1100-1700. (K7)*

Braintree
Blake House Craft Centre
Blake End
Tel: (01376) 552553
The courtyard of Listed farm buildings, which have been converted into craft shops and units as specialised businesses. *Open all year, Tue-Sun, Bank Hol Mon, 1030-1700. Closed 25 Dec-3 Jan. (G4/5)*

Braintree
⦾ **Braintree District Museum**
Manor Street Tel: (01376) 325266
Threads of Time is a permanent exhibition housed in a converted Victorian school, telling the story of Braintree district and its important place in our history. *Open 4 Jan-30 Sep, Mon-Sat, Bank Hol Mon, 1000-1700; 1 Oct-31 Dec, Mon-Sat, 1000-1700; Sun, 1400-1700; closed 24-26, 31 Dec, 1 Jan. £2.00/£1.00. (G4/5)*

Braintree
The Town Hall Centre
Market Square
Tel: (01376) 557776
Art gallery in Grade II* listed building with tourist information centre on site. Situated in historic market square dating back to 1199. *Open all year, Mon-Fri, 0900-1700, Sat, 1000-1600. Closed 29 Mar-1 Apr, 24 Dec-3 Jan. (G4/5)*

Brentwood
Brandler Galleries
1 Coptfold Road Tel: (01277) 222269
A gallery selling exhibitions of work by major British artists and prints by European masters at affordable prices. *Open all year, Tue-Sat, 1000-1730; closed 13 Apr, 1 Jan, please phone to confirm not closed for an outside show. (D/E9/10)*

Tymperleys Clock Museum, Colchester

Essex

Brentwood
Brentwood Museum
Cemetery Lodge, Lorne Road
Tel: (01277) 224012

A small cottage museum covering social and domestic history with special reference to Brentwood. It includes a 1930s kitchen, toys, games and memorabilia from 2 world wars. *Open 7 Apr, 5 May, 2 Jun, 7 Jul, 4 Aug, 1 Sep, 6 Oct, Sun, 1430-1630. (D/E9/10)*

Brentwood
⊛ **Kelvedon Hatch** Q
Nuclear Bunker
Kelvedon Hall Lane, Kelvedon Hatch
Tel: (01277) 364883

A large, 3-storey, ex-government regional headquarters buried some 100ft below ground, complete with canteen, BBC studio, dormitories, plant room and plotting floor. *Open 3 Jan-28 Feb, Thu-Sun, 1000-1600; 1 Mar-31 Oct, Mon-Fri, 1000-1600; Sat, Sun, Bank Hol Mon; 1000-1700; 1 Nov-29 Dec, Thu-Sun, 1000-1600. £5.00/£3.00. (D/E9/10)*

Brightlingsea
Brightlingsea Museum
1 Duke Street

The maritime and social history museum of Brightlingsea (a limb of the Cinque Port of Sandwich) showing collections relating to the town's Cinque Port connections. *Open 30 Mar-28 Sep, Mon, Thu, 1400-1700; Sat, 1000-1600. 50p/25p/25p. (L6)*

Broxted
Church Hall Farm Antique and Craft Centre
Church End Tel: (01279) 850858

A magnificent 16thC barn in beautiful surroundings offering a wide variety of antiques, crafts and collectables. Plus top-quality tearooms, car parking and toilets. *Open all year, Tue-Sun, Bank Hol Mon, 1000-1700. Closed 25-27 Dec. (D4)*

Burnham-on-Crouch
Burnham-on-Crouch and District Museum
Tucker Brown Boathouse,
Coronation Road

A small museum devoted to local history with maritime and agricultural features of the Dengie Hundred. *Please contact for details of opening times. 50p/20p/50p. (J9)*

A 2000 Year Adventure

See history
Some of the most important historical finds in Britain can be seen here

Hear history
Audio visual dramas explain Colchester's involvement in some of the most important events in British history

Touch history
Try on a toga, catch up with medieval fashions and touch real Roman pottery

Discover history
A variety of events take place during

A visit to **Colchester Castle Museum** takes you through 2000 years of some of the most important events in British history. Once capital of Roman Britain, Colchester has experienced devastation by Boudica *(Boadicea)*, invasion by the Normans and siege during the English Civil War.

Since the 16th century, the Castle has been a ruin, a library and a gaol for witches. Today it is an award–winning museum featuring many hands-on displays to help explain the townspeople's experience of Colchester's varying fortunes.

The Castle itself is the largest keep ever built by the Normans. It was constructed on the foundations of the Roman Temple of Claudius, which can still be seen today.

EAST OF ENGLAND TOURIST BOARD
ALITY ASSURED FOR ATTRACTION

OLCHESTER

ColchesterCastleMuseum

lephone: 01206 282939

Sir Alfred Munnings Art Museum, Dedham

Canvey Island
Dutch Cottage Museum
Canvey Road Tel: (01268) 794005
An early 17thC cottage of one of Vermuyden's Dutch workmen who was responsible for drainage schemes in East Anglia. *Open 1 Apr, 6 May, Bank Hol Mon, 1430-1700; 2-30 Jun, Sun, Bank Hol Mon, 1430-1700; 3 Jul-28 Aug, Wed, Sun, Bank Hol Mon, 1430-1700; 1-8 Sep, Sun, 1430-1700. (H11)*

Canvey Island
Heritage Centre
Canvey Village, Canvey Road
Tel: (01268) 512220
The Heritage Centre is housed in the now redundant parish church of St Katherine, built in 1876. It contains an art and craft centre and a folk museum. *Open 5 Jan-7 Apr, Sat, Sun, 1200-1500; 20 Apr-27 Oct, Sat, Sun, 1100-1600; 2 Nov-15 Dec, Sat, Sun, 1200-1500. Please telephone for Easter openings. (H11)*

Chelmsford
⊛ **Chelmsford Museum**
Oaklands Park, Moulsham Street
Tel: (01245) 615100
Permanent collections of fossils and rocks, archaeology, costume, decorative arts, glass, natural history and the Essex Regiment Museum. Temporary exhibition programmes. *Open all year, Mon-Sat, 1000-1700; Sun, 1400-1700; closed 29 Mar, 25, 26 Dec. (F7)*

DID YOU KNOW
At Great Dunmow, Lionel Lukin demonstrated the world's first unsinkable lifeboat on the Doctors Pond in 1784.

Chelmsford
Moulsham Mill
Parkway
Tel: (01245) 608200
A mill on the site of an ancient watermill, dating back to Domesday. The watermill is not working and has been restored to a retail craft and business centre. *Open all year, Mon-Fri, 0900-1730, Sat, 0900-1700. Closed 25, 26 Dec, Bank Hol Mon. (F7)*

Coggeshall
Coggeshall Heritage Centre
St Peter's Hall, Stoneham Street
Tel: (01376) 563003
Ever-changing historical depiction of this medieval wool and market town. *Open 31 Mar-27 Oct, Sun, Bank Hol Mon,1415-1645. (I5)*

Colchester
⊛ **Colchester Castle** Q
Tel: (01206) 282931
A Norman keep on the foundations of a Roman temple. The archaeological material includes much on Roman Colchester (Camulodunum). *Open all year, Mon-Sat, 1000-1700, Sun, 1100-1700. Closed 25, 26 Dec, 1 Jan. £3.90/£2.60/£2.60. (K4)*

Essex

Colchester
● Firstsite - The Minories Art Gallery Q
74 High Street Tel: (01206) 577067

A Grade A gallery showing a programme of temporary exhibitions of contemporary art and housed in a converted Georgian house. *Open 2 Jan-29 Jun, Mon-Sat, 1000-1700; 1 Jul-31 Aug, Mon-Wed, 1000-1700, Thu, 1000-2000, Fri, Sat, 1000-1700, Sun, 1100-1700; 2 Sep-31 Dec, Mon-Sat, 1000-1700. (K4)*

Colchester
● Hollytrees Museum Q
High Street Tel: (01206) 282931

A collection of toys, costume and decorative arts from the 18th-20thC, displayed in an elegant Georgian town house, built in 1718. *Open all year, Mon-Sat, 1000-1700, Sun, 1100-1700. Closed 25, 26 Dec, 1 Jan. (K4)*

DID YOU KNOW

The turf maze in Saffron Walden is the largest one in the world, said to be around 800 years old.

CHELMSFORD MUSEUM & ESSEX REGIMENT MUSEUM

Oaklands Park, Moulsham Street,
Chelmsford CM2 9AQ
Tel: (01245) 615100

Admission Free
Open Mon - Sat 1000-1700
Sundays 1400-1700 Mar 20 Oct
(1300-1600 to 24 Mar and from 27 Oct)
Closed 29 Mar (Good Friday), 25 & 26 Dec.

Local and Society History from prehistory to the present; Essex Regiment history; Natural History (including live beehive), Coins, Ceramics, Costume, Glass. Temporary Exhibitions and Events. Wheelchair access to ground floor only (not including temporary exhibitions).

Barleylands Farm, Billericay

Colchester
● Natural History Museum Q
All Saints Church, High Street
Tel: (01206) 282932

Many hands-on displays and events giving the whole family an interesting perspective on the local natural history of Essex. *Open all year, Mon-Sat, 1000-1700, Sun, 1100-1700. Please contact for opening for Easter and Christmas. (K4)*

Colchester
Pam Schomberg Gallery
12 St Johns Street
Tel: (01206) 769458

Gallery situated in centre of town with changing exhibition program. Featuring a wide range of ceramics, glass, jewellery, wood textiles, prints and paintings. *Open all year, Mon-Sat, 1000-1700. Closed 25-28 Dec. (K4)*

Colchester
● Tymperleys Clock Museum Q
Trinity Street Tel: (01206) 282931

A fine collection of Colchester-made clocks from the Mason collection, displayed in a 15thC timber-framed house which Bernard Mason restored and presented to the town. *Open all year, Mon-Sat, 1000-1700, Sun, 1100-1700. Closed 25, 26 Dec, 1 Jan. (K4)*

DID YOU KNOW

The Electric Palace Cinema in Harwich, is the oldest unaltered, purpose-built cinema in Britain, dating from 1911

Dedham

◉ The Sir Alfred Munnings Art Museum
Castle House, Castle Hill
Tel: (01206) 322127

The house, studio and grounds where Sir Alfred Munnings, KCVO, lived and painted for 40 years. The collection also includes pictures on loan from private collections. *Open 31 Mar-31 Jul, Sun, Wed, Bank Hol Mon, 1400-1700; 3-31 Aug, Sat, Sun, Wed, Thu, Bank Hol Mon, 1400-1700; 1 Sep-6 Oct, Sun, Wed, Bank Hol Mon, 1400-1700. £3.00/50p/£2.00. (L3)*

Finchingfield

Finchingfield Guildhall and Heritage Centre
Church Hill
Tel: (01371) 810456

The Guildhall is open for exhibitions, lectures and meetings. Heritage Centre is open for details of Guildhall, church and other ancient property in village. *Open 29 Mar-29 Sep, Sun, Bank Hols, 1400-1700. (F3)*

Grays

Thurrock Museum
Thameside Complex, Orsett Road
Tel: (01375) 382555

Thurrock Museum contains over 1500 artefacts interpreting 250000 years of Thurrock's Heritage. From prehistory through to our recent industrial developments. *Open all year, Mon-Sat, 0900-1700; closed Bank Hols. (E12)*

Museum of Power, Langford

Great Bardfield

Bardfield Cage
Bridge Street

Great Bardfield cage is a 19thC village lock-up. There is a figure of a man in the cage and an audio tape player. *Open 30 Mar-29 Sep, Sat, Sun, Bank Hol Mon, 1400-1730. (F3/4)*

Great Bardfield

Cottage Museum
Dunmow Road

A 16thC charity cottage with a collection of 19th and 20thC domestic and agricultural artefacts and some rural crafts. Mainly straw plaiting and corn dollies. *Open 30 Mar-29 Sep, Sat, Sun, Bank Hol Mon, 1400-1730. (F3/4)*

Great Warley

◉ Hazle Ceramics Workshop
Stallion's Yard,
Codham Hall
Tel: (01277) 220892

Learn how to cast clay and watch demonstrations of the award-winning collectable ceramic wall plaques, A Nation of Shopkeepers. *Open all year, Fri-Sun, Bank Hol Mon, 1100-1700. Closed 24 Dec-4 Jan. (D10)*

Halstead

Townsford Mill Antiques Centre
The Causeway
Tel: (01787) 474451

Over 60 antique and collectable units housed in mill dating back to 1740 on 3 floors. The mill featured in Lovejoy straddles the River Colne. *Open all year, Mon-Sat, 1000-1700; Sun, Bank Hol Mon. 1100-1700; closed 25, 26, 31 Dec, 1 Jan. (H3)*

Harlow

The Playhouse
Playhouse Square, The High
Tel: (01279) 431945

Main 419 seat auditorium. National touring comedy, drama, music, dance and children's performances throughout the year. Theatre tours by appointment. *Open all year, Mon-Sat, 1100-2300. Closed 25 Dec, 1 Jan. Please contact for details of admission prices. (B7)*

Harwich

Ha'penny Pier Visitor Centre
The Quay

Visitor information centre for everything in Harwich and includes a small Harwich and the New World exhibition. *Open 1 May-31 Aug, daily, 1000-1700. (O3)*

Essex

Ha'Penny Pier Visitor Centre, Harwich

Harwich
Harwich Lifeboat Museum
Timberfields, off Wellington Road
The Harwich Lifeboat Museum contains the last Clacton off-shore 37ft lifeboat, the Oakley class and a fully-illustrated history of lifeboat service in Harwich. *Open 7 May-28 Aug, daily, 1000-1700; 1-22 Sep, Sun, 1000-1200, 1400-1700. 50p/50p. (O3)*

Harwich
Harwich Maritime Museum
Low Lighthouse, Harbour Crescent
Tel: (01255) 503429
A museum with special displays related to the Royal Navy and commercial shipping with fine views over the unending shipping movements in the harbour. *Open 7-28 Apr, Sun, 1000-1200, 1400-1700; 1 May-31 Aug, daily, 1000-1700; 1-22 Sep, Sun, 1000-1200, 1400-1700. 50p. (O3)*

Kelvedon
Feering and Kelvedon
Local History Museum
Maldon Road Tel: (01376) 571206
A museum containing artefacts from the Roman settlement of Camonium, manorial history, agricultural tools and bygones. *Open 5 Jan-23 Feb, Sat, 1000-1230; 2 Mar-26 Oct, Mon, 1400-1700, Sat, 1000-1230; 2 Nov-21 Dec, Sat, 1000-1230; closed 1 Apr, 27 May. (I5)*

Langford
Museum of Power
Steam Pumping Station,
Hatfield Road
Tel: (01621) 843183
Housed in an impressive 1920s building. A large triple-expansion steam engine is the main exhibit with many other sources of power on show. *Open all year, Wed-Sun, 0930-1730; closed 23-31 Dec. £1.50/75p/75p. (H/17)*

Linford
Walton Hall Farm Museum
Walton Hall Road Tel: (01375) 671874
The main collection is housed in a 17thC English barn and other farm buildings. *Open 23 Mar-23 Dec, Thu-Sun, 1000-1700. Please phone for school holiday opening times. £3.00/£1.50. (F12)*

Lindsell, nr Dunmow
⊛ Lindsell Art Gallery
Tel: (01371) 870777
An art gallery specialising in paintings, prints, sculptures and greeting cards by local artists. The pictures are largely of local interest. *Open all year, daily except Wed, 0930-1730; closed 26-31 Dec. (E4)*

Maldon
Maeldune Heritage Centre
Plume Building
Tel: (01621) 851628
The Maeldune Centre houses the celebrated Maldon embroidery and exhibitions of paintings and local history. Large archive of old Maldon photographs with prints available. *Open 3 Jan-30 Mar, Thu-Sat, 1200-1500; 1 Apr-30 Sep, Mon-Sat, 1330-1630; 3 Oct-28 Dec, Thu-Sat, 1200-1500. Please phone to confirm opening times. (H/7)*

*Southchurch Hall Museum,
Southend-on-Sea*

Colchester Castle Museum

Maldon
Maldon District Museum
47 Mill Road Tel: (01621) 842688
A small museum devoted to Maldon town with
many articles of a general and domestic nature in
a charming building. *Open 1 Apr-27 Oct, Wed-Fri;
1400-1600, Sat, Sun; Bank Hol Mon, 1400-1700.
£1.00/25p. (H/I7)*

Manningtree
**Manningtree and District Local History
Museum**
Manningtree Library, High Street
Tel: (01206) 392747
A local history museum with displays of old
photographs, artefacts, books, local maps and
plans. Some permanent displays with 2 major
exhibitions of local interest yearly. *Open all year,
Wed, 1000-1200, Fri, 1400-1600; Sat, 1000-1200;
closed 29, 30 Apr, 26-29 Dec. (L/M3)*

Mistley
⊛ Essex Secret Bunker
Crown Building, Shrubland Road
Tel: (01206) 392271
Vast concrete bunker hides over 16,000sq ft of
operational space. Explore the maze of rooms and
passages and the site comes to life with sound
effects, cinemas and displays. *Open 5 Jan-24 Feb,
Sat, Sun, 1030-1630; 2 Mar-31 July, daily, 1030-
1700; 1-31 Aug, daily, 1030-1800; 1-29 Sep, daily,
1030-1700. Please phone for Oct-Dec opening times.
£4.95/£3.75/£4.45. (M3)*

Purfleet
Purfleet Heritage and Military Centre
Royal Gunpowder Magazine,
Centurion Way Tel: (01708) 866764
The Royal Gunpowder Magazine dates from 1760.
The heritage centre displays local history,
photographs, artefacts and 1939-1945
memorabilia. *Please contact for details of opening
times. £2.00/75p. (D12)*

Essex

Rayleigh
Lower Barn Farm Craft and Cultural Centre
Lower Barn Farm,
London Road
Tel: (01268) 780991
A tearoom with over 20 craft studios, regular cultural events, antique fayres, toy fayres and school educational visits. *Open all year, daily, 1000-1700. (H10)*

Romford
Norpar Flowers
Navestock Hall,
Navestock
Tel: (01277) 374968
Beautiful timbered shop set in ancient farmyard, with historic buildings. Dried flowers are grown and dried on the premises and then made up for retailing in the shop. *Open all year, Mon-Sat, 0900-1700. Please phone for Christmas opening. (C10)*

Saffron Walden
Fry Public Art Gallery
Bridge End Gardens, Castle Street
Tel: (01799) 513779
Permanent exhibition of 20thC British artists who have lived and worked in north west Essex. Two or three changing exhibitions additionally are on show in parallel. *Open 29 Mar-30 Jun, Sat, Sun, Bank Hols, 1430-1730; 2 Jul-24 Sep, Tue, Sat, Sun, Bank Hol Mon, 1430-1730; 28 Sep-27 Oct, Sat, Sun, 1430-1730. (C/D2)*

Saffron Walden
⊛ Saffron Walden Museum
Museum Street Tel: (01799) 510333
A friendly, family-sized museum of local history, decorative arts, ethnography, archaeology and natural history. Good disabled access. *Open 363 days of the year - please contact for details. £1.00/free/50p. (C/D2)*

Southend-on-Sea
⊛ Central Museum and Planetarium
Victoria Avenue Tel: (01702) 215131
An Edwardian building housing displays of archaeology, natural history, social and local history. Also housing the only planetarium in south east England outside London. *Open all year, Tue-Sat, except Tue following Bank Hol, 1000-1700; closed 29 Mar. Please contact for Christmas opening. £2.50/£1.60/£1.60. (I10/11)*

Southend-on-Sea
Focal Point Gallery
Southend Central Library, Victoria Avenue
Tel: (01702) 612621
A regularly changing exhibition programme of the best of contemporary photography, digital and video art. Artists' talks and workshops accompany most shows. *Open all year, Mon-Fri, 0900-1900, Sat, 0900-1700. Closed Bank Hols, 25 Dec, 1 Jan. Closed between exhibitions, please phone for details. (I10/11)*

Southend-on-Sea
⊛ Prittlewell Priory
Priory Park, Victoria Avenue
Tel: (01702) 342878
The remains of a 12thC priory with later additions housing displays of natural history, medieval religious life, radios, gramophones and televisions. *Open all year, Tue-Sat, 1000-1300, 1400-1700. (I10/11)*

Southend-on-Sea
Southend Pier Museum
Southend Pier, Marine Parade
Tel: (01702) 611214
Situated in redundant pier workshops underneath the pier station. Depicts the history of the longest pier in the world from 1830. Pictures and antique slot machines. *Open 6 May-27 Oct, Tue, Wed, Sat, Sun, 1100-1700; school hols, 1100-1800; 26 Dec, 1 Jan, 1200-1600. 50p. (I10/11)*

House on the Hill Museums Adventure, Stansted Mountfitchet

Essex

Southend-on-Sea
Southend Planetarium
Central Museum, Victoria Avenue
Tel: (01702) 215131

The projector provides a clear illusion of the night sky with stars and the Milky Way which lasts 40 minutes. No children under 5 please. *Open all year, Wed-Sat, performances, 1100, 1400, 1600. Pre-booked groups have priority. Closed 29, 30 Mar. Please phone for Christmas closure. £2.25/£1.60. (I10/11)*

Southend-on-Sea
⊚ Southchurch Hall Museum
Southchurch Hall Gardens, Southchurch Hall Close
Tel: (01702) 467671

A moated, timber-framed 14thC manor-house with Tudor extensions set in attractive gardens. *Open all year, Tue-Sat, 1000-1300, 1400-1700. Preference given to schools in the morning. Closed 29 Mar, 2 Apr, 25, 26 Dec, 1 Jan, Tue following Bank Hol Mon. (I10/11)*

Stansted Mountfitchet
House on the Hill Museums Adventure
Tel: (01279) 813237

An exciting, animated toy museum covering 7,000 sq ft and featuring a huge collection of toys from Victorian times to the 1970s. Offers a nostalgic trip back to childhood. *Open all year, daily, 1000-1600. Please phone for winter openings. £3.80/£2.80/£3.50. (C4)*

Thaxted
Glendale Forge
Monk Street
Tel: (01371) 830466

Forge with a comprehensive range of wrought ironwork, gates, lanterns, fireguards, blacksmith work and a small collection of unusual half-size vehicles. *Open all year, Mon-Sat, 0900-1700, Sun, 1000-1200. Closed 23 Dec-2 Jan. Train shed open, Wed, 1400-1700, Sun, 1000-1200. (E3)*

Thaxted
Thaxted Guidhall
Town Street Tel: (01371) 830226

A 15thC building housing a permanent display of old photographs and relics, mainly relating to the history of Thaxted. Exhibitions on some weekends and a small museum. *Open 29 Mar-22 Sep, Sat, Sun, Bank Hol Mon, 1400-1730. 25p/10p/25p. (E3)*

Tiptree
Tiptree Tearoom, Museum and Shop Ⓠ
Wilkin and Sons Ltd
Tel: (01621) 814524

Tearoom and shop with a museum displaying how life was and how the art of jam-making has advanced over the years at Tiptree. *Open 2 Jan-31 May, Mon-Sat, 1000-1700; 1 Jun-31 Aug, Mon-Sat, 1000-1700; Sun, 1200-1700; 2 Sep-24 Dec, Mon-Sat, 1000-1700. (I6)*

Southchurch Hall Museum, Southend-on-Sea

Waltham Abbey
Epping Forest District Museum
39-41 Sun Street Tel: (01992) 716882
Tudor and Georgian timber-framed buildings with a herb garden, a Tudor-panelled room, temporary exhibitions, the social history of Epping Forest and many special events. *Please contact for details of opening times. (A8)*

Waltham Abbey
⊛ Royal Gunpowder Mills
Beaulieu Drive Tel: (01992) 767022
Combining fascinating history, exciting science and 175 acres of natural parkland, the Royal Gunpowder Mills offers a truly unique day out for the family. *Open 16 Mar-27 Oct, daily, 1000-1800 (last admission 1700). £5.90/£3.25/£5.25. (A8)*

Walton-on-the-Naze
Walton Maritime Museum
East Terrace
A 100-year-old former lifeboat house, carefully restored with exhibitions of local interest particularly maritime, urban, geological seaside and development. *Open Easter (29 Mar-1 Apr), 4-6, 25-27 May, Sat-Bank Hol Mon, 1400-1600; 1 Jul-29 Sep, daily, 1400-1600. 60p. (O5)*

Westcliff-on-Sea
⊛ Beecroft Art Gallery
Station Road Tel: (01702) 347418
An Edwardian building with panoramic estuary views which houses a permanent collection of works of art plus a varied programme of temporary exhibitions. *Open all year. Tue-Sat, 1000-1330, 1400-1700. Closed 29 Mar. Open Sun in Jun-Aug, 1100-1300, 1400-1700. Please phone for Christmas opening. (I11)*

West Mersea
Mersea Island Museum
High Street Tel: (01206) 385191
Museum of local, social and natural history with displays of methods and equipment used in fishing and wildfowling. Fossils and a mineral display. Also special exhibitions. *Open 4 May-29 Sep, Wed-Sun, Bank Hol Mon, 1400-1700. 50p/25p/25p. (K6)*

Witham
Dorothy L Sayers Centre
Witham Library, 18 Newland Street
Tel: (01376) 519625
A reference collection of books by and about Dorothy L Sayers. *Open all year, Thu, 1400-1700. Closed 26, 27 Dec, 2 Jan. (H6)*

Mountfitchet Castle, Stansted Mountfitchet

Essex

machinery & transport

Audley End
Audley End Miniature Railway
Tel: (01799) 541354
Steam and diesel locomotives in 10.5 gauge, running through attractive woodland for 1.5 miles. The railway crosses the River Cam twice. *Open 23 Mar-27 Oct, Sat, Sun, 1400-1700, daily in school hols and Bank Hols, 1400-1700; 14-22 Dec, daily 1100-1600. Please contact for details of admission prices. (C/D2)*

Billericay
Barleylands Farm
See entry in Museums section.

Burnham-on-Crouch
Mangapps Railway Museum
Tel: (01621) 784898
A large collection of railway relics, 2 restored stations, locomotives, coaches and wagons with a working railway line of 0.75 miles. *Please contact for details of opening times. £4.00/£2.00. (J9)*

Canvey Island
Canvey Railway and Model Engineering Club
Waterside Farm Leisure Centre
Two miniature railways. One live steam and one live steam and diesel over 1 mile of track. *Open 7 Apr-6 Oct, Sun, 1000-1700. (H11)*

DID YOU KNOW

The railway station platform at Colchester is the longest in England, whilst the platform at nearby Manningtree is the second longest!

Canvey Island
Castle Point Transport Museum Society
105 Point Road
Tel: (01268) 684272
A 1935 museum housing a collection of buses, coaches and commercial vehicles in restored and unrestored condition. Some examples of these vehicles are unique. *Open 7 Apr-27 Oct, Sun, 1000-1700. (H11)*

Castle Hedingham
◎ Colne Valley Railway
Yeldham Road
Tel: (01787) 461174
An award-winning station. Ride in the most pleasant part of the Colne Valley. A large, interesting collection of operational heritage rolling stock. *Open 31 Mar-31 Oct, daily, 1000-1600. Please contact for details of admission prices. (H2/3)*

East Anglian Railway Museum, Colchester

Essex

Colchester
East Anglian Railway Museum
Chappel Station
Tel: (01206) 242524

A large and varied collection of working and static railway exhibits from the age of steam, set in original surroundings of a once important Victorian country junction station. *Open all year, daily, 1000-1700; closed 24 Dec-7 Jan. £6.00/ £3.00/ £4.50. (event days), £3.00/£2.00/£2.50 (non-event days). (K4)*

Goldhanger
Maldon and District Agricultural and Domestic Museum
47 Church Street
Tel: (01621) 788647

An extensive collection of farm machinery, domestic items of every kind, products of Maldon Ironworks, printing machines from 1910, a display of photographs and stuffed birds. *Open 31 Mar-1 Dec, Wed, 1000-1800; Sun, 1400-1800. £1.50/£1.00. (I/J7)*

North Weald
North Weald Airfield Museum
Ad Astra House, Hurricane Way
Tel: (01992) 523010

A fine old house at the former main gate of North Weald Airfield standing adjacent to an impressive memorial. *Open 31 Mar-27 Oct, Sat, Sun, 1200-1700; 3 Jul-28 Aug, Wed, 1200-1700. £1.50/£1.00/ £1.00. (C8)*

Pitsea
National Motorboat Museum
Wat Tyler Country Park
Tel: (01268) 550077

A museum devoted to the history and evolution of the motorboat in the sports and leisure field. *Open all year, Thu-Sun, 1000-1630; daily during school hols; closed 23 Dec-4 Jan. (F10)*

St Osyth
East Essex Aviation Society and Museum
Martello Tower, Point Clear

An exhibition of aircraft parts from local recoveries. There are also displays from World War I up to the late 1940s housed in a 19thC Martello tower. *Open all year, Mon, 1900-2200; 3 Feb-2 Jun, Sun, 1000-1400, 5 Jun-29 Sep; Wed, Sun, 1000-1400. 6-27 Oct, Sun 1000-1400. Open additional hours on Bank Hol Mon. (H6)*

Barleylands Farm, Billericay

Essex

mills

Aythorpe Roding
◉ Aythorpe Roding Postmill
Tel: (01245) 437663

An 18thC postmill restored to working order. It is winded by a fantail arrangement which runs along a stone track around the mill. *Open 28 Apr, 26 May, 30 Jun, 28 Jul, 25 Aug, 29 Sep, Sun 1400-1700. (D6)*

Bocking
Bocking Windmill
Church Street

Postmill built in 1721. Small collection of historic agricultural items. *Open 6, 27 May, 23 Jun, 21 Jul, 26 Aug, Sun, Bank Hol Mon, 1400-1700 (G4/5).*

Colchester
◉ Bourne Mill
Bourne Road   Tel: (01206) 572422

The mill was originally built as a fishing lodge in 1591 and features stepped Dutch Gables. There is a mill pond and some of the machinery including the waterwheel is working. *Open: 30, 31 Apr; 2, 6, May; 2 Jun-27 Aug, Sun, Tue, Bank Hol Mons, 1400-1700. £2.00/£1.00. (K4)*

Finchingfield
◉ Finchingfield
(Duck End) Postmill
Tel: (01245) 437663

A small, simple, mid-18thC feudal or 'estate'-type postmill with a wooden wind shaft and 1 pair of stones. *Open 21 Apr, 19 May, 16 Jun, 21 Jul, 18 Aug, 15 Sep, Sun, 1400-1700. (F3)*

Mountnessing
◉ Mountnessing Windmill
Roman Road   Tel: (01245) 437663

An early 19thC postmill restored to working order. Visitors may climb the windmill and see the fascinating wooden machinery. *Open 19 May, 16 Jun, 21 Jul, 18 Aug, 15 Sep, 20 Oct, Sun. 1400-1700. (E9)*

Rayleigh
Rayleigh Windmill and Museum
Rear of Mill Hall, Bellingham Lane
Tel: (01268) 771072

A windmill with sails but no mechanism. On the ground floor, the museum has bygones and local artefacts. The upper floors of the mill are not open. *Open 6 Apr-28 Sep, Sat, 1030-1300. 20p/10p/20p. (H10)*

Stansted
Stansted Mountfitchet Windmill
Millside

Brick tower windmill built 1787. Not working but contains most of original machinery. Scheduled ancient monument. *Open 31 Mar, 1, 7 Apr, 5, 6, 26, 27 May, 2 Jun, 7 Jul, 4, 25, 26 Aug, 1 Sep, 6 Oct, Sun, Bank Hols, 1400-1800. 50p/25p (C/D4/5).*

Stock
◉ Stock Towermill
Mill Lane Tel: (01245) 437663

A 19thC towermill, recently restored to working order and typical of the latest in millwrights techniques just before windmills became obsolete. *Open 12 May, 9 Jun, 14 Jul, 11 Aug, 8 Sep, 13 Oct, Sun 1400-1700. (F9)*

Thaxted
John Webb's Windmill
Mill Row Tel: (01371) 830285

The windmill has 4 floors of mill which can be explored. The main machinery is intact and on view. There is a rural museum on the two lower floors. *Open 4 May-29 Sep, Sat, Sun and Bank Hol Mon, 30 Sep, 1400-1800. 50p/25p. (E3)*

Thorrington
◉ Thorrington Tidemill
Brightlingsea Road Tel: (01245) 437663

An early 19thC tidal watermill, restored by Essex County Council. Visitors may climb to the top of the mill. *Open 28 Apr, 26 May, 30 Jun, 28 Jul, 25 Aug, 29 Sep, 1400-1700. (M5)*

Essex

Gardens & Vineyards

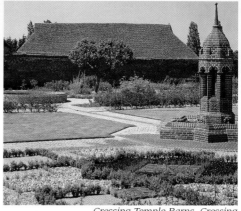

Cressing Temple Barns, Cressing

Abridge
BBC Essex Garden
Ongar Road Tel: (01708) 688581
Garden with lawn, borders, small vegetable area, linked to Ken's programme Down to Earth on Sats. Also farmyard pets, teashop, superb plants and clematis on sale. *Open all year, daily, 0900-1730; closed 24-30 Dec. (C9)*

Bocking
Roundwood
Bocking Church Street
Tel: (01376) 551728
Set in 7 acres, delightful area for tea in the tearooms. Unusual plants and crafts for sale all year round. *Open all year, Mon, 0900-1630, Tue, Wed, 0900-1730, Thu, 0900-1630, Fri, 0900-1600 or dusk if earlier; 5 May-23 Jun, Sun, 1000-1600. (G4/5)*

Boxted
Carter's Vineyards Q
Green Lane Tel: (01206) 271136
Vineyards and a winery with an alternative energy project and a conservation area. Fishing facilities (day licence) are available. *Open 24 Apr-30 Sep, Tue-Sun, Bank Hol Mon, 1100-1700. £2.50. (K3)*

Braintree
The Original Great Maze
Blake House Craft Centre
Tel: (01376) 553146
This challenging maize maze is known as one of the biggest mind benders in the world. Now set in over 10 acres of the idyllic northern Essex countryside. *Open 13 Jul-8 Sep, daily, 1000. Last admission 1700. £4.00/£2.50/£2.50. (G4/5)*

Coggeshall
⊛ Grange Barn
See entry in Historic Houses section.

Coggeshall
⊛ Markshall Estate and Arboretum
The Thomas Phillips Price Trust,
Estate Office, Marks Hall
Tel: (01376) 563796
Garden, arboretum, woodlands and visitor centre with a teashop, gift sales, ornamental grounds, lakes, cascades, mature avenues and waymarked walks. *Car charge £3.50. Walks open at any reasonable time. Visitor Centre and Arboretum open 2-31 Mar, Sat, Sun, 1030-dusk; 2 Apr-31 Oct, Tue-Sun, 1030-1700; 2-30 Nov, Sat, Sun, 1030-dusk. (I5)*

Coggeshall
⊛ Paycockes
See entry in Historic Houses section.

Cressing
⊛ Cressing Temple Barns
See entry in
Ancient Monuments section.

Dedham
⊛ Gnome Magic
New Dawn, Old Ipswich Road
Tel: (01206) 231390
Gnome Magic is an unusual treat. Enjoy the delightful garden which blends into an amazing wood where the growing number of 500 gnomes and their friends live. *Open 1 Apr-20 Sept, daily, 1000-1730. £3.00/£1.50/£2.50. (L3)*

Visit
COLCHESTER
Castle park

COLCHESTER'S CASTLE PARK is an oasis of horticultural splendour in the town centre. This award winning classic Victorian park is a delight for the senses all the year round. But it's not just the gardens that makes the park such a delight to visit. Castle Park's 23 gently sloping acres (9.3ha) provide the perfect venue for fairs, festivals, open-air concerts and displays.

Variety is the essence of Castle Park. There are formal flower beds and gardens, a Sensory Garden, a children's playground, the newly planted herb beds and rhododendron borders, the new Hollytrees museum where you can discover life in Colchester over the last 300 years and summertime Pitch & Putt. A magnificent weeping willow provides an impressive backdrop to the children's boating lake and you can take picturesque walks along the river. Stroll through the park to the oldest Roman wall in Britain, for a treat in the café near the Victorian bandstand or bring your own picnic.

No trip to Castle Park is complete without a visit to the award-winning Castle Museum, popular for its hands-on displays and holiday events. Visit the Castle Museum and its Roman foundations and discover the major historical events which took place in and around the Castle almost 2000 years ago.

EAST OF ENGLAND TOURIST BOARD
QUALITY ASSURED VISITOR ATTRACTION

COLCHESTER

*f*OR FURTHER INFORMATION ABOUT COLCHESTER AND EVENTS IN CASTLE PARK
☞ PLEASE CALL THE COLCHESTER VISITOR INFORMATION CENTRE
1 QUEEN STREET · COLCHESTER · ESSEX · CO1 2PG ☎ 01206 282920

Carters Vineyard, Boxted

East Mersea
Mersea Vineyard
Rewsalls Lane
Tel: (01206) 385900
Established 10-acre site overlooking the Blackwater and Colne estuaries. Free admission, tasting and vineyard walk. Conducted tours of winery and vineyard by appointment only. *Open all year, Mon-Sat, except Tue, 1100-1700, Sun, 1200-1600. Closed 24 Dec-2 Jan. (L6)*

Elmstead Market
The Beth Chatto Gardens Ltd
Tel: (01206) 822007
Drought tolerant plants furnish the gravel garden throughout the year, the dappled wood garden is filled with shade lovers, while the water garden fills the spring fed hollow. *Open 3 Jan-28 Feb, Mon-Fri, 0900-1600; 1 Mar-31 Oct, Mon-Sat, 0900-1700; 1 Nov-20 Dec, Mon-Fri, 0900-1600. Closed Bank Hol Mons. £3.00. (L4/5)*

Feering
Feeringbury Manor
Tel: (01376) 561946
A large 6-acre garden with a stream, ponds and the River Blackwater at the bottom of the garden. There are many rare and interesting plants. *Open 4 Apr-26 Jul, Thu, Fri, 0800-1600. £2.50. (I5)*

Felsted
Felsted Vineyard
The Vineyards, Crix Green
Tel: (01245) 361504
Showing wine and cider making and vineyard work. Wine and vines may be bought along with other local produce. *Open all year, Sat, Sun, 1000-dusk. Closed 24 Dec-1 Jan. (F5)*

Gosfield
Gosfield Hall
See entry in Historic Houses section.

Great Dunmow
The Gardens of Easton Lodge
Warwick House, Easton Lodge
Tel: (01371) 876979
Gardens created since 1971 on the foundations of Easton Lodge with a courtyard, dovecote, pergolas and forgotten gardens designed by Peto (1903) and now being restored. *Open 29 Mar-27 Oct, Fri-Sun, 1200-1800; please contact to confirm snowdrops opening times. £3.80/£1.50/£3.50. (E5)*

Harlow
The Gibberd Garden
Marsh Lane, Gilden Way
Tel: (01279) 442112
Important 20thC garden designed by Sir Frederick Gibberd, master planner for Harlow New Town. With some 50 sculptures. *Open 6 Apr-29 Sep, Sat, Sun, Bank Hol Mon, 1400-1800. Please contact for details of admission prices. (B7)*

Ingatestone
⊛ Ingatestone Hall
See entry in Historic Houses section.

Layer Marney
⊛ Layer Marney Tower
See entry in Historic Houses section.

Seafront Gardens, Clacton-on-Sea

RHS Garden, Rettendon

Little Easton
**Little Easton Manor
and Barn Theatre**
Park Road Tel: (01371) 872857
Little Easton Manor has gardens, lakes and fountains, The Barn Theatre, angling, a caravan and rally site and refreshments. *Open 6 Jun–26 Sep, Thu, 1300–1700. £2.00/free. (E4/5)*

Messing
Red House
School Road
Tel: (01621) 815219
Wildlife gardens, pond and children's play area. Greenhouses and polytunnels with a large display of shrubs and bedding plants. Coffee shop, picnic area and conference venue. *Open 8 Jan–30 Apr, Mon-Fri, 0930-1600; 1 May-30 Sep, Mon-Fri, 0930-1600, Sat, Sun, 1000-1600; 1 Oct-17 Dec, Mon-Fri, 0930-1600. (J5)*

Purleigh
New Hall Vineyards
Chelmsford Road
Tel: (01621) 828343
Guided tours of the vineyards with a trail through the vines and the cellars where wine can be tasted. Also visit the press house with slide shows. See fermentation and bottling. *Open all year, Mon-Fri, 1000-1700; Sat, Sun, 1000-1330. (H/I8)*

Rettendon
⊛ **R H S Garden**
Hyde Hall Tel: (01245) 400256
An eight acre garden with all year round interest including greenhouses, roses, flowering shrubs, perennial borders and alpines. *Open 30 Mar-31 Aug, daily, 1100-1800; 1 Sep-27 Oct, daily, 1000-1700. Please contact for details of admission prices. (G9)*

Saffron Walden
⊛ **Audley End House and Park** Q
See entry in Historic Houses section.

Saffron Walden
⊛ **Bridge End Gardens**
Tel: (01799) 510445
Victorian garden featuring fine trees, garden ornaments, a rose garden, Dutch garden, pavilions and a hedge maze. Contact Tourist Centre (refundable deposit £10.00 for key). *Open all year by appointment only, daily, dawn-dusk. (D/E2)*

Stock
Great Stocks Vineyard
Downham Road Tel: (01277) 841122
A 10-acre vineyard set in 20 acres of peaceful countryside. Two coarse fishing lakes near the village of Stock, just off the B1007. *Open all year by appointment. £5.00/£5.00. (F9)*

Widdington
⊛ **Priors Hall Barn**
See entry in Historic Houses section.

Writtle
⊛ **Hylands House
Park and Gardens**
See entry in Historic Houses section.

Essex

nurseries & garden centres

Coggeshall
The Dutch Nursery
Garden Centres
West Street, Coggeshall, Essex CO6 1NT
Tel: (01376 561287)

In picturesque Coggeshall, The Dutch Nursery is well worth a visit. The large shop has a wide range of cut flowers, houseplants, silks, gift items, pots, garden furniture and seasonal bulbs direct from Holland. In the Plant Area you will find many different varieties of trees, shrubs, climbing plants, roses and seasonal bedding. Our terracotta and glazed pots and containers are excellent value. Sit down and relax in our new Coffee Shop which serves delicious home-made cakes and snacks daily. Coach parties welcome by appointment. Finally, visit the water gardens and other shops adjacent to the large car park. *(I5)*

Ardleigh
Notcutts Garden Centres
Station Road, Ardleigh, Essex
Tel: (01206) 230271

Discover a world of ideas and inspiration around every corner for you, your home and your garden. From fabulous plants to gifts and treats galore, there's so much to see. Gift ideas from around the world, houseplants, books, 3,000 varieties of hardy plants (with a 2 year replacement guarantee), expert friendly advice about seasonal and bedding plants, garden furniture and barbecues. Keep an eye open for regular offers on key garden products. *Notcutts open 7 days a week, free car-parking plus children's play area. (L3/4)*

Essex

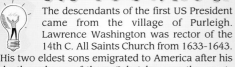

Clacton-on-Sea
Clacton Pier
E and M Harrison (Clacton) Ltd
1 North Sea   Tel: (01255) 421115
Fun pier with 13 fairground rides, arcades, shops, cafes, restaurants, side shows, a pub with children's play area and sea aquarium. *Open all year, daily, from 1000; closed 25 Dec. (N6)*

Clacton-on-Sea
Rascals Children's Indoor Play Centre
Rascals House, Telford Rd, Gorse Lane Ind Est
Tel: (01255) 475755
Soft play centre with seating for 100 in the restaurant area. Full menu available. *Open all year, daily, summer 1000-2100; winter 1000-1900. Closed 24-26 Dec. Please contact for details of admission prices. (N6)*

Colchester
Childsplay Adventureland Ｑ
Clarendon Way
Tel: (01206) 366566
Premier indoor play facility for under 9's. ROSPA inspected for safety. Ball pools, slides and a special area for babies and toddlers. Coffee shop and restaurant. *Open all year, daily, 0930-1830. Closed 25, 26 Dec. Child £3.20. (K4)*

Colchester
⊛ **Colchester Zoo** Ｑ
Maldon Road, Stanway
Tel: (01206) 331292
Zoo with 200 species and some of the best cat and primate collections in the UK, 60 acres of gardens and lakes, award-winning animal enclosures and picnic areas. *Open all year, daily, winter, 0930-1 hour before dusk; summer, 0930-1830; closed 25 Dec. Please contact for details of admission prices. (K4)*

Colchester
Go Bananas Ｑ
9-10 Mason Road, Cowdray Centre
Tel: (01206) 761762
Children's indoor adventure playground with a 3-storey adventure frame for 5-12 year-olds, an under 5's village, climbing wall, spaceball ride and cafeteria. *Open all year, daily, 0930-1830 except Fri, 0930-2030. Closed 1 Apr, 25, 26 Dec, 1 Jan. Child (under 5) £3.20. (K4)*

Colchester
⊛ **Quasar at Rollerworld**
Eastgates   Tel: (01206) 868868
East Anglia's largest quasar arena. *Please contact for details of opening times and prices. (K4)*

Halstead
⊛ **Tumblewood**
Whitehouse Business Park, Whiteash Green
Tel: (01787) 474760
Childrens' indoor adventure playground with facilities for parties. There are 3 separate play areas, baby area, toddler area and large play area. *Open all year, daily, 1000-1800. Closed 25, 26 Dec. Under 5: £2.95, over 5: £3.45. (H/I 3/4)*

DID YOU KNOW

The longest pleasure pier in the world can be found at Southend-on-Sea. Opened in 1899, it stretches 1.33 miles into the Thames estuary. Whilst Clacton-on-Sea boasts the largest pleasure pier in the world - built in 1871, it was widened in the 1930's to over 300 feet wide!

Colchester Zoo

Essex

Mistley
Mistley Place Park
New Road Tel: (01206) 396483

Twenty five acres of woodlands and lakeside walks with goats, horses, sheep, rabbits, ducks, hens, a tearoom, gift shop and a nature trail. *Open all year, Tue-Sun, Bank Hol Mon, 1000-1800, or dusk, if earlier. Open daily in school hols. £2.50/£1.50/£2.00. (M3)*

Nazeing
Ada Cole Rescue Stables
Broadlands, Broadley Common
Tel: (01992) 892133

A horse rescue charity with 47 acres of paddocks and stables with a gift shop and information room. *Open all year, daily, 1400-1700 or dusk in winter; closed 25, 26 Dec, 1 Jan. £1.50/free/£1.50. (B7)*

Rayleigh
◉ Megazone Laser Arena
The Warehouse Centre, 7 Brook Road
Tel: (01268) 779100

A game of stealth, strategy and skill played in the laser arena in Essex with the most advanced laser system. *Open all year, Mon-Fri, 1630-2300, Sat, Sun, 0930-2200, School Hols, Mon-Fri, 0930-2300, Sat, Sun, 0930-2200, Closed 29 Mar, 25, 26 Dec, 1 Jan. £3.50/£3.50/£3.50. (H10)*

Southend-on-Sea Ｑ
Adventure Island
Sunken Gardens West,
Western Esplanade Tel: (01702) 468023

Rides and attractions include the big wheel, fantasy dome, giant pirate ship and Dragon Claw with fast food kiosks. *Open 5 Jan-31 Mar, Sat, Sun, from 1100; 1 Apr-30 Sep, daily, from 1100; 5 Oct-29 Dec, Sat, Sun, from 1100. Closed 25 Dec. (I10/11)*

Southend-on-Sea
Mr B's Space Chase Quasar
5/8 Marine Parade Tel: (01702) 603947

A quasar arena situated within a family entertainment centre with prize bingo and video games. *Open all year, Mon-Fri, 1200-2300; Sat, Sun, Bank Hol Mon, summer school half terms, 1000-2300; closed 25 Dec. £2.00/£2.00. (I10/11)*

Southend-on-Sea
◉ Southend-on-Sea Pier
Western Esplanade Tel: (01702) 215620

Train ride along the pier. Pier Museum at North Station, amusements novelty shop, restaurant, licensed public house. Guided tours at Lifeboat House. *Please contact for details of opening times and admission prices. (I10/11)*

Southend-on-Sea
Southend Sea Life Centre
Eastern Esplanade Tel: (01702) 601834

The very latest in marine technology brings the secrets of the mysterious underwater world closer than ever before. An amazing underwater tunnel allows an all-round view. *Open all year, daily, from 1000; last admission, 1700; closed 25 Dec. £4.95/£3.50/£3.50. (I10/11)*

South Weald
Old MacDonalds
Educational Farm Park
Weald Road Tel: (01277) 375177

We tell the whole story of British livestock farming, keeping rare breeds, cattle, pigs, sheep, shire horses and poultry, red squirrels, owls, otters and lots more. *Open all year, daily, 1000-dusk in winter; 1000-1800 in summer; closed 25, 26 Dec. £3.25/£2.00/£2.75. (D9)*

South Woodham Ferrers
Tropical Wings Butterfly and Bird Gardens
Wickford Road
Tel: (01245) 425394

Over 6,000sq ft of tropical house which is home to free-flying birds. Outdoor bird gardens and mini-beast display. *Open 16 Feb-17 Nov, daily, summer, 0930-1730, winter 0930 - 1 hour before dusk. £3.50/£2.25/£3.00. (H9)*

Adventure Island,
Southend-on-Sea

Essex

South Woodham Ferrers
Marsh Farm Country Park
Marsh Farm Road Tel: (01245) 321552
A farm centre with sheep, a pig unit, free-range chickens, milking demonstrations, an indoor and outdoor adventure play area, nature reserve, walks, picnic area and pet's corner. *Open 16 Feb-end Oct school hol, Mon-Fri, 1000-1630, Sat, Sun, Bank Hols, 1000-1730; Oct school hol-15 Dec, Sat, Sun, 1000-1730. Please contact for details of admission prices. (H9)*

Theydon Garnon
Hobbs Cross Open Farm
Tel: (01992) 814764
A working livestock farm with pigs, beef cattle, hens, sheep, goats, playbarn playground, toddlers playroom, a licensed restaurant and a farm shop. *Open all year, daily, 0900-1700; closed 18 Dec-13 Jan. £2.75/£2.25/£2.25. (B9)*

Vange
Basildon Zoo
London Road Tel: (01268) 553985
Big cats, meerkats, otters and birds of prey. Sand pit and swings. Feed and touch domestic animals. Cafe and picnic area. *Open all year, daily, from 1000; winter closes 1 hour before dusk. Closed 25, 26 Dec. £3.50/£2.00. (F11)*

Waltham Abbey
Lee Valley Park Farms
Hayes Hill and Holyfield Hall, Stubbings Hall Lane, Crooked Mile
Tel: (01992) 892781
Two farms in one. Hayes Hill, a traditional-style farm with visitor facilities including tearooms and play area. Holyfield Hall, a modern arable farm. *Open all year, Mon-Fri, 1000-1630; Sat, Sun, Bank Hol Mon, 1000-1800; tearooms closed 25 Dec, 1 Jan. £3.10/£2.05/£2.05. (A8)*

Walton-on-the-Naze
Walton Pier
Pier Approach Tel: (01255) 672288
Pier with arcade, prize bingo, diner, tenpin bowling centre, fishing, adult and junior rides and Pirate Pete's indoor soft play area. Gala days, including firework display. *Please contact (01255) 682400 for details of opening times. (O5)*

Wethersfield
Boydells Dairy Farm
Boydells Farm Tel: (01371) 850481
A small dairy farm where you can watch the milking of cows, sheep and goats. *Open 24 Mar-29 Sep, Fri-Sun, 1400-1700, daily during Essex school holidays. Closed 29 Mar. £3.00/£1.75. (F3)*

Widdington
Mole Hall Wildlife Park
Tel: (01799) 540400
Park with otters, chimps, guanaco, lemurs, wallabies, deer, a butterfly pavilion, attractive gardens, picnic play areas, pet's corner and 3-acre maize maze. *Open all year, daily, 1030-1800; closed 25 Dec. £5.00/£3.50/£4.00. (D3)*

Brightlingsea

Countryside

Country Parks & Nature Reserves

Abberton Reservoir Visitor Centre Q
Layer-de-la-Haye Tel: (01206) 738172
This Essex Wildlife Trust nature reserve provides superb bird-watching with over 1200 acres. Shop with toilets and displays. Adult and children's activities. *Open all year, Tue-Sun, 0900-1700; closed 25, 26 Dec. (J5)*

Belfairs Nature Reserve
Leigh-on-Sea Tel: (01702) 520202
Woodland gardens and walks. Golf course, pitch and putt and 92-acre nature reserve. *Open all year, daily, 0730-dusk. (I11)*

Copt Hall Marshes
Little Wigborough, Colchester
Site of Specific Scientific Interest. Salt marshes rich in overwintering wildfowl and wading birds. (NT) *Open at any reasonable time. (K6)*

Cudmore Grove Country Park
Bromans Lane Tel: (01206) 383868
Situated next to the entrance of the Colne estuary, the Park consists of grassland and a sandy beach, ideally suited to walking, picnics, informal games and wildlife watching. *Open all year, daily, 0800-dusk. (K/L6)*

Danbury and Lingwood Commons
Danbury, Chelmsford
Danbury Common is composed of a mixture of woodland, shrub, grassland and heath. Napoleonic defences are evidence of Danbury's military past. (NT) *Open at any reasonable time. (H7/8)*

Fingringhoe Wick Nature Reserve Q
Fingringhoe Tel: (01206) 729678
One hundred and twenty five acres of woodland, lakes and saltmarsh on the Colne estuary, with nature trails and 8 hides. Observation room, tower and gift shop (EWT). *Open all year, Tue-Sun, 0900-1700. Closed 25, 26 Dec. Admission £1.00/50p. (L7)*

Lee Valley Park

Flitch Way and Rayne Station Centre
Rayne Tel: (01376) 340262
Fifteen miles of linear country park along the old Bishop's Stortford to Braintree railway. Rayne Station Centre has been renovated and now has an exhibition of local heritage. *Open all year, daily, dawn-dusk; Rayne Station Centre open all year, daily, 0900-1700; Exhibition Room open all year, Sun, 1300-1600. (G4/5)*

Hainault Forest Country Park
Romford Road, Chigwell
Tel: (020) 8500 7353
Six hundred acres of ancient woodland, a lake and rare breeds farm. Managed by the London Borough of Redbridge and the Woodland Trust for Essex County Council. *Open all year, 0730-dusk. (B9)*

Hylands Park, Chelmsford

Hanningfield Reservoir Visitor Centre
Hawkswood Road
Tel: (01268) 711001

The visitor centre has refreshments, toilets, gift shop and full disabled access. It will help you discover the 100-acre nature reserve, birds, hides and walks. *Open all year, Tue-Sun, Bank Hol Mon, 0900-1700. (G9)*

High Woods Country Park Q
Colchester   Tel: (01206) 853588

A 330-acre (134-hectare) country park situated to the north of central Colchester with a variety of landscape and wildlife, visitor's centre, toilets, bookshop and small shop. *Open at any reasonable time; Visitors Centre, 6 Jan-31 Mar, Sat, Sun, 1000-1600; 1 Apr-30 Sep, Mon-Sat, 1000-1630; Sun, Bank Hol Mon, 1100-1730; 6 Oct-29 Dec, Sat, Sun, 1000-1600. Closed 22 Dec. (K4)*

Hockley Woods
High Road, Hockley
Tel: (01702) 203078

Ancient semi natural woodland, 300 acres, freedom to roam, picnic area, play area and 2 self guide trails. Horse routes. Rare animals, birds, insects. Local nature reserve. *Open at any reasonable time. (I10)*

Holland Haven Country Park
Holland Haven
Tel: (01255) 253235

Marshes with footpaths through meadows. Cliff-top walks to Frinton-on-Sea. Bird-watching hides. Access to beaches. *Open at any reasonable time. (N/O 5/6)*

Essex

Stour Estuary Nature Reserve
Great Oakley Tel: (01255) 886043
Unique mix of managed woodland, threatened salt marsh and mudflats which provide ample opportunity to see and experience a wide range of wildlife. (RSPB) *Open at any reasonable time; closed 25 Dec. (N/04)*

Thorndon Country Park
Brentwood Tel: (01277) 211250
Fishing lake, horse and cycle rides, 2 WC and visitor centre, barbecue and picnic areas in 540 acres of country park. *Please contact for details of opening times. (D/E9/10)*

Wat Tyler Country Park
Pitsea Tel: (01268) 550088
A nature reserve with additional attractions including a marina, museum, arts and crafts studios and a heritage area. Miniature railway and cafe. Play equipment. *Open all year, daily, 0900-dusk. (F10)*

Langdon Hills Country Park
Corringham Tel: (01268) 542066
Country park consisting of Westley Heights and One Tree Hill. Picnic areas, wildflower, meadows and ancient woodlands overlooking the Thames estuary. *Open all year, daily, 0800-dusk. (F/G11)*

◉ Weald Country Park
Weald Road, South Weald Tel: (01277) 261343
Visitor Centre giftshop, light refreshmnets, deer paddock, country walks, fishing, lakes and horse-riding. *Open all year, daily, 0800-dusk. Visitor centre 2 Apr-31 Oct, Tue-Sun, Bank Hol Mon, 1000-1600; 2 Nov-29 Dec, Sat, Sun, 1000-1600. (D9)*

◉ Lee Valley Park Information Centre
Waltham Abbey Tel: (01992) 702200
The centre provides information and advice on facilities in the 25 miles of Lee Valley Park including the River Lee Country Park with opportunities for bird-watching and such. *Open Park at any reasonable time; Information Centre 1 Jan-28 Mar, daily, 1000-1600; 29 Mar-31 Oct, daily, 0930-1700; 1 Nov-31 Dec, daily, 1000-1600. (A8)*

◉ Marsh Farm Country Park
See entry in Family Fun section.

Naturalists' Organisations & Other Abbreviations used in this section

EWT	Essex Wildlife Trust, Fingringhoe Wick Nature Reserve, South Green Road, Fingringhoe, Colchester CO5 7DN. Tel: (01206) 729678.
◉ NT	The National Trust, Blickling, Norwich, Norfolk NR11 6NF. Tel: (01263) 738030.
◉ RSPB	Royal Society for the Protection of Birds, HQ: The Lodge, Sandy, Beds SG19 2DL. Tel: (01767) 680551. East Anglia Regional Office, Stalham House, 65 ThorpeRoad, Norwich NR1 1UD. Tel: (01603) 660066.
SSSI:	Site of Special Scientific Interest

DID YOU KNOW
Britain's second largest flock of mute swans can be found at Mistley.
The River Stour is the longest river in the East of England, covering 50 miles/80kms.

Essex

Activities & Sport

Maldon

Boat Hire and Regular Excursions

⊛ Blackwater Boats
on the Chelmer and Blackwater Navigation
Tel: (01206) 853282

2 and 4 berth luxury narrow boats. Day hire, short breaks and long holidays. Short trips from Chelmsford for up to 10 people. Trip boat also available. *(F-L7/8)*

⊛ Chelmer Cruises
Paper Mill Lock, Hatfield Road,
Little Baddow, Chelmsford
Tel: (01245) 225520 Email: cruises@cbn.co.uk

A 48 passenger canal cruiser on the picturesque Chelmer and Blackwater navigation between Maldon and Chelmsford. Bar, toilet and meals by arrangement. *Open from April-October for cruising and static venue for the rest of the year. (H7)*

Golf Courses

⊛ Five Lakes Hotel, Golf, Country Club & Spa
Colchester Road, Tolleshunt Knights,
Maldon CM9 8HX
Tel: (01621) 868888 Fax: (01621) 869696

Set in 320 acres of dramatic countryside including two 18 hole golf courses. The hotel is situated just south of Colchester, 36 miles from the M25 and easily accessible from the A14. Boasting 4 star luxury, 114 tastefully decorated and generously proportioned en-suite bedrooms (including some four posters and suites), many with spectacular views over the golf courses. An award winning restaurant 'Camelot' offers a mixture of international cuisine and English speciality dishes or try a more relaxed buffet style carvery in the Brasserie. Outstanding health and beauty facilities include a pool, squash, tennis courts and extensive other leisure facilities. Special two night breaks available. *(J6)*

Essex

Stoke By Nayland Club

Keepers Lane, Leavenheath,
Colchester, Essex CO6 4PZ
Tel: (01206) 262836 Fax: (01206) 263356
Email: info@golf-club.co.uk
www.stokebynaylandclub.co.uk

The superb accommodation and facilities, open all year, are enhanced by the beauty of the surrounding area. Set amidst 300 acres of undulating golf courses and lakes, the hotel is ideally suited to leisure and golf breaks. Two impressive 18-hole golf courses offer challenging play and Peake Fitness health club boasts a hi-tech gymnasium, stunning indoor pool, spa and solarium. All 30 bedrooms and suites are luxuriously appointed with stunning views and offer satellite television and ISDN terminals. Dining locations range from the casual Spike Bar or Peakes Bistro and A La Carte dining in the Gainsborough restaurant. *(J/K2)*

Stoke By Nayland Golf Club

Leavenheath Tel: (01206) 262769
Email: info@golf-club.co.uk
(See entry above)

River Stour, Dedham

Leisure Centres and Indoor Activities

Blackwater Leisure Centre

Maldon Tel: (01621) 851898
Leisure pool with flumes, baby/toddlers pool, health and fitness area and cafeteria. *(H/I7)*

Leisure World

Cowdray Avenue, Colchester
Tel: (01206) 282000
www.colchesterleisureworld.co.uk
Comprising leisure pool with flumes, fitness pool, sports hall, squash courts, activity hall and floodlit artificial sports pitch. Facilities for the disabled. *Open 06.00-22.30. (K4)*

Peake Fitness at Stoke-By-Nayland Club

Keepers Lane, Leavenheath,
Colchester, Essex CO6 4PZ
Tel: (01206) 265820 Fax: (01206) 263356
Email: info@golf-club.co.uk
www.stokebynaylandclub.co.uk
Superb Health and Fitness club, 18 meter indoor pool, sauna, Jacuzzi, treatment rooms and 40 station 'Technogym' gymnasium. *Special 'Pamper Packages' from £20. (J/K2)*

Riverside Ice and Leisure Centre

Victoria Road, Chelmsford
Tel: (01245) 615050
Ice rink, 3 pools, 6 court sports hall, Wellness Vision techno gym, squash courts and childrens' adventure playground. *(F7)*

Rollerworld

Eastgates, Colchester
Tel: (01206) 868868
Great Britain's largest roller-skating rink, 25m x 50m maple floor. RollerHire, RollerCafe and RollerBar - stunning sound and light show. Also Quasar at Rollerworld, the earths favourite laser game. *(K4)*

DID YOU KNOW

The town of Maldon was home to Edward Bright. He died in 1750, reputedly the biggest man in England at 44 stones. He is buried in All Saints Church.

Essex ————————————————————————

restaurants

High Street, Manningtree

Colchester
Crispin's
The Street, Messing, Near Colchester CO5 9TR
Tel: (01621) 815868

Crispin's built around 1475 is an oak-beamed, candlelit restaurant with en-suite rooms with four-poster beds. B&B for two is £55.00. Our international cuisine is outstanding and the restaurant is open from 1930 Wednesday-Saturday and for lunch on Sunday. We are just a few miles from the A12 south of Colchester. *(15)*

Castle Hedingham
❀ The Old Moot House Restaurant
1 St. James Street, Castle Hedingham CO9 3EJ
Tel: (01787) 460342

Michael and Maureen Medcraft, proprietors since 1979, have seen their business grow on their reputation for good food, service and value for money. Attractive bar and lounge area. A la Carte and vegetarian menu, lunch and evening special menus available. Patio Garden. *Closed Monday and Tuesday. (H2/3)*

Great Tey
❀ The Barn Brasserie
Great Tey, Colchester CO6 1JE
Tel: (01206) 212345
Fax: (01206) 211522

Just five minutes from Colchester, The Barn Brasserie is one of the premier restaurants in the area. The visually stunning conversion of this 16th century barn is amazing, offering an extremely spacious and relaxed dining experience. An extensive Á la carte menu is available for lunch and dinner seven days a week, with set menus at most sittings for under £10. Outside dining is available all day with a courtyard menu offering light lunches and snacks. Also on offer is an extensive wine list with top quality wines and champagne available by the glass or bottle. *(I4)*

Stoke-by-Nayland

THE Barn BRASSERIE 2

VALUE
EXCELLENCE
TASTE

Choose from our extensive á la carte menu or our special priced menus.

Open 7 days a week for lunch and dinner

Tel: 01206 212345

THE BARN BRASSERIE ◆ GREAT TEY

Great Yeldham
The White Hart
Poole Street (A1017), Great Yeldham, Halstead,
Essex CO9 4HJ
Tel: (01787) 237250

An imposing 16th century building with full a la carte menu available in restaurant and in bar, where lighter meals and snacks are also served. 100 wines on list, several served by the glass. Bar offers ever-changing range of quality real ales and bottled beers, an impressive range of cognacs and malt whiskies. Patio overlooking riverside garden. Ideal venue for weddings and special occasions, equally popular for those wanting just a relaxing drink. John Dicken is one of the country's most accomplished chefs. *Open seven days a week; telephone booking essential for restaurant at weekends, but bar always available. (G2)*

afternoon teas

Aldham
◉ Mill Race Nursery Coffee Shop
New Road, Aldham, Colchester
(just off the A1124, formerly
A604 at Ford Street)
Tel: (01206) 242521
www.millracenursery.co.uk

Enjoy home-made and speciality cakes, cream teas or light lunches in our conservatory style coffee lounge or courtyard garden. Riverside garden and boat hire, large plant centre, silk and dried flower shop and giftware. *Open daily including Sundays 0930-1700. (14)*

Pleshey

Walton-on-the-Naze
Harbour Lights (Walton-on-the-Naze) Ltd.
Titchmarsh Marina, Coles Lane,
Walton-on-the-Naze CO14 8SL
Tel: (01255) 851887

Sail or drive, for freshly prepared food with award winning service and fine views overlooking the Marina. Open seven days a week, through the summer and winter, our experienced team of chefs serve a wide range of traditional English fayre. Full English and Continental breakfasts, extensive bar meals, traditional Sunday lunches, seafood and vegetarian dishes, summer evening barbecues, a la carte restaurant and exciting flambé desserts. Christmas parties and special occasions are also catered for. Easy parking and all on one level, Harbour Lights provides good access for disabled customers. *(O5)*

Essex

Colchester
GREYFRIARS BOOKS
Rare and Secondhand
92b East Hill, Colchester CO1 2QN
Tel: (01206) 563138
www.gfbooks-colchester.co.uk

This surprisingly large basement bookshop located at the top of East Hill, near to the Minories Art Gallery, Colchester Castle and Hollytrees Museums, sells a wide range of sensibly priced and interesting secondhand books specialising in literature, art, philosophy, history, science and local interest. *Open: Monday to Saturday, 10am-5.30pm. (K4)*

West Thurrock
⊛ Lakeside Shopping Centre
West Thurrock Way, West Thurrock,
Grays RM20 2ZP
Tel: (01708) 869933 Fax: (01708) 865870
Website: www.lakeside.uk.com

As the largest retail area in Europe, Lakeside offers unrivalled choice of retail and leisure facilities. Over 300 shops, including four large department stores, popular high street names plus a selection of boutiques; 32 places to eat; 7 screen cinema; watersports lake and award winning children's facilities. Customer service facilities include free pushchair, free Shopmobility scheme, shopping lockers, sale of Lakeside Gift Vouchers. 13,000 free car park spaces, dedicated parent and child bays and a free 250 space coach park. The Centre opens seven days a week, 10am-10pm on weekdays. Located at Junction 30/31, off M25, direct trains to Lakeside's Chafford Hundred Station connect with Fenchurch Street (London), Barking and Upminster. *(D12)*

DID YOU KNOW

Manningtree is England's smallest town. It is 22 acres (9 hectares) at low tide, but only 17 (7 hectares) at high tide. It is so small that one end of the high street is in Lawford, the other in Mistley.

*High Street,
Colchester*

discovery tours

Bloomin' Beautiful

Enjoy the spectacular colours and delicate fragrances of some of England's finest gardens.

Tour 1

Starting point: Chelmsford, Essex *(F/G7)*
Mileage: Hylands House, Cressing Temple Barns and Marks Hall Estate 23m/37km
Hylands House, Cressing Temple Barns and The Gardens of Easton Lodge 30m/48km

Morning - enjoy a stroll in the parkland of *Hylands House*, then take the A12 to Witham. Follow the B1018 to *Cressing Temple Barns* and its Tudor walled garden.
Afternoon - remain on the B1018 to Braintree. Two choices, either take the A120 east for 6m, then the B1024 to the landscaped parkland of the *Marks Hall Estate*. Or take the A120 west for 10m to Gt. Dunmow. Follow the B184 for 2m, then turn left to Little Easton and *The Gardens of Easton Lodge*.

Tour 2

Starting point: Southend-on-Sea, Essex *(I10)*
Mileage: 12m/19km
Morning - enjoy a floral tour of *Southend-on-Sea*, famous for its award-winning parks and gardens.
Afternoon - leave on the A127 towards Basildon. After 7 miles, turn right onto the A130. 5 miles later in the village of Rettendon, follow signs to the *RHS Hyde Hall Garden* with its roses and waterlilies.

Southend-on-Sea Pier

Coggeshall

Raptors, Romans and Roundabouts

A fun-packed family tour, based around Britain's oldest recorded town.

Starting point: Colchester, Essex *(K4)*
Mileage: 22m/35km
Morning - leave the town on the B1022 to visit the excellent *Colchester Zoo*, one of Europe's finest.
Afternoon - return to Colchester, and discover the *Castle Museum*, where mum can try on a Roman toga! End the day by taking the A133 to *Clacton-on-Sea*, and its fun-packed pier. Smash into dad on the dodgems and scare your little sister in the haunted house.

Antiques, Auctions, Bids and Bargains

Explore priceless antique towns and stately homes filled with heirlooms.

Starting point: Halstead, Essex *(H3)*
Mileage: 29m/47km
Morning - explore *Halstead's* speciality shops and weather-boarded antiques centre. Then take the A1124 to Earls Colne, where you turn right onto the B1024 to historic *Coggeshall*, a mecca for antiques lovers.
Afternoon - remain on the B1024 south to *Kelvedon* (with more shops to enjoy), then join the A12 south towards London. After 12m, take the A130 to the antiques village of *Battlesbridge*.

Essex

A Taste of Essex

If you are in search of culinary adventure, then this tour is full of tasty surprises.

Starting point: Southend-on-Sea, Essex *(I10)*
Mileage: 30m/48km
Morning - start the day with a cockle or two in the fishing village of *Leigh-on-Sea*. Then enjoy a stroll along the world's longest pier at *Southend*, with some delicious fish and chips.
Afternoon - follow the A127 for 7m, before turning right onto the A130. 3m later (at the roundabout), turn right onto the A132. At South Woodham Ferrers, turn left onto the B1418. Then 5m later (at the roundabout) join the A414 to the hilltop town of *Maldon*, noted for its sea salt production. End the day by taking the B1022 to *Tiptree*, and enjoy afternoon tea at the jam factory.

Country Classics

Discover the historic houses and castles of the rich and famous.

Starting point: Saffron Walden, Essex *(C/D2)*
Mileage: 19m/31km
Morning - explore charming *Saffron Walden*, then follow signs to the Jacobean *Audley End House*.
Afternoon - take the B1053 via *Finchingfield* (a picture postcard village) to Wethersfield, where you turn left onto the unclassified road to Sible Hedingham. At the T-junction with the A1017, turn left to reach *Castle Hedingham*, and its magnificent castle keep.

The Witchfinder's Way

Watch out for black cats and broomsticks in Witch Country!

Starting point: Harwich, Essex *(O3)*
Mileage: 18m/29km
Morning - explore the medieval seafaring town of *Harwich*. Then take the B1352 (with its spectacular river views) to *Mistley* and *Manningtree*, the former haunt of Matthew Hopkins, The Witchfinder General.
Afternoon - take the A137 south to *Colchester*. If you dare, visit the dungeons of the *Castle Museum*, where the screams of the witches can still be heard!

Finchingfield

Stand and Deliver!

Visit the haunts and hideaways of Britain's most famous highwayman Dick Turpin (1705-39).

Starting point: Saffron Walden, Essex *(C/D2)*
Mileage: 42m/68km
Morning - follow the B1053/B1054 to *Hempstead*, birthplace of Turpin. Then take the B1053/B1051 to the medieval town of *Thaxted*, where his house stands in Stoney Street. Now head south along the B184 to 'The Rodings', a group of attractive villages where Turpin found safe places to hide.
Afternoon - remain on the B184 to Chipping Ongar, then turn right onto the A414. After 3 miles, turn left onto the B181/B1393 to *Epping*. Take a walk in the famous forest, where Turpin held up the passing coaches. Then take the A121 to *Waltham Abbey*, reputedly the burial place of King Harold.

Defence of the Realm

Explore the military defences of the area, built to safeguard against invasion and attack.

Starting point: Waltham Abbey, Essex *(A8)*
Mileage: 38m/61km
Morning - trace the evolution of gunpowder technology at the *Royal Gunpowder Mills*.
Afternoon - join the M25 to junction 28, then take the A1023/A128 (via Brentwood) to *Kelvedon Hatch*. Go underground to explore the *Nuclear Bunker*. Then head back along the A128 (via Brentwood) and onto the junction with the A13, where you turn right. Just over a mile later, turn left onto the A1089 to 17th C. *Tilbury Fort*.

Norfolk

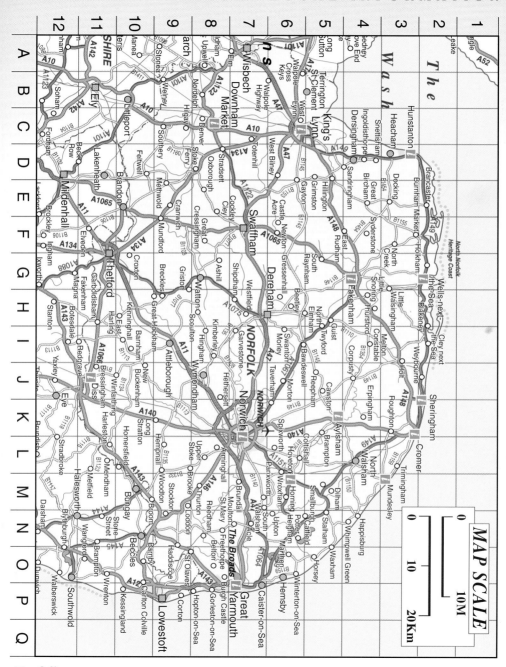

MAP SCALE

| 0 | | 10M |
| 0 | 10 | 20Km |

Norfolk

County Town: Norwich
Population: 796,000 approx.
Highest Point: Roman Camp, Sheringham 336 feet.
Rivers: Ant, Babingley, Burn, Bure, Chet, Glaven, Great Ouse, Little Ouse, Nar, Ouse, Stiffkey, Tas, Thet, Waveney, Wensum, Wissey, Yare.
Landmarks: Blakeney Point, The Norfolk Broads, Norwich Cathedral, Sandringham, Thetford Forest Park, The Wash.

Industry Past & Present:

Noted for its rich *agricultural* heritage, Norfolk has led the way in farming developments. In the Middle Ages, pastures supported vast flocks of sheep, and this local wool started the important *weaving* industry. The wealth generated can be seen in medieval guildhalls, merchants' houses and churches. On the coast, Great Yarmouth (home of North Sea *gas/oil production*) had a huge *herring* industry, which reached its peak at the start of the 20th C. Today *shellfish* is more important - with *cockles/shrimps* from the Wash, *mussels/whelks* from North Norfolk, and *crabs/lobsters* at Cromer and Sheringham. *Smoked* fish *(bloaters/kippers)* have also long been a specialty. The port of King's Lynn was chosen by the Hanseatic merchants as a base for their warehouses. Similarly Norwich has traded its goods throughout Europe, noted for its *banking/insurance* (Norwich Union), *brewing, printing* (Jarrolds), *shoe making* and *mustard* (Colman's). To the north, the Norfolk Broads were created, when *peat* (used for fuel) diggings of the 12-14th C. became flooded. Here *reed/sedge* are cut for thatch. While to the south, the vast Thetford Forest provides valuable *timber*. Famous names include - Bernard Matthews *(poultry)*, Del Monte Foods *(fruit drinks)*, Group Lotus *(sports cars)* and Jeyes Pharmaceuticals.

Famous People:

Henry Blogg *(Cromer lifeboatman)*, Anne Boleyn *(Henry VIII's second wife)*, George Borrow *(author)*, Thomas Browne *(author)*, Nurse Edith Cavell, The Coke Family *(Holkham)*, John Crome & John Sell Cotman *(Norwich School of painting)*, William Cowper *(poet)*, Edward VII, Elizabeth Fry *(social reformer)*, Richard Lincoln *(Abraham Lincoln's ancestor)*, Admiral Lord Nelson, Thomas Paine *(political writer)*, Arthur Ransome *(author)*, Humphry Repton *(landscape gardener)*, John Rolfe *(married Red Indian princess Pocahontas)*, Anna Sewell *(author)*, Captain George Vancouver *(seafarer)*, Sir Robert Walpole *(Britain's first Prime Minister)*.

Cities
towns &
Villages

MD: Market Day	
EC: Early Closing	
i Tourist Information Centre	

Acle *(N7)*
This small town, situated halfway between Norwich and Great Yarmouth, sits on the edge of the Halvergate Marshes. It originally stood on the coast, until the reclamation of the river estuaries. The large green is surrounded by 17/18th C. buildings, while the church has a detached, round Saxon tower. Acle is noted for its regular auctions. **MD**: Thurs.

Attleborough *(I9)*
Pleasant market town. It was once famous for its cider works (depicted on the town sign) and for producing turkeys, which used to make the journey to the London markets on foot. The small shopping centre is set around an attractive green, while the parish church was once the centre of a much larger building, whose remains can be seen. **MD**: Thurs. **EC**: Wed.

Attleborough

Aylsham *(K5)*
For 500 years, this picturesque small town was a important centre for the manufacture of linen, then worsted cloth. The open market place is surrounded by handsome 18th C. buildings. Humphry Repton, the famous 18th C. landscape gardener is buried in the churchyard. The town is noted for its regular antique auctions. **MD**: Mon and Fri. **EC**: Wed. *i*

Burnham Market *(F3)*
This is the largest of the seven 'Burnham' villages. Attractive main street and green, with elegant 18th C. houses and pretty flint cottages. Antique, book and craft shops. Bolton House was the home of Lord Nelson's sister, while his daughter was married at St. Mary's Church in 1823.

Caister-on-Sea *(O/P7)*
Popular seaside resort, with a wide sandy beach and famous volunteer lifeboat service. Remains of fortified Roman town/port. Ruins of 15th C. castle, built by Sir John Fastolf, who features in Shakespeare's Henry VI. Several holiday centres, caravan and chalet parks.

Cromer *(K/L3)*
Dominated by the tower of its parish church (the tallest in the county), this sedate seaside town stands on a cliff top, with wide sandy beaches running down to the sea. Cromer is famous for its crabs, caught by its little fishing boats which still work from the beach. The fine pier is noted for its end-of-the-pier theatre and lifeboat station. **MD**: Fri. **EC**: Wed. *i*

Diss *(J11)*
Set in the Waveney Valley, this thriving market town borders a six acre mere, home to a variety of wildfowl. Diss still retains much of its picturesque old world charm, with a maze of streets clustered around St. Mary's Church, its tower dating from 1300. 16th C. timber-framed houses, and later buildings of the 18/19th C. surround the market place. **MD**: Fri (also auction). **EC**: Tues. *i*

Downham Market *(C8)*

Dating back to Saxon times, this small hillside settlement is one of Norfolk's oldest market towns. Lying on the edge of the Fens, Downham Market is noted for its 19th C. black and white clock tower and local carrstone buildings, some showing a Dutch influence. 15th C. church with unusual spire. **MD**: Fri. **EC**: Wed. *i*

East Dereham *(H6/7)*

Lively market town, established as a religious community by St. Withburga in the 7th C. 18th C. buildings surround the market place, while the partly Norman church has a detached bell tower. Bishop Bonner's Cottages are noted for their pargetting. The poet William Cowper lived here from 1796 until his death. **MD**: Tues and Fri. **EC**: Wed. *i*

Fakenham *(G4)*

Thriving market town set on the River Wensum. The large market place is surrounded by handsome 18/19th C. buildings, interesting courtyards and tiny lanes. The patronage of the partly 15th C. church has rested with Trinity College in Cambridge since 1547. The town boasts one of the finest National Hunt courses in the country. **MD**: Thurs. **EC**: Wed.

Gorleston *(P8)*

Sitting on the other side of the River Yare from its more busy neighbour, Great Yarmouth, Gorleston is ideal for those looking for a quieter holiday. The town has interesting 19th C. villas, and its own theatre, lifeboat station and inshore fishing fleet. The sandy beach is backed by low cliffs to form a bay.

Great Yarmouth *(O/P7)*

One of Britain's most popular seaside resorts with wide sandy beaches, colourful gardens and traditional seaside attractions and entertainment. Built on a spit of sand, between the sea and River Yare, the town's wealth comes from its port, and the former herring industry. The historic quayside has old merchants houses and 'rows' (narrow medieval alleys). Remains of the town wall and the largest parish church in England. **MD**: Wed, Fri (summer only) and Sat. **EC**: Thurs. *i*

Harleston *(L11)*

Lying in the Waveney Valley, this old-fashioned market town borders countryside made famous by the local painter, Sir Alfred Munnings. Harleston has fine timber-framed buildings, and Georgian town houses. In the Old Market Place are courtyards where weavers and basketmakers once lived. **MD**: Wed. **EC**: Thurs.

Norfolk

Hingham *(I8)*
Pretty market town, with two splendid greens bordered by Georgian period houses and linked by narrow streets. The large church contains a bust of Abraham Lincoln, a descendant of Samuel Lincoln, a local weaver and Quaker, who sailed to religious freedom in the America's in 1637.

Holt *(I/J3)*
One of the most attractive small towns in Norfolk, with a main street lined with elegant Georgian buildings, mostly built after the fire of 1708. The town is best known for Greshams, a public school founded in 1555 by Sir John Gresham, a former Lord Mayor of London. Holt is a mecca for antique and bric-a-brac collectors. Nostalgic horse drawn carriage rides. **EC**: Thurs.

Hunstanton *(D3)*
This is England's only east coast resort which faces west. Hunstanton is a traditional seaside town with a range of attractions, large sandy beaches and gardens. Ornate Victorian and Edwardian houses overlook wide open greens. To the north is Old Hunstanton, a residential village with distinctive red and white striped cliffs.
MD: Wed and Sun. **EC**: Thurs (out of season). *i*

King's Lynn *(C5/6)*
Historic port and market town, dating back to the 12th C. and steeped in maritime history. Two magnificent market places and two medieval guildhalls; one is the largest in Britain, the other houses the town's regalia. Former merchant's houses, hidden courtyards and attractive waterfront area with 18th C. Custom House. 12th C. church with rare moon/tide dial. **MD**: Tues, Fri and Sat. *i*

Little Walsingham *(G/H3)*
Picturesque village, a famous pilgrimage centre since 1061, when the Lady of the Manor had a vision of the Virgin Mary. The subsequent shrine became one of the most important in Europe. Timber-framed buildings and Georgian facades line the High Street and Market Place, with its 16th C. pump-house. Also extensive ruins of Augustinian abbey set in attractive parkland.

Loddon *(M9)*
Broadland market town on the River Chet, with an imposing and beautiful 15th C. church. The town is a popular boating centre, with Georgian and Victorian houses lining the main street. Its small shopping centre has a waterside picnic area. Loddon was once a commercial port, and there are old warehouses and a watermill still remaining. **MD**: Fri. **EC**: Wed.

Long Stratton *(K9)*
This large village, almost a small town, has a long main street bordered by 16/17th C. half-timbered buildings. St. Mary's Church has a round tower and very rare sexton's wheel. Preserved 19th C. ice house which once served the demolished Manor House. **EC**: Wed.

Mundesley *(M3)*
Built at the mouth of the tiny river Mund, this is one of Norfolk's best kept secrets. The town prospered at the start of the 12th C. when the railway arrived, and for a time it was something of a health resort with two sanatoriums. Today Mundlesey is a quiet holiday town with a clean 'Blue Flag' beach, and shallow pools left by the turning tide. **EC**: Wed. *i*

North Walsham *(L4)*
This busy market town became a centre for the wool industry in the late medieval ages. The wealth generated enabled the local people to build St. Nicholas Church, which dates back to 1330. The 16th C. market cross is the focal point of the town. Lord Nelson spent his schooldays at 'The Paston School'. **MD**: Thurs. **EC**: Wed.

Guildhall of the Holy Trinity,
King's Lynn

Norfolk

Norwich (K/L7)

East Anglia's capital, and the most complete medieval city in Britain. Surrounded by its old walls are over 1,500 historic buildings, and a intricate network of winding streets and lanes, such as cobbled Elm Hill. Norwich is dominated by its magnificent cathedral, and impressive 12th C. castle keep. Lively cultural scene with museums, galleries, theatres, restaurants and pubs. Excellent shopping centre, including the Castle Mall, famous Mustard Shop and colourful open air market. **MD**: Mon to Sat (cattle market on Sat). **i**

Reepham (J5)

Attractive market town, with narrow winding streets lined with Georgian/half-timbered buildings. Dominating the market place is 'The Dial House', so called because of the sun-dial over the door. Reepham is unique in having three churches in one churchyard (although one is now a ruin). **MD**: Wed. **EC**: Thurs.

Sheringham (J/K2/3)

This traditional seaside town grew up around its old fishing village, and a band of little boats still bring in the daily catch. A mixture of Edwardian and Victorian buildings, Sheringham is home of the North Norfolk Railway (The Poppy Line), which operates steam train rides to Holt. At low tide the large sandy beach reveals rock pools. **MD**: Wed, Sat. **EC**: Wed. **i**

Stalham (M/N5)

Peaceful little market town on the edge of the Norfolk Broads. Still a centre for boat building, Stalham has pretty Georgian houses, shops, inns and cafes. The large 15th C. church contains a magnificent richly carved font. The staithe, once busy with the wherry trade, is built on an artificial cut (or dyke) leading from the river. **MD**: Tues. **EC**: Wed. **i**

Swaffham (F7)

Charming old market town, once a fashionable centre for the gentry in the 18th C. The triangular-shaped market place has handsome Georgian buildings (such as the Assembly Rooms) and a butter market. The 15th C. church is one of the finest in the region, with its double hammerbeam angel roof, and memorial to the famous Pedlar of Swaffham. **MD**: Sat. **EC**: Thurs.

Thetford (F/G11)

Thriving market town, which a thousand years ago was the capital of East Anglia. Its importance continued during the early Middle Ages, and has left a legacy of historic sites, such as the Iron Age earthworks, a Norman castle mound and the remains of the 12th C. priory. The town centre is a conservation area with fine medieval and Georgian buildings. **MD**: Tues and Sat. **EC**: Wed.

Wells-next-the-Sea

Norfolk

Watton *(G8)*

Busy rural centre with an unusual clock tower dated 1679. The wide High Street has late 18/19th C. houses offering many family-run shops. Watton has the only church in the country that is wider than it is long. To the south is Wayland Wood, which is connected to the famous story of the 'Babes in the Wood'. This is depicted on the town sign. **MD**: Wed. **EC**: Thurs.

Wells-next-the-Sea *(G2)*

Picturesque small town, a busy port for coasters and the local whelk and shrimp boats. Not quite on the sea, but sitting on an estuary, Wells has narrow streets lined with traditional flint buildings. While on the green (The Buttlands) is a series of Georgian houses. A little railway takes visitors from the port to the nearby sandy beach.
MD: Wed (summer only). **MD**: Thurs. *i*

Wroxham and Hoveton *(L/M6)*

The adjoining villages of Wroxham and Hoveton are known as the 'capital of the Broads'. Linked together by a hump-backed bridge over the River Bure, Hoveton offers the main shopping and tourist centre with its boatyards, chandleries and 'Roys' (the largest village store in the world). Various boat excursions available. **EC**: Wed (partial).

Wymondham *(J8)*

Wymondham (pronounced "Win-dum") retains all the character of a historic market town. The town has more listed buildings than any similar sized town in the county, including the 17th C. octagonal market cross. The twin towers of the beautiful abbey dominate the skyline, and are the result of a 14th C. dispute between the townspeople and the monks. **MD**: Fri. **EC**: Wed.

Pull's Ferry, Norwich

Pick of the villages

1 **Beachamwell** - ancient village set around its green and thatched church. *(E8)*
2 **Binham** - flint cottages and elegant houses. 11th C. priory remains. *(H3)*
3 **Blakeney** - narrow streets, flint houses, medieval guildhall and boat trips to see the seals. *(H/I2)*
4 **Brancaster** - fisherman's cottages, sailing boats and earthworks of Roman fort. *(E2)*
5 **Burnham Thorpe** - wide open green with brick/flint buildings. Birthplace of Lord Nelson. *(F3)*
6 **Castle Acre** - flint-built village with castle mound, priory ruins and 13th C. bailey gate. *(F6)*
7 **Caston** - small and pretty village with thatched church, green and windmill. *(H9)*
8 **Cley-next-the-Sea** - once important port. Narrow streets, flint cottages and windmill. *(I2)*
9 **The Creakes (North and South)** - two riverside villages. Flint houses and 13th C. abbey ruins. *(F3)*
10 **Coltishall** - former wherry port. 18th C. buildings, thatched church and green. *(L6)*
11 **Denver** - famous sluice controls vast Fenland waterways. 19th C. restored windmill. *(C8)*
12 **Great Massingham** - huge village green with flint houses and three large ponds. *(E5)*
13 **Happisburgh** - seaside village with flint houses and red/white striped lighthouse. *(N4)*
14 **Heydon** - attractive, privately owned village. Used in numerous TV/film productions. *(J5)*
15 **Horning** - ancient village. Gardens/lawns sweep down to river. Thatched houses. *(M6)*
16 **Letheringsett** - set in wooded Glaven valley. 18th C. hall and water mill. *(I3)*
17 **East Lexham** - tiny hamlet. Butter market, round-towered church and 17th C. hall. *(F6)*
18 **Litcham** - handsome village on banks of River Nar. Elegant 18th C. town houses. *(G6)*
19 **Neatishead** - Broadland village at head of wooded creek. Georgian houses. *(M6)*
20 **Martham** - wide open green with Georgian houses. Splendid church tower. *(O6)*
21 **New Buckingham** - planned medieval village. 17th C. market house and castle ramparts. *(J10)*
22 **North Elmham** - ecclesiastical centre of Saxon Norfolk. Remains of Norman chapel. *(H6)*
23 **Outwell/Upwell** - adjoining Fenland villages. 'Dutch-style' houses, gardens and boats. *(A8)*
24 **Pulham Market** - green with 16/17th C. colour-washed houses. Airship connections. *(K10)*
25 **Ranworth** - 'cathedral of the Broads' (views from tower) and floating conservation centre. *(M6)*
26 **Surlingham** - thatched cottages beside River Yare. 'Wherry graveyard'. *(M7)*
27 **Stiffkey** - narrow winding street with fishermen's cottages. Famous for its shellfish. *(H2)*
28 **Walpole St. Peter** - 'Marshland' village, noted for one of the finest churches in Britain. *(B6)*
29 **Woodbastwick** - estate village with thatched cottages and church. *(M6)*
30 **Worstead** - medieval weaving centre. 15th C. wool church and elegant 17th C. houses. *(M5)*

Tourist Information
Centres

With so much to see and do in this area, it's impossible for us to mention all of the places you can visit. You will find Tourist Information Centres (TICs) throughout Norfolk, with plenty of information on all the things that you can do and the places you can visit. TICs can book accommodation for you, in their own area, or further afield using the 'Book A Bed Ahead Scheme'. They can be the ideal place to purchase locally made crafts or gifts, as well as books covering a wide range of local interests. A list of the TICs in this area can be found below, together with a map reference to help you locate them.

* Not open all year.

Aylsham (K4/5), Bure Valley Railway Station, Norwich Road, Tel: (01263) 733903
Email:aylsham.tic@broadland.gov.uk
Cromer (K/L2/3), Prince of Wales Road,
Tel: (01263) 512497
Email: jn@north-norfolk.gov.uk
Diss (J11), Meres Mouth, Mere Street,
Tel: (01379) 650523
Email: disstic@dial.pipex.com
Web: www.south-norfolk.gov.uk
Downham Market (C8), The Priory Centre 78 Priory Road. Tel: (01366) 387440
Email: downham-market.tic@west-norfolk.gov.uk
* **Great Yarmouth** (O/P7), Marine Parade,
Tel: (01493) 842195
Email: tourism@great-yarmouth.gov.uk
Web: www.great-yarmouth.co.uk
* **Hoveton** (M6), Station Road,
Tel: (01603) 782281
Hunstanton (D3), Town Hall, The Green,
Tel: (01485) 532610
Email: hunstanton.tic@west-norfolk.gov.uk
Web: www.west-norfolk.gov.uk
King's Lynn (C6), The Custom House,
Purfleet Quay, Tel: (01553) 763044
Email: kings-lynn.tic@west-norfolk.gov.uk
Web: www.west-norfolk.gov.uk
* **Mundesley** (M3), 2 Station Road,
Tel: (01263) 721070
Email: jn@north-norfolk.gov.uk
Norwich (K/L7), The Forum, Millennium Plain,
Tel: (01603) 727927
Email: tourism.norwich@gtnet.gov.uk
Web: www.norwich.gov.uk
* **Sheringham** (J/K2/3), Station Approach,
Tel: (01263) 824329
Email: jn@north-norfolk.gov.uk

* **Wells-next-the-Sea** (G2), Staithe Street,
Tel: (01328) 710885
Email: jn@north-norfolk.gov.uk

Wymondham (J8), Market Cross, Market Place,
Tel: (01953) 604721
Email: wymondhamtic@aol.com

Blue Badge Guides:

There are also experts available to help you explore some of our towns and cities. These Registered Blue Badge Guides have all attended a training course sponsored by the East of England Tourist Board. Below are some of the tours offered by these Guides - you can obtain further information by contacting the appropriate Tourist Information Centre, unless otherwise indicated. Some Blue Badge Guides have a further qualification to take individuals or groups around the region for half day, full day or longer tours if required.

King's Lynn
● **Regular Town Tours:** Individuals may join the tours, which leave the Tales of the Old Gaolhouse, May-Jul and Oct, Wed, Sat, 1400 and Sun, 1430. Aug, Sep, daily except Tue and Thu, 1400. Sun, 1430.
● **Group Tours:** Guided tours can be arranged for groups by contacting the King's Lynn Town Guides on Tel: (01553) 765714.

Norwich
● **Regular City Tours** 'Norwich - City of Century' walking tours lasting 1½ hours leave from the Tourist Information Centre in the Forum at 1400 from April – Oct. Sun only Jun – Oct at 1100.
● **Evening Tours** A variety of Themed Tours leave twice weekly at 1900 Jun – Sep.
● **Group Tours** A variety of Themed Walking Tours are available for pre-booked groups, alternatively a 'Panoramic Norwich' Coach tour can be arranged.
Itineraries can also be arranged for longer half or full days tours, including the Broads or North Norfolk Coast.
Please contact the Tourist Information Centre for full information. Tel: (01603) 666071 Fax: (01603) 765389 email tourism@norwich.gov.uk

Walsingham
Walking guided tours round the historic village of Walsingham. Bookings and Information: (01328) 820250. 1 Apr-30 Sept, Wed & Thu, 1100; Jun, Jul, Aug, Sept, Wed & Thu, 1100, Sat 1400. Group tours throughout year by arrangement.

Norfolk

historic houses

DID YOU KNOW

Houghton Hall was the 18th C. home of England's first prime minister, Sir Robert Walpole. He was born in 1676, becoming prime minister from 1715-1742. He is buried at Houghton. It was Robert who bequeathed 10 Downing Street to the nation.

Blakeney
⊛ Blakeney Guildhall
Tel: (01604) 730320

The remains of the 14thC basement to a merchant's house which was most likely used for storage. *Open at any reasonable time. (H/I2)*

Blickling
⊛ Blickling Hall Q
Tel: (01263) 738030

A Jacobean redbrick mansion with garden, orangery, parkland and lake. There is also a display of fine tapestries and furnitur. *House open 23 Mar-3 Nov, Wed, Sun, Bank Hol, 1300-1630; Garden open 1015-1715. Please contact for details of admission prices.(K4/5)*

Downham Market
⊛ The Collectors World of Eric St John-Foti
Hermitage Hall, Bridge Farm
Tel: (01366) 383185

The Collectors World contains unique collections amassed by Eric St John-Foti and the Magical Dickens Experience takes you back in time. *Open 1 Jan-31 Dec, daily, 1100-1700. Closed 24-26 Dec. £3.50/£2.50/£3.00. (C8)*

Felbrigg
⊛ Felbrigg Hall
Tel: (01263) 837444

A 17thC country house with original 18thC furniture and pictures. There is also a walled garden, orangery, park and woodland with way marked walks, shops and catering. *Please contact for details of opening times and admission prices. (K3)*

Houghton
⊛ Houghton Hall
Tel: (01485) 528569

A hall built in the early 18thC with superb state rooms, a collection of 20,000 model soldiers, a picnic area, gift shop and a newly-restored walled garden. *Open: Gates, Soldier Museum, Gardens, Tearooms 31 Mar-29 Sep, Thu, Sun, Bank Hol Mon, 1300-1730. House open: Thu, Sun, Bank Hol Mon, 1400-1730. Please contact for details of admission prices. (E4)*

Felbrigg Hall

Sandringham, (by gracious permission of HM The Queen)

Norwich
🏵 **Dragon Hall**
115-123 King Street
Tel: (01603) 663922

Medieval merchant's hall with outstanding timber-framed structure. The 15thC Great Hall has a crown post roof with an intricately carved and painted dragon. *Open 2 Jan-31 Mar, Mon-Fri, 1000-1600; 2 Apr-31 Oct, Mon-Sat, 1000-1600; 1 Nov-31 Dec, Mon-Fri, 1000-1600; closed 29 Mar, 1 Apr, 20 Dec-1 Jan. £2.50/£1.00/£2.00. (K/L7)*

Norwich
🏵 **Mannington Gardens and Countryside**
See entry in
Gardens & Vineyards section

Oxborough
🏵 **Oxburgh Hall** Q
Tel: (01366) 328258

A 15thC moated redbrick fortified manor-house with an 80ft gatehouse, Mary Queen of Scot's needlework, a Catholic priest's hole, garden, woodland walks and a Catholic chapel. *Please contact for details of opening times. £5.50/£2.80. (K/L7)*

Norfolk

Holkham Hall

Sandringham
⊛ **Sandringham**
Tel: (01553) 772675

The country retreat of HM The Queen. A delightful house and 60 acres of grounds and lakes. There is also a museum of royal vehicles and royal memorabilia. *Please contact for details of opening times and admission prices. (D4/5)*

Thetford
⊛ **Euston Hall**
Euston Estate Office
Tel: (01842) 766366

Hall housing paintings by Van Dyck, Lely and Stubbs with pleasure grounds designed by John Evelyn and 'Capability Brown' and the 17thC church of St Genevieve. *Open 6 Jun-26 Sep, Thu, 1430-1700; 30 Jun, 1 Sep, Sun, 1430-1700. See page 170 for more information. £3.50/£1.00/£3.00. (F/G10/11)*

Thetford
⊛ **Thetford Warren Lodge**
Tel: (01604) 730320

The ruins of a small 2-storey medieval gamekeeper's lodge which can only be viewed from the outside. *Open at any reasonable time. (F/G10/11)*

Wells-next-the-Sea
⊛ **Holkham Hall** [Q]
Tel: (01328) 710227

A classic 18thC Palladian-style mansion. Part of a great agricultural estate and a living treasure house of artistic and architectural history along with a bygones collection. *Open 31 Mar, 1 Apr, 5, 6 May, 2-4 Jun, 25, 26 Aug, 1130-1700. Open 26 May-30 Sep, Sun-Thu, 1300-1700. Closed 22 Sep. £8.00/£4.00. See left for further information. (G2)*

Oxburgh Hall

Ancient Monuments

Baconsthorpe
⊛ Baconsthorpe Castle
A 15thC part-moated, semi-fortified house. The remains include the inner and outer gatehouse and the curtain wall. Baconsthorpe Post Office sells guide books and postcards. *Open all year, daily, 1000-1600. (J3)*

Binham
⊛ Binham Priory
Tel: (01604) 230320
Extensive remains of an early 12thC Benedictine priory. The original nave of the church is still used as the parish church. *Open at any reasonable time. (H3)*

NORWICH CATHEDRAL

Built in the bow of the River Wensum and surrounded by a beautiful Close, Norwich Cathedral is a magnificent building. The 315 foot spire stands proudly over the largest monastic cloister in England and a building containing over 1,000 roof bosses, one of the greatest medieval art treasures in Europe.

For further information on services or tours please contact the Visitor's Officer on

(01603) 218321

Burnham Market
⊛ Creake Abbey
Remains of an abbey church dating from 13thC, including presbytery and north transept with chapels. *Open at any reasonable time. (F2/3)*

Castle Acre
Castle Acre Castle Q
The remains of a Norman manor-house which became a castle with earthworks, set by the side of a village. *Open at any reasonable time. (F6)*

Castle Acre
⊛ Castle Acre Priory Q
Stocks Green Tel: (01760) 755161
The impressive ruins of a Cluniac priory built by William de Warenne in about 1090 with a church and decorated 12thC west front and 16thC gatehouse and a prior's lodgings. *Open 2 Jan-31 Mar, Wed-Sun, 1000-1600; 1 Apr-30 Sep, daily, 1000-1800; 1-31 Oct, daily, 1000-1700; 1 Nov-31 Dec, daily, 1000-1600. Closed 24-26 Dec, 1 Jan. £3.50/£1.80/£2.60. (F6)*

Castle Rising
⊛ Castle Rising Castle
Tel: (01553) 631330
Castle Rising Castle is a fine example of a Norman castle. The rectangular keep, one of the largest, was built around 1140 by William D'Albini. *Open 2 Jan-31 Mar, Wed-Sun, 1000-1600; 1 Apr-30 Sep, daily, 1000-1800; 1-31 Oct, daily, 1000-1700; 1 Nov-29 Dec, Wed-Sun, 1000-1600. Closed 24-26 Dec. £3.25/£1.60/£2.50. (C/D5)*

Great Yarmouth
⊛ Burgh Castle Church Farm
Burgh Castle
The remains of a 3rdC Roman fort overlooking the River Waveney. The monument is only approached on foot. There is information and a tearoom available from Easter to October. *Open at any reasonable time. (O/P7)*

Great Yarmouth
⊛ Caister Roman Site
The remains of a Roman commercial port which was possibly a fort. The footings of walls and buildings are seen all along the main street. *Open at any reasonable time. (O/P7)*

Norfolk

Great Yarmouth
⚜ North West Tower
North Quay Tel: (01493) 332095

Medieval tower originally part of the town walls. Exhibition about trading wherries, the cargo craft once used on the Broads and information centre. *Open 1 Jul-30 Sep, daily, 1000-1545. (O/P7)*

Lynford
⚜ Grimes Graves
The Exhibition Building Tel: (01842) 810656

Neolithic flint mines. Four thousand years old and first excavated in the 1870s with over 300 pits and shafts. *One open to the public, and a 30ft deep, 7 radiating gallery. Open 2 Jan-28 Mar, Wed-Sun, 1000-1300, 1400-1600; 1 Apr-30 Sep, daily, 1000-1300, 1400-1800; 1-31 Oct, daily, 1000-1300, 1400-1700; 1 Nov-29 Dec, Wed-Sun, 1000-1300, 1400-1600. Closed 25, 26 Dec, 1 Jan. £2.10/£1.10/£1.60. (F10)*

New Buckenham
New Buckenham Castle
Tel: (01953) 860374

A Norman motte-and-bailey castle and chapel keep, said to be the largest in diameter in England. *Open all year, Tue, Wed, 0800-1800, Thu, 0800-1300, Fri-Sun, 0800-1800. Closed 25, 26 Dec, 1 Jan. £1.00/50p/50p. (I/J10)*

North Elmham
North Elmham Chapel
High Street

The remains of a Norman chapel, later converted into a house and enclosed by earthworks. *Open at any reasonable time. (H5/6)*

Norwich
⚜ Norwich Cathedral
The Close Tel: (01603) 218321

A Norman cathedral from 1096 with 14thC roof bosses depicting bible scenes from Adam and Eve to the Day of Judgement, cloisters, cathedral close, shop and restaurant. *Open 1 Jan-14 May, daily, 0730-1800; 15 May-30 Sep, daily, 0730-1900; 1 Oct-31 Dec, daily 0730-1800. (K/L7)*

Norwich
Roman Catholic Cathedral of St John The Baptist
Unthank Road Tel: (01603) 624615

A fine example of a 19thC Gothic-style building. *Open all year, daily, 0700-2000. (K/L7)*

Norwich
Saint Peter Mancroft Church
Haymarket Tel: (01603) 610443

A church with a Norman foundation (1075). The present church consecrated in 1455, a font (1463), Flemish tapestry (1573), an east window with medieval glass, Thomas Browne memorial. *Open all year, Mon-Fri, 1000-1530; summer 1000-1600, Sat, 1000-1230; please contact for Bank Hol opening times. (K/L7)*

Thetford
Thetford Priory
Tel: (01604) 730320

The 14thC gatehouse is the best preserved part of this Cluniac priory, built in 1103. The extensive remains include a plan of the cloisters. *Open at any reasonable time. (F/G10/11)*

Walsingham
Shrine of our Lady of Walsingham
Holt Road Tel: (01328) 820239

A pilgrimage church containing the Holy House, standing in extensive grounds. *Open all year, daily, dawn-dusk. (G/H3)*

Walsingham
Slipper Chapel Catholic National Shrine
Houghton St Giles Tel: (01328) 820217

The Roman Catholic national shrine of Our Lady. A small 14thC chapel. Plus the new Chapel of Reconciliation. Bookshop and tearoom. *Open all year, daily, dawn-dusk. (G/H3)*

Weeting
⚜ Weeting Castle
Tel: (01604) 730320

The ruins of an early medieval manor-house within a shallow rectangular moat. *Open at any reasonable time. (E10)*

DID YOU KNOW

Norwich Cathedral boasts the second tallest spire in England at 315ft, whilst 12th C. St Nicholas Church in Great Yarmouth is the largest parish church in England. St Andrew's church in East Lexham has the oldest (9th C.) round tower in Britain

museums, heritage & Craft Centres

Cromer Museum

Burston Strike School

Tel: (01379) 741565

A building erected to house a school for scholars of the strike. An interpretative exhibit of artefacts, documents and photographs. *Open all year, daily, dawn-dusk. Except for local and national polling days. (J11)*

Iceni Village and Museums

Tel: (01760) 724588

Iceni tribal village reconstruction, believed to be on the original site. Medieval cottage and forge with museum, Saxon church AD 630, carriage, vintage engine and farm museum. *Open 31 Mar-31 Oct, daily, 1100-1730. £3.50/£2.00/£2.50. (E8)*

⊛ Cromer Museum

East Cottages, Tucker Street
Tel: (01263) 513543

A late-Victorian fisherman's cottage with displays of local history (fishing, bathing resort), geology, natural history and archaeology. *Open all year, Mon-Sat, 1000-1700; Sun, 1400-1700; closed 29 Mar, 23-26 Dec, 1 Jan. £1.80/90p/£1.40. (K/L3)*

Henry Bloggs Museum

The Old Boathouse, The Promenade
Tel: (01263) 511294

World War II Watson Class lifeboat 'H.F Bailey', Bloggs boat which saved 500 lives between 1935-1945. *Open 7 Apr-31 Oct, daily, 1000-1600. (K/L3)*

Hobbies Museum of Fretwork and Craft Centre

34-36 Swaffham Road
Tel: (01362) 692985

A museum of fretwork machines dating back to 1900 with magazines and hobbies weeklies from 1895 and samples of old fretwork designs. *Open 2 Apr-30 Aug, Mon-Fri, 1000-1200, 1400-1600. (H6/7)*

100th Bomb Group Memorial Museum

Common Road Tel: (01379) 740708

A museum housed in an original World War II control tower with other buildings, showing the history of the 100th Bomb Group plus 8th Air Force exhibits and a visitor's centre. *Open 3 Feb-28 Apr, Sat, Sun, Bank Hol Mon, 1000-1700; 1 May-7 Sep, Wed, Sat, Sun, Bank Hol Mon, 1000-1700; 29 Sep-27 Oct, Sat, Sun, 1000-1700. (K11)*

Diss Museum

Market Place Tel: (01379) 650618

Housed in the historic Shambles building, award-winning Diss Museum provides visitors with a variety of changing displays on local history and prehistory. *Open 13 Mar-4 May, Wed, Thu, 1400-1600, Fri, Sat, 1030-1630; 5 May-28 Jul, Wed, Thu, 1400-1600, Fri, Sat, 1030-1630, Sun, 1400-1600; 31 Jul-21 Dec, Wed, Thu, 1400-1600, Fri, Sat, 1030-1630. (J11)*

⊛ The Collectors World of Eric St John-Foti

See entry in Historic Houses Section.

Norfolk

East Dereham
Bishop Bonners Cottage Museum
St Withburga Lane

A timber-framed building, built in 1502 with walls of brick, flint, wattle and daub. It has a thatched roof, coloured pargetting, local artefacts and bygones from local trades. *Open 30 Apr-28 Sep, Tue, Thu-Sat, 1430-1700. (H6/7)*

Erpingham
⊛ Alby Crafts
Cromer Road
Tel: (01263) 761590

A large set of converted farm buildings containing gallery, gift shop and 7 working craftsmen involved in different crafts. Bottle and lace museum, tearooms and gardens. *Open 12 Jan-10 Mar, Sat, Sun, 1000-1700; 12 Mar-19 Dec, Tue-Sun, Bank Hol Mon, 1000-1700. (K4)*

Fakenham
Fakenham Museum
of Gas and Local History
Hempton Road Tel: (01328) 863150

A complete small-town gasworks with a local history section and displays of working gas meters and working exhausters. Open by appointment for small groups only. *Open 23 May-5 Sep, Thu, 1030-1530. Last admission 1500. £1.50/25p/£1.00. (G4)*

Glandford
Shell Museum and
Saint Martins Church
Tel: (01263) 740081

The museum has exhibits of shells, fossils, pottery and objects of local history. The church has beautiful carvings and a clock with twelve bell carillon. *Open 1 Mar-31 Oct, Tue-Sat, 1000-1230, 1400-1630. £1.50/50p/£1.00. (I3)*

Great Yarmouth
⊛ Elizabethan House Museum
4 South Quay Tel: (01493) 855746

A 16thC merchant's house displaying rooms as though still lived in by families in the past. Includes Victorian kitchen/scullery, tudor bedroom and conspiracy room. *Open 29 Mar-1 Nov, Mon-Fri, 1000-1700, Sat, Sun, 1315-1700. £2.00/£1.00/£1.50. (O/P7)*

Great Yarmouth
⊛ Maritime Museum
Marine Parade Tel: (01493) 842267

The maritime history of Norfolk with herring fishery, a large collection of ship models, World War II and home-front exhibitions. *Open 25 Mar-7 Apr, Mon-Fri, 1000-1700, Sat, Sun, 1315-1700; 1 May-27 Sep, Mon-Fri, 1000-1700, Sat, Sun, 1315-1700. £1.10/70p/90p. (O/P7)*

Norfolk

Great Yarmouth
Old Merchant's House Q
Row III House and Greyfriars Cloisters
South Quay Tel: (01493) 857900

Typical 17thC town houses, one with splendid plaster ceilings containing local original architectural and domestic fittings salvaged from other 'Row' houses. *Open 1 Jan-28 Mar, daily, 1000-1300, 1400-1700; 1 Apr-31 Oct, daily, 1000-1300, 1400-1700; 1 Nov-31 Dec, daily, 1000-1300, 1400-1700. (O/P7)*

Great Yarmouth
Tolhouse Museum
Tolhouse Street Tel: (01493) 858900

One of the oldest municipal buildings in England, once the town's courthouse and gaol. Prison cells can still be seen with displays illustrating the long history of the town. *Open 1 Jul-27 Sep, Mon-Fri, 1000-1700, Sat, Sun, 1315-1700. Please phone to confirm dates. £1.10/70p/90p. (O/P7)*

Gressenhall
Roots of Norfolk at Gressenhall Q
Rural Life Museum
Tel: (01362) 860563

Museum of rural and Norfolk life housed in a former workhouse farm with rare breed animals. A 50-acre site, interactive displays and wide range of events. *Open 24 Mar-3 Nov, daily, 1000-1700. £4.70/£3.30/£4.00. (H6)*

Harleston
Harleston Museum
King Georges Hall, Broad Street

A museum housing an exhibition of items of historical interest relating to Harleston and the district. *Open 11 May-28 Sep, Wed, 1000-1200, 1400-1600; Sat, 1000-1200. (L11)*

Holt
Bircham Contemporary Arts
14 Market Place
Tel: (01263) 713312

Exhibitions of contemporary paintings, prints, ceramics, sculpture and jewellery by the finest artists and craftspeople. *Open all year, Mon-Sat, 0900-1700. Closed 25-27 Dec, 1 Jan. (I/J3)*

Holt
Picturecraft of Holt
North Norfolk's Art Centre, 23 Lees Courtyard,
Off Bull Street Tel: (01263) 711040

The main art gallery exhibits 19 artists' work which change every 3 weeks. Picture-framing specialists and an artists' material centre. *Open all year, Mon-Wed, Fri, Sat, 0900-1700; Thu, 0900-1300; Bank Hols, 1000-1600. (I/J3)*

Horning
Dinosaur Discs
35 Lower Street
Tel: (01692) 631540

Small museum showing the development of Edison's phonograph to the demise of the 78RPM record in 1960. *Open 27 Mar-21 Dec, Wed, Thur, Sat, 1030-1700. Donations appreciated. (M6)*

Hoveton
Wroxham Barns Q
Tunstead Road
Tel: (01603) 783762

Rural craft centre with 13 resident craftsmen, tearooms, gift and clothes shop, food and fudge shops. Junior Farm, Williamsons Family Fair and Cycle Hire Centre. *Open all year, daily, 1000-1700. Closed 25, 26 Dec, 1 Jan. Junior Farm £2.25/£2.25. (L/M6)*

Bursten Strike School

Cromer Museum

Hunstanton
Le Strange Old Barns
Antiques, Arts and Craft Centre,
Golf Course Road Tel: (01485) 533402
Antiques, arts and craft centre in a lovely location, 200 yards from the beach. The largest centre of its type in Norfolk. *Open 1 Jan-25 May, daily, 1000-1700; 26 May-29 Oct, daily, 1000-1800; 30 Oct-31 Dec, daily, 1000-1700; closed 25 Dec. (D3)*

Ickburgh
Iceni Brewery
3 Foulden Road
Tel: (01842) 878922
Tours of the brewery, featuring traditional and new methods of brewing and the history of brewing. Free tasting sessions. Hop Garden now open. *Open 2 Jan-23 Dec, Mon-Fri, 0900-1700, Sat, 1000-1400. Closed 29 Mar-1 Apr. Tours £6.00. Children free. (F9)*

King's Lynn
⊛ Caithness Crystal Visitor Centre Q
8-12 Paxman Rd, Hardwick Ind Est.
Tel: (01553) 765111
See glass making at close quarters, watching the skill of our glass makers as they shape and blow the glass in the manner used for centuries. The factory shop sells giftware. *Open all year, Mon-Sat, 0900-1700, Sun, 1015-1615. Please ring for details of glassmaking demonstration times. Closed 31 Mar, 25, 26 Dec. (C5/6)*

King's Lynn
Guildhall of St George
27-29 King Street Tel: (01553) 765565
A regional arts centre, the medieval Guildhall now houses a theatre with a regular programme of daytime and evening events: film, concerts and galleries. *Open all year, Mon-Sat, 1000-1700; closed Bank Hol Mon, 25 Dec. (C5/6)*

King's Lynn
⊛ Lynn Museum Q
Market Street Tel: (01553) 775001
Housed in a Victorian church. Lynn Museum has displays on natural history, archaeology and local history. *Open all year, Tue-Sat, 1000-1700; closed on public and Bank Hols. £1.00/60p/80p. (C5/6)*

King's Lynn
⊛ Tales of the Old Gaol House Q
The Old Gaol House,
Saturday Market Place
Tel: (01553) 774297
A personal stereo tour of the Old Gaol House tells the true stories of Lynn's infamous murderers, highwaymen and even witches. *Open 4 Jan-29 Mar, Fri-Tue, 1000-1700; 30 Mar-1 Nov, daily, 1000-1700; Last admission 1615. Please contact for details of admission prices. (C5/6)*

Norfolk

King's Lynn
⊛ Town House
Museum of Lynn Life
46 Queen Street Tel: (01553) 773450
The past comes to life in this newly-opened museum with historic room displays including costumes, toys, a working Victorian kitchen and a 1950s living room. *Open 3 Jan-30 Apr, Mon-Sat, 1000-1600; 1 May-30 Sep, Mon-Sat, 1000-1700, Sun 1400-1700; 1 Oct-31 Dec, Mon-Sat, 1000-1600; closed Bank and Public Hols. £1.80/90p/£1.40. (C5/6)*

King's Lynn
⊛ True's Yard Heritage Centre
3-5 North Street Tel: (01553) 770479
Two fully-restored fisherman's cottages with research facilities for tracing ancestry in King's Lynn. There is a museum, gift shop and tearoom. *Open all year, daily, 0930-1545; closed 24 Dec-2 Jan. £1.90/£1.00/£1.50. (C5/6)*

Langham
⊛ Langham Glass Q
The Long Barn
North Street
Tel: (01328) 830511
Glassmakers can be seen working with molten glass from the furnace using blowing irons. Situated in a lovely flint faced Norfolk barn complex. New 6.5 acre maize maze. *Open all year, daily, 1000-1700. Closed 25, 26 Dec, 1 Jan. £3.00/£2.00/£2.00. (H/13)*

Litcham
Litcham Village Museum
'Fourways' Tel: (01328) 701383
A local village museum and underground lime kiln. The Museum houses local artifacts from Roman times to date and a local photograph collection with 1000 photographs. *Open 31 Mar-29 Sep, Sat, Sun, 1400-1700. (F/G6)*

Little Dunham
Dunham Museum
Tel: (01760) 723073
An exhibition building showing collections of old working tools, bygones and machinery. There is a leathersmith and shoemakers. *Open 1 Apr-29 Aug, Sun-Thu, 1100-1500. 50p per car. (F7)*

Little Walsingham
⊛ Shirehall Museum
and Abbey Grounds
Common Place Tel: (01328) 820510
A Georgian country courthouse, local museum and Tourist Information Centre. Ruins of the Augustinian abbey, peaceful gardens, woodland walks set in approximately 20 acres. *Open 1 Apr-31 Oct, daily, 1000-1630; 2 Nov-22 Dec, Sat, Sun, 1000-1630. Please phone for opening during snowdrop season and opening of grounds out of season and admission prices. (G/H3)*

Ludham
Toad Hole Cottage Museum
How Hill Tel: (01692) 678763
A small 18thC cottage with a Broads information area. Museum giving the impression of the home and working life of a family on the marshes. *Open 25 Mar-31 May, Mon-Fri, 1100-1300, 1330-1700; Sat, Sun, 1100-1700; 1 Jun-30 Sep, daily, 1000-1800; 1-31 Oct, Mon-Fri, 1100-1300, 1330-1700; Sat, Sun, 1100-1700. (N6)*

North Walsham
Cat Pottery
1 Grammar School Road
Tel: (01692) 402962
Pottery cats with glass eyes, plant pots in the shape of classical heads. Casting, painting, glazing and firing and a collection of railwayana. *Open all year, Mon-Fri, 0900-1700; Sat, Bank Hol Mon, 1100-1300. Closed 25, 26 Dec, 1 Jan. (L4)*

Inspire Discovery Centre, Norwich

Norwich
Bridewell Museum
Bridewell Alley Tel: (01603) 667228
A museum with displays illustrating local industry during the past 200 years with a re-created 1920s pharmacy and a 1930s pawnbroker's shop. There are also temporary exhibits. *Open all year, Mon-Sat, 1000-1700. Closed 25, 26 Dec, 1 Jan. £2.00/£1.00/ £1.50. (K/L7)*

Norwich
Inspire Discovery Centre
St Michael's Church, Coslany Street
Tel: (01603) 612612
Inspire is a hands-on science centre housed in a medieval church. Suitable for all ages, it allows everyone to explore and discover the wonders of science for themselves. *Open all year, Tue-Sun, 1000-1730; closed 24 Dec-1 Jan. £3.50/£2.90/£2.50. (K/L7)*

Norwich
Mustard Shop
15 The Royal Arcade Tel: (01603) 627889
A decorated 19thC-style shop which houses a museum with a series of displays illustrating the history of Colman's Mustard. *Open all year, Mon-Sat, 0930-1700, Bank Hol Mon, 1100-1600. Closed 25, 26 Dec. (K/L7)*

Norwich
Norwich Castle
Shirehall
Market Avenue
Tel: (01603) 493625
Ancient Norman keep of Norwich Castle dominates the city and is one of the most important buildings of its kind in Europe. *Please contact for details of opening times and admission prices. (K/L7)*

Roots of Norfolk at Gressenhall

Norwich
The Norwich Gallery
Norwich School of Art and Design,
St Georges Street
Tel: (01603) 610561
Gallery showing temporary exhibitions of contemporary art, design and crafts. *Open all year, Mon-Sat, 1000-1700; closed Bank Hols. (K/L7)*

Norwich
Origins
The Forum, Millennium Plain, Theatre Street
Tel: (01603) 727955
Discover the latest state-of-the-art visitor attraction containing unforgettable features that are unique in England - see it, touch it, hear it at Origins in Norwich. *Please contact for details of opening times and admission prices. (K/L7)*

Norwich
The Royal Air Force Air Defence [Q] Radar Museum
RAF Neatishead
Tel: (01692) 633309
Winner of
Excellence in England regional Award 2001
History of the development and use of radar in the UK and overseas from 1935 to date. Display rooms and a gallery of original RAF unit badges. *Open 12 Jan, 9 Feb, 9 Mar, 2nd Sat in month, 1000-1500; 2 Apr-26 Sep, Tue, Thu, 2nd Sat in month and Bank Hol Mon, 1000-1500; 12 Oct, 9 Nov, 7 Dec, Sat, 1000-1500. £3.00/£2.00/£3.00. (K/L7)*

Norwich
Royal Norfolk Regimental Museum
Shirehall, Market Avenue
Tel: (01603) 223649
A modern museum with displays about the county regiment from 1685, includes a reconstructed World War I communication trench. *Open all year, Mon-Sat, 1000-1700; closed 25-26 Dec, 1 Jan. £1.80/90p/£1.40. (K/L7)*

Norwich
Sainsbury Centre for Visual Arts
University of East Anglia
Tel: (01603) 456060
Housing the Sainsbury collection of works by Picasso, Bacon and Henry Moore alongside many objects of pottery and art. Also a cafe and an art bookshop with activities monthly *Open all year, Tue-Sun, 1100-1700. £2.00/£1.00/£1.00. (K/L7)*

The Collectors World of Eric St John-Foti, Downham Market

Norwich
Strangers' Hall Museum
Charing Cross
Tel: (01603) 667229
Medieval town house with period room. Displays from Tudor to Victorian times. Toy collection on display. *Open all year, Wed, Sat, guided tours 1100, 1300, 1500. Guided tour £2.50/£1.50/£2.00. (K/L7)*

Norwich
⊛ Sutton (Windmill) Pottery
Church Road,
Sutton
Tel: (01692) 580595
A pottery producing thrown and hand-made stoneware pottery, tableware, lamps, outdoor pots and special items. Visitors are welcome to view and buy in the workshop. *Open all year, Mon-Fri, 0900-1300, 1400-1800. Restricted hours at weekends, please phone for details. Closed 31 Mar, 25, 26 Dec, 1 Jan. (K/L7)*

Seething
Seething Airfield Control Tower
Station 146, Seething Airfield
Tel: (01508) 550787
A renovated original wartime control tower holding the 448th Bomb Group honour roll and World War II exhibits, also pictures and stories from 448th veterans from 1943-1945. *Open 5 May, 2 Jun, 7 Jul, 4 Aug, 1 Sep, 6 Oct, 1000-1700. (M9)*

Sheringham
Sheringham Museum
Station Road Tel: (01263) 822895
A local history museum housing all things to do with the social history and life of the town plus lifeboat history and a new art gallery. *Open 26 Mar-31 Oct, Tue-Sat 1000-1600, Sun 1400-1600. £1.00/50p. (J/K2/3)*

Stalham
The Museum of the Broads
Stalham Staithe
Tel: (01692) 581681
Displays of tools from the traditional Broads industries and many Broads boats. *Open 29 Mar-25 Oct, Mon-Fri, 1100-1700, daily during school hols. £2.00/£1.00/£1.00. (M/N5)*

Stokesby
⊛ The Candlemaker Workshop
Mill Road
Tel: (01493) 750242
Candles manufactured. Candle dipping during school holidays. *Open 1 Feb-17 Mar, Thu-Sun, 1000-1600; 19 Mar-31 Oct, Tue-Sun, Bank Hol Mon, 0900-1800; 3 Nov-22 Dec, Thu-Sun, 1000-1600. (N7)*

Strumpshaw
⊛ Strumpshaw Old Hall Steam Museum and Farm Machinery Collection
Strumpshaw Old Hall,
Low Road
Tel: (01603) 714535
Many steam engines, beam engines, mechanical organs, narrow gauge railway and a working toy train for children. There is also a cafe, gift shop, picnic area and free parking. *Open 2 Jul-2 Oct, daily except Sat, 1100-1600. £3.00/free/£2.00. (M7)*

Ancient House Museum, Thetford

Permanent Collection, Sainsbury Centre for Visual Arts, University of East Anglia

Swaffham
⊛ Ecotech
Turbine Way
Tel: (01760) 726100
Discovery centre, grounds and ecotricity wind turbine. Environmental visitor attraction within unique EcoTech building. UK's largest wind turbine and organic garden. *Open 29 Mar-31 Oct, daily, 1000-1700. Please phone for winter opening times. £4.50/£3.25/£3.80. (F7)*

Swaffham
Swaffham Museum
Town Hall, London Street
Tel: (01760) 721230
An 18thC building, formerly a brewer's home. Small social history museum for Swaffham and the surrounding villages. Annual exhibitions plus displays from Stone Age to 20thC. *Open 30 Mar-2 Nov, Tue-Sun, 1100-1600. £1.00/free. (F7)*

Thetford
⊛ Ancient House Museum [Q]
White Hart Street Tel: (01842) 752599
A museum of Thetford and Breckland life in a remarkable early-Tudor house. Displays on local history, flint, archaeology and natural history. *Open 2 Jan-25 May, Mon-Sat, 1000-1230, 1300-1700; 26 May-25 Aug, Mon-Sat, 1000-1230, 1300-1700; Sun, 1400-1700; 27 Aug-31 Dec, Mon-Sat, 1000-1230, 1300-1700; closed 29 Mar, 23-26 Dec. £1.00/60p/80p. (F/G10/11)*

Thetford
⊛ Charles Burrell Museum
Minstergate Tel: (01842) 751166
The Charles Burrell Steam Museum draws together an impressive collection of exhibits to tell the story of Charles Burrell and Son (1770-1932). *Open 31 Mar-27 Oct, Sat; Sun, Bank Hol Mon, 1000-1700. £1.25/70p/70p. (F/G10/11)*

Wells-next-the-Sea
Wells Maritime Museum
Old Lifeboat House, The Quay
Tel: (01328) 711646
The maritime history of Wells, housed in the old lifeboat house. *Please contact for details of opening times. 75p/25p. (G2)*

Woodbastwick
Woodforde's Brewery Shop and Visitor Centre
Broadland Brewery
Tel: (01603) 722218
Woodforde's cask ale brewery, shop and visitor centre. The Fur and Feather Inn is located next door, which is the brewery tap and restaurant. *Please contact for details of opening times. (M6)*

Wymondham
Wymondham Heritage Museum
Bridewell, Norwich Road
Tel: (01953) 600205
The museum is housed in a prison built in 1785, telling the story of the Bridewell as a prison, police station and courthouse. Many local history displays. *Open 1 Mar-30 Nov, Mon-Sat, 1000-1600; Sun, 1400-1600. £2.00/50p/£1.50. (J8)*

Caithness Crystal, King's Lynn

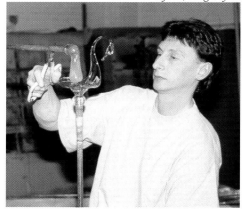

machinery & transport

Thursford Collection

Aylsham
⚙ Bure Valley Railway
Aylsham Station, Norwich Road
Tel: (01263) 733858

A 15-inch narrow-gauge steam railway covering 9 miles of track from Wroxham in the heart of the Norfolk Broads to Aylsham which is a bustling market town. *Open 24 Mar-5 Apr, daily, 1000-1730; 5-23 May, Sun-Thu, 1000-1730; 25 May-6 Jun, daily, 1000-1730; 9-27 Jun, Sun-Thu, 1000-1730; 30 Jun-5 Sep, daily, 1000-1730; 8-29 Sep, Sun-Thu, 1000-1730; 19-27 Oct, daily, 1000-1730. £4.40/£3.00/£4.00. (K5)*

Bressingham
⚙ Bressingham Steam Experience and Gardens
Tel: (01379) 687386

Steam rides through 5 miles of woodland. Six acres of the Island Beds plant centre. Mainline locomotives, the Victorian Gallopers and over 50 steam engines. *Steam Experience and Garden open 31 Mar-31 Oct, daily, 1030-1730. Dads Army National Collection open 1 Jan-31 Mar, daily, 1030-1600; 1 Apr-30 Sep, daily, 1030-1730; 1 Oct-31 Dec, daily, 1030-1600. Please contact for details of admission prices. (I/J11)*

Dereham
⚙ Mid Norfolk Railway (Dereham to Wymondham Line)
The Railway Station, Station Road
Tel: (01362) 690633

Victorian railway station at Dereham undergoing restoration. Selection of class 50, class 20 and Gloucester bubble car. Other vehicles undergoing restoration. *Open all year, Sun, 1030-1600, for timetable telephone (01362) 690633. Train: £5.00/£2.50. (H6/7)*

Dickleburgh
100th Bomb Group Memorial Museum
See entry in Museums section.

Forncett St Mary
Forncett Industrial Steam Museum
Low Road
Tel: (01508) 488277

A unique collection of large industrial steam engines including one that used to open Tower Bridge. Seven engines can be seen working on steam days. *Open 5 May, 2 Jun, 7 Jul, 4 Aug, 1 Sep, 6 Oct, 3 Nov, Sun, 1100-1700. £4.00/free/£3.50. (K9/10)*

Horsham St Faith
City of Norwich Aviation Museum
Old Norwich Road
Tel: (01603) 893080

A collection of aircraft and memorabilia showing the aviation history of Norfolk. The collection features many aircraft which have flown from Norfolk. *Open 5 Jan-31 Mar, Sat, Sun, Wed, 1000-1600; 1 Apr-31 Oct, Tue-Sun, 1000-1700; Bank Hol Mon, 1200-1700; 2 Nov-22 Dec, Wed, Sat, 1000-1600, Sun 1200-1600. Please contact for details of admission prices. (K/L6)*

North Elmham
Mid-Norfolk Railway
County School Station, Holt Road
Tel: (01362) 668181

Station built in 1884 is northern outpost of Mid-Norfolk Railway. Situated in the heart of the unspoilt Wensum Valley. Tearoom, small exhibition and walks. *Please contact for details of opening times and admission prices. (H5/6)*

Norfolk

North Walsham
Norfolk Motor Cycle Museum
Railway Yard Tel: (01692) 406266
A museum displaying a wide collection of motor cycles dating from 1920 to 1960. *Open 2 Jan-30 Mar, Mon-Sat, 1000-1630; 31 Mar-2 Nov, daily, 1000-1630; 4 Nov-31 Dec, Mon-Sat, 1000-1630; closed 25, 26 Dec, 1 Jan. £2.50/£1.50/ £2.00. (L4)*

Sheringham
⊛ **North Norfolk Railway**
Sheringham Station, Station Approach
Tel: (01263) 820800
A 5-mile long steam railway with stations at Sheringham, Weybourne and Holt. Also a museum of railway memorabilia, static exhibits, a station buffet and souvenir shop. *Station open daily, trains run daily May-Sep, contact the railway for details. £7.50/£4.00/£6.50. (J/K2/3)*

⊛ Strumpshaw
Strumpshaw Old Hall Steam Museum and Farm Machinery Collection
See entry in Museums section.

⊛ Thetford
Charles Burrell Museum
See entry in Museums section.

Thursford
⊛ **Thursford Collection** [Q]
Thursford Green
Tel: (01328) 878477
Musical evenings some Tuesdays from mid-July to the end of September. A live musical show with 9 mechanical organs and a Wurlitzer show starring Robert Wolfe daily 29 Mar-mid Oct. *Open 29 Mar-20 Oct, daily, 1200-1700. £4.90/£2.40/£4.60. (H4)*

Norfolk

Wells-next-the-Sea
Wells Harbour Railway
c/o Pinewoods,
Beach Road Tel: (01328) 710964
This 10.25 inch narrow gauge railway of approximately 1 mile runs adjacent to the beach road, carrying passengers to the beach or harbour. Late trains available. *Open 29 Mar-7 Apr, daily, 1030-1730; 13 Apr-4 Jun, Sat, Sun, 1030-1730; 5 Jun-15 Sep, daily, 1030-1730; 21-29 Sep, Sat, Sun, 1030-1730. Single fare 80p/60p. (G2/3)*

Wells-next-the-Sea
Wells Walsingham Railway
Stiffkey Road Tel: (01328) 710631
Four miles of railway; the longest 10.25-inch railway in the world with a new steam locomotive 'Norfolk Hero' now in service, the largest of its kind ever built. *Open 29 Mar-31 Oct, daily, please phone for train times and admission prices. (G2)*

West Walton
Fenland and West Norfolk Aviation Museum
Bambers Garden Centre,
Old Lynn Road Tel: (01945) 584440
Vampire T11, Lightning aircraft, uniforms, aero engines, aircraft components, artefacts, memorabilia, radio equipment, souvenirs, models and a replica Spitfire. *Open 2 Mar-27 Oct, Sat, Sun, Bank Hol Mon, 0930-1700. £1.50/75p/75p. (A6/7)*

Weybourne
Muckleburgh Collection **Q**
Weybourne Old Military Camp
Tel: (01263) 588210
Collection of over 136 military vehicles and heavy equipment used by the allied armies during and since World War II including fighting tanks, armoured cars and artillery. *Open 17 Feb-27 Oct, daily, 1000-1700. £4.95/£2.50. (J2/3)*

Wroxham
Barton House Railway
Hartwell Road, The Avenue Tel: (01603) 782470
A 3.5-gauge miniature steam passenger railway and a 7.25-gauge steam and battery-electric railway. Full-size M and GN accessories including signals and signal boxes. *Open 21 Apr, 19 May, 16 Jun, 21 Jul, 18 Aug, 15 Sep, 20 Oct, Sun, 1430-1730. 50p/25p. (L/M6)*

Norfolk

Acle
Stracey Arms Drainage Mill
Stracey Arms

An exhibition of photos and the history of drainage mills in Broadland. A restored drainage mill with access by 2 ladders to the cap showing the brakewheel and gears. *Please contact for details of opening times and admission prices. (N7)*

Cley Mill

Stracey Arms Drainage Mill

Billingford
Billingford Windmill
Tel: (01379) 740743

Nineteenth century tower cornmill with Norfolk boat shaped cap restored to full working order. *Please contact for details of opening times and admission prices. (K11)*

Cley-next-the-Sea
Cley Mill
Tel: (01263) 740209

A towermill used as a flourmill until 1918 and converted to a guesthouse in 1983. Built in the early 1700s, it is an outstanding example of a preserved mill with sails. *Open 28 Mar-1 Oct, daily, 1400-1700. £1.50/75p/75p. (I2)*

Denver
⊛ Denver Windmill Q
Sluice Road   Tel: (01366) 384009

A fully restored windmill and all its internal machinery with a splendid Blackstone Oil Engine. Unique guided tours to the top of the tower. *Open 2 Jan-31 Mar, Mon-Sat, 1000-1600, Sun, 1200-1600; 1 Apr-31 Oct, Mon-Sat, 1000-1700, Sun, 1200-1700; 1 Nov-31 Dec, Mon-Sat, 1000-1600, Sun, 1200-1600. Closed 25, 26 Dec, 1 Jan. £2.75/£2.50/£2.50. (C8)*

Billingford Windmill

Great Bircham
⊛ Bircham Mill Q
Tel: (01485) 578393
A Norfolk cornmill with working machinery and a small working bakery museum. There are also tearooms, ponies and cycle hire. *Open 6 Apr-30 Sep, daily, 1000-1700. Please contact for details of admission prices. (E4)*

Halvergate Marsh
⊛ Berney Arms Windmill
c/o 8 Manor Road, Great Yarmouth
Tel: (01604) 730320
A most splendid and the highest remaining Norfolk marshmill in working order with 7 floors. Built in the late 19thC by millwrights Stolworthy and situated on Halvergate Marsh. *Open 1 Apr-31 Oct, daily, 0900-1300, 1400-1700. £1.60/80p/£1.20. (O9/10)*

DID YOU KNOW
St. George's Guildhall in King's Lynn is the largest surviving medieval guildhall in England. Built 1410-1420, it has now been converted into an arts centre. It is reputed to be the oldest performing arts venue still in use today, and Shakespeare is rumoured to have performed here.

Horsey
⊛ Horsey Windpump
Tel: (01493) 393904
This windmill is 4 storeys high and the gallery affords splendid views across the marshes. *Open 1 Apr-1 Oct, daily, 1100-1700. £1.30/65p. (O5)*

Letheringsett
Letheringsett Watermill
Riverside Road   Tel: (01263) 713153
An historic working watermill with an iron water wheel and main gearing restored with an additional vintage Ruston Hornsby oil engine. Flour, animal and pet feed are for sale. *Please contact for details of opening times. From £2.50/£1.50. (I3)*

Old Buckenham
Old Buckenham Mill
Green Lane
The largest diameter cornmill in the country built in 1818. The mill is static but contains much machinery. It had 5 sets of stones when operating. *Please contact for details of opening times and admission prices. (I10)*

Starston
Starston Windpump
Tel: (01379) 852393
A restored windpump. *Open at any reasonable time. (L10/11)*

Norfolk

gardens & Vineyards

Attleborough
⊛ Peter Beales Roses
London Road   Tel: (01953) 454707
Two and a half acres of display rose garden set in rural surroundings. *Open all year, Mon-Fri, 0900-1700, Sat, 0900-1630; Sun, Bank Hols, 1000-1600. (I9)*

Beeston Regis
Priory Maze and Gardens
Cromer Road
Tel: (01263) 822986
Ten acres of gardens with beech hedge maze and various demonstration gardens. *Open 25 May, Sat, 1000-1700; 26 May-29 Sep, Tue-Fri, Sun, Bank Hol Mon, 1000-1700. £3.00/£1.50/£3.00. (K2/3)*

Blickling
⊛ Blickling Hall Q
See entry in Historic Houses section.

Dereham
⊛ Norfolk Herbs
Dereham   Tel: (01362) 860812
Specialist growers of culinary, medicinal and aromatic herb plants. Herb shop and hand thrown garden terracotta. Display garden and plant sales area. Herbal advice, information and garden design. *Open 1 Feb-30 Mar, Wed-Sat, 0900-1700; 1 Apr-31 Jul, daily, 0900-1800; 1-31 Aug, Tue-Sun, 0900-1800; 4 Sep-21 Dec, Wed-Sat, 0900-1700. (H6/7)*

Downham Market
⊛ The Collectors World of Eric St John-Foti
See entry in Historic Houses section.

DID YOU KNOW

Norfolk Lavender at Heacham, is England's only commercial lavender farm (founded in 1932).

Blickling Hall

Cottage Garden, Blakeney

East Ruston
⊛ East Ruston
Old Vicarage Garden
Norwich
Tel: (01603) 650432
A 16-acre exotic garden separated into sections including the Tropical Border, Mediterranean Garden, Sunken Garden, Autumn Borders, Kitchen Garden and Wildflower Meadows. *Open 31 Mar-25 Oct, Wed, Fri, Sun, Bank Hol Mon, 1400-1730. £3.80/£1.00/£3.80. (M4/5)*

Felbrigg
⊛ Felbrigg Hall
See entry in Historic Houses section.

Grimston
⊛ Congham Hall Herb Garden
Lynn Road   Tel: (01485) 600250
Garden with over 650 varieties of herbs in formal beds with wild flowers and a potager garden. Over 250 varieties of herbs for sale in pots. *Open 1 Apr-30 Sep, Sun-Fri, 0900-1630. (D/E5)*

Heacham
⊛ Norfolk Lavender Limited Ｑ
Caley Mill   Tel: (01485) 570384
Lavender is distilled from the flowers and the oil made into a wide range of gifts. There is a slide show when the distillery is not working. *Open all year, daily, 1000-1700; closed 25, 26 Dec, 1 Jan. (D3)*

Houghton
⊛ Houghton Hall
See entry in Historic Houses section.

King's Lynn
West Acre Gardens
West Acre
Tel: (01760) 755562
D-shaped walled garden with extensive display beds with year-round interest and beauty. *Open 1 Feb-30 Nov, daily, 1000-1700. (C5/6)*

Neatishead
Willow Farm Flowers
Cangate   Tel: (01603) 783588
One of the largest displays of dried, silk and parchment flowers in the region situated in a magnificent 300-year-old thatched barn in the heart of the Broads. *Open all year, Mon-Sat, 1000-1600. Please contact for Christmas closure. (M5/6)*

Norwich
⊛ Dragon Hall
See entry in Historic Houses section.

Norwich
⊛ Mannington Gardens
and Countryside
Mannington Hall   Tel: (01263) 584175
Gardens with a lake, moat, woodland and an outstanding rose collection. There is also a Saxon church with Victorian follies, countryside walks and trails with guide booklets. *Open: Walks all year, daily, from 0900; Gardens 28 Apr-29 Sep, Sun 1200-1700, 5 Jun-28 Aug, Wed-Fri, 1100-1700. £3.00/free/£2.50. (K/L7)*

Norfolk Lavender, Heacham

Norwich
The Plantation Garden
4 Earlham Road

A rare surviving example of a private Victorian town garden, created between 1856-1897 in a former medieval chalk quarry and undergoing restoration by volunteers. *Open all year, daily, 1000-1600. Teas served mid Apr-mid Oct, Sun, 1430-1630. £1.50. Special Events £2.00/£1.00. (K/L7)*

Oxborough
⊛ Oxburgh Hall Q
See entry in Historic Houses section.

Raveningham
Raveningham Gardens
The Stables   Tel: (01508) 548480

Extensive gardens surrounding an elegant Georgian house provide the setting for many rare, variegated and unusual plants and shrubs with sculptures, parkland and a church. *Open 1 Apr-29 Sep, Sun, Wed, Bank Hol Mon, 1400-1730. £2.50/free/£2.00. (M/N9)*

Sandringham
⊛ Sandringham
See entry in Historic Houses section.

South Creake
South Creake Maize Maze
Compton Hall
Tel: (01328) 823224

An amazing maize maze. Acres of maze and paths. *Open 14 Jul-16 Sep, daily, 1000-1800. Last admission 1700. £3.50/£2.50/£2.00. (F/G 3/4)*

South Walsham
⊛ Fairhaven Woodland and Water Garden
School Road   Tel: (01603) 270449

One hundred and eighty acres of woodland and water gardens including a private inner broad and separate wildlife sanctuary. Tearoom, giftshop and plant sales. *Open all year, daily, 1000-1700; 2 May-31 Aug, Wed, Thu, 1000-2100; closed 25 Dec. £3.50/£1.25/£3.00. (N6/7)*

Thetford
⊛ Euston Hall
See entry in Historic Houses section.

Wells-next-the-Sea
⊛ Holkham Hall Q
See entry in Historic Houses section.

Wroxham
⊛ Hoveton Hall Gardens
Tel: (01603) 782798

Approximately 10 acres of gardens in a woodland setting with a large walled herbaceous garden and a Victorian kitchen garden. There are also woodland and lakeside walks. *Open 31 Mar-28 Apr, Wed, Fri, Sun, Bank Hol, 1100-1730; 1-31 May, Wed-Fri, 1100-1730, Sun, Bank Hol, 1100-1730; 2 Jun-22 Sep, Wed, Fri, Sun, Bank Hol, 1100-1730. £3.50/£1.00/£2.00. (L/M6)*

Fairhaven Woodland and Water Garden, South Walsham

nurseries
& garden
centres

Attleborough
⊛ Peter Beales Roses
Peter Beales Roses, London Road,
Attleborough, NR17 1AY
Tel: (01953) 454707 Fax: (01953) 456845
E-mail: Sales@classicroses.co.uk
www.classicroses.co.uk

A large and world famous collection of roses featuring over 1100 rare, unusual and beautiful varieties of which 250 are unique. The National Collection of Rosa Species is held here. Browse through 2.5 acres of gardens, container roses available in the summer months, or order for winter delivery. Experts are always on hand for advice or help in the selection of new varieties. *Open Mon-Fri. 0900-1700, Sat. 0900-1630, Sun and Bank Hols 1000-1600. Catalogue free on request (I9)*

DID YOU KNOW
The largest medieval brick barn in England can be found at 'Read's Nursery and Gardens' in Hale.

Bressingham
Blooms of Bressingham
Bressingham, Diss, Norfolk
Tel: (01379) 688585

Three miles west of Diss on A1066. Designed to excite and inspire 21st century gardeners this unique two acre Plant Centre adjacent to world famous Bressingham Gardens and Bressingham Steam Experience featuring the "Dad's Army Exhibition", gives bigger, better choice for creative gardeners. The famous Blooms range of quality plants and an increased product range incorporates a new "life-style" approach to gardening. Add a Garden Design Service and the innovative "Into-Food" Café all set in a striking structure and it's a must for a great day out. *Open: Daily 0900-1800 March to October; 0900-1700 November to February except Christmas Day/Boxing Day. See also entry for Bressingham Steam Museum and Gardens under Machinery & Transport on page (182) and Into Food Café under Afternoon Teas on page (208). (I/J11)*

Norfolk

Gressenhall
⊛ Norfolk Herbs
Blackberry Farm, Dillington,
Nr Gressenhall, Dereham NR19 2QD
Tel: (01362) 860812

(Approx. 1 mile north of Dereham on the B1110, now signed as the B1146, take the first left to Dillington and we are approx. 1.5 miles on right). Norfolk's specialist Herb Farm, in a beautiful wooded valley renowned for its wildlife. Visitors may browse through a vast array of aromatic, culinary and medicinal herb plants and learn all about growing and using herbs. *Open Apr-Jul, daily, Aug, Tue-Sun, 0900-1800; Sep-Mar, Wed-Sat, 0900-1700. Closed Dec 24-Jan 31. For group visits or visiting outside of these hours, please telephone for an appointment. (H6)*

Hickling Broad

Fairhaven Woodland and Water Garden, South Walsham

Grimston
⊛ Congham Hall Herb Gardens
Grimston, King's Lynn PE32 1AH
Tel: (01485) 600250

Reminiscent of a traditional country house garden, with over 700 varieties of herbs to see and 200 for sale in pots. Group tours including lunch, dinner or afternoon tea and a talk on herbs, by prior arrangement. *Gardens open 2.00pm-4.00pm, Sunday to Friday from April to September. (D/E5)*

Heacham
⊛ Norfolk Lavender Ltd. Q
Caley Mill, Heacham, Norfolk (on A149)
Tel: (01485) 570384
Fax: (01485) 571176

The Fragrant Plant Meadow and Conservatory offer a wide selection of scented plants to add to our lavenders, herb plants and garden collection. Also Tours (May-Sep) - Learn about the harvest and ancient distillation process. The Gift Shop stocks the full range of Norfolk Lavender's famous fragrant products with a wide choice of other gifts to suit all pockets. Miller's Cottage Tearoom - Specialising in locally baked cakes, scones, cream teas and lunches The National Collection of Lavenders. *FREE ADMISSION. Open daily 1000-1700 (closed Dec 25, 26 and Jan 1). (D3)*

King's Lynn
⊛ The African Violet Centre Q
Terrington St Clement, King's Lynn, Norfolk
Tel: (01553) 828374
www.africanvioletcentre.ltd.uk

The African Violet and Garden Centre offers a wide variety of plants for any enthusiast. Known for our African Violets we boast the best in Britain. A winner of many Chelsea Gold Medals, we place ourselves as the perfect venue, whatever the weather. Our Visitor Centre enables visitors to share in the secrets and discover the wonderful world of African Violets. Spacious Garden and Gift Shop, Café serving light lunches, children's play area. Ample parking, coach parties welcome. Talks/demonstrations by appointment. Situated by the A17, five miles King's Lynn. *FREE ADMISSION! Open daily: 0900-1700 Sun 1000-1700. Closed Christmas/New Years day only. (C5/6)*

Norwich
⊛ Notcutts Garden Centres
Daniels Road (Ring Road),
Norwich, Norfolk Tel: (01603) 453155

Discover a world of ideas and inspiration around every corner for you, your home and your garden. From fabulous plants to gifts and treats galore, there's so much to see. Gift ideas from around the world, houseplants, books, fresh cut & silk flowers, 3,000 varieties of hardy plants (with a 2 year replacement guarantee), pet centre, coffee shop, plus expert friendly advice about seasonal and bedding plants, garden furniture and barbecues. Keep an eye open for regular offers on key garden products. *Notcutts open 7 days a week, free car-parking plus children's play area. (K/L7)*

Blickling Hall Gardens

Reymerston
Thorncroft Clematis Nursery
The Lings, Reymerston, Norwich,
Norfolk NR9 4QG
Tel: (01953) 850407
www.thorncroft.co.uk

Come and visit our nursery and garden in the 'heart' of the Norfolk countryside where these beautiful, versatile climbers can be seen growing in a natural setting. Our nursery stocks many beautiful, and unusual varieties. Send 5 x 2nd class stamps for catalogue. *Open 1 Mar-31 Oct, 1000-1630. Closed Wednesdays. (Visits Nov-Feb by appointment).* On B1135 exactly halfway between Wymondham and Dereham (not in village). *(I8)*

Taverham
Taverham Nursery Centre
Fir Covert Road, Taverham, Norwich
Tel: (01603) 860522

Taverham Garden Centre is set in 15 acres of beautiful countryside, 7 miles from Norwich on the A1067 Norwich/Fakenham road. We offer a riot of colour all year round. Acres of greenhouses packed with beautiful flowers and pot plants, grown to the highest standards. There's an unrivalled choice of plants, shrubs, trees; an extensive range of bulbs and seeds; attractive garden furniture and ornaments, terracotta pots, planters, paving slabs, pools and conservatories. Plus dried and silk flowers, books, pet food, coffee bar, craft complex. Fully trained staff. Disabled facilities, coach parties welcome. Parking for 1000 cars. *Open Mon-Sat, 0900-1730. Sun, 1000-1730. (J6)*

Norfolk ⎯⎯⎯⎯⎯⎯⎯⎯⎯⎯⎯⎯⎯⎯⎯⎯⎯⎯⎯⎯⎯⎯⎯⎯⎯⎯⎯⎯

Sealife Centre, Great Yarmouth

Attleborough
Kool Kidz
34-35 Haverscroft Industrial Estate,
New Road   Tel: (01953) 457333
Indoor activity centre including large soft play area, educational equipment, cafe bar, satellite TV and refreshments. Birthday parties available and free parking. *Open all year, daily, 1000-1900; closed 25, 26 Dec, 1 Jan. Child £2.95. (I9)*

Banham
⊛ Banham Zoo Q
The Grove Tel: (01953) 887771
Wildlife spectacular which will take you on a journey to experience tigers, leopards and zebra some of the worlds most exotic, rare and endangered animals. *Open all year, daily 1000-1700. Closed 25, 26 Dec, 1 Jan. Closing times have seasonal variations. £7.95/£5.95/£5.50. (I10)*

Cromer
Funstop
Exchange House, Louden Road
Tel: (01263) 514976
A children's indoor adventure centre with a giant slide, ball pond, tubes, scrambling nets, a special under-3's area, a super snack bar and lots more. *Open 5 Jan-21 Apr, Fri-Sun, daily during school hols, 1000-1800; 1 May-30 Jun, Wed-Sun, 1000-1800; 1 Jul-30 Sep, daily, 1000-1800; 5 Oct-24 Dec, Fri-Sun, daily during school hols, 1000-1800.   Child from £1.90. (K/L3)*

Fleggburgh
⊛ The Village Experience Q
Burgh St Margaret Tel: (01493) 369770
Over 35 acres of fun. Working steam, live shows, traditional fairground, adventure area and Compton-Christie organ. Crafts, shops, rides and shows included in price. *Open 24 Mar-27 Oct, daily, 1000-1700. Please phone for Christmas opening. £5.95/£4.95/£5.45. (N/O6)*

Filby
⊛ Thrigby Hall Wildlife Gardens Q
Tel: (01493) 369477
A wide selection of Asian mammals, birds, reptiles, tigers, crocodiles and storks. A 250-year-old landscaped garden with play area and willow pattern gardens. *Open all year, daily, 1000-1700. £5.90/£3.90/£4.90. (O6/7)*

Frettenham
Hillside Animal Sanctuary
Hill Top Farm,
Hall Lane
Tel: (01603) 891227
Visit our rescued farm animals. Information centre and gift shop. *Open 29 Mar-1 Apr, daily, 1300-1700; 7 Apr-30 Jun, Sun, 1300-1700; 1 Jul-26 Aug, Sun, Mon, 1300-1700; 1 Sep-27 Oct, Sun, 1300-1700. £2.00/£1.00/£1.00. (L6)*

Fritton
Redwings Visitor Centre
Caldecott Hall
Tel: (01493) 488531
A sanctuary for horses, ponies and donkeys. Stroll along the paddock walks, visit the gift shop and information centre or adopt a rescued horse. *Please contact for details of opening times and admission prices. (O8)*

Great Ellingham
⊛ The Tropical Butterfly World
Long Street
Tel: (01953) 453175
Vibrant free flying tropical butterflies in landscaped gardens. Bird park, giant maze, flying displays, conservation walk, garden centre, gift shop and cafe. *Open 15 Feb-30 Oct, Mon-Sat, 0900-1800, Sun, 1100-1630. Closed 31 Mar. Please contact for details of admission prices. (H/I9)*

Norfolk

Thetford Forest

Great Yarmouth
Louis Tussauds House of Wax
18 Regent Road
Tel: (01493) 844851

A waxworks exhibition with torture chambers, a chamber of horrors, a hall of funny mirrors and a family amusement arcade. *Open 1 Mar-30 Apr, daily, 1100-1600; 1 May-31 Aug, daily, 1030-1830; 1 Sep-31 Oct, daily, 1100-1600. £3.00/£2.00/£1.50. (O/P7)*

Great Yarmouth
The Mint
31 Marine Parade Tel: (01493) 842968

Family entertainment centre including 'Quasar' the live action laser game. *Open all year, daily, 0900-2300. £2.99/£2.99. (O/P7)*

DID YOU KNOW

Great Yarmouth's Pleasure Beach is home to one of the oldest (1033) and most historic roller-coasters in the world.

Norfolk

Heavy horse rides at Fritton Park

Great Yarmouth
◉ Pleasure Beach
South Beach Parade
Tel: (01493) 844585
Rollercoaster, Terminator, log flume, Twister, monorail, galloping horses, caterpillar, ghost train, fun house. Height restrictions are in force on some rides. *Please contact for details of opening times. (O/P7)*

Great Yarmouth
Sea-Life Centre
Marine Parade Tel: (01493) 330631
Walk through the underwater tropical reef shark tank, a sand tank with ray fish and British sharks plus 25 themed displays depicting British marine life and local settings. *Open all year, daily, from 1000. Closed 25 Dec. £5.95/£3.95. (O/P7)*

Hunstanton
Jungle Wonderland
C H S Amusements
1st Floor Pier Entertainment Centre,
The Green   Tel: (01485) 535505
An adventure playground catering for children aged 2-12 with a soft play area, a giant ball pool, Kenny the Croc slide, many more safe play items and an 80-seater diner. *Open 1 Jan-29 Mar, Fri-Sun, daily during school hols, 1000-1800; 30 Mar-31 Oct, daily, 1000-1800; 1 Nov-31 Dec, Fri-Sun, daily during school hols, 1000-1800. Closed 25, 26 Dec. Please contact for details of admission prices. (D3)*

Hunstanton
Hunstanton Sea-Life and Marine Sanctuary
Southern Promenade
Tel: (01485) 533576
Ocean tunnel. See a world which experienced divers see. See and touch rock pool creatures. Also a seal rehabilitation centre for unwell or abandoned seals and otter sanctuary. *Open all year, daily, from 1000; closed 25 Dec. £4.99/£3.50/£3.95. (D3)*

Larling
◉ Overa House Farm: Equine Recovery and Rehabilitation Centre
Tel: (01953) 717309
Visit the centre for horses and ponies in beautiful countryside. See the work of the International League for the Protection of Horses. Visit the coffee and gifts shops. *Open all year, Wed, Sat, Sun, Bank Hols, 1100-1600. Closed 25 Dec, 1 Jan. (H10)*

Lenwade
◉ The Dinosaur Adventure Park Q
Weston Estate   Tel: (01603) 870245
A unique family day out. Attractions include the dinosaur trail, woodland maze, new secret animal garden, Climb-a-Saurus, adventure play areas and education centre. *Please contact for details of opening times and admission prices. (J6)*

Norfolk

Poringland
⊛ The Playbarn
West Green Farm, Shotesham Road
Tel: (01508) 495526

Children's indoor and outdoor play centre. Designed for under 7's. Large barn and courtyard, beach barn, children's farm, riding school and animal centre. *Open all year, Mon-Fri, 0930-1530; Sun, 1000-1700; closed 25, 26 Dec, 1 Jan. £1.00 /£4.00. (L8)*

Reedham
⊛ Pettitt's Animal Adventure Park
Camphill   Tel: (01493) 700094

A family park, which includes animals galore including birds of prey, chickens, ducks, miniature Fallabella horses, goats, monkeys, parrots, peacocks, rheas and wallabies. *Please contact for details of opening times and admission prices. (N8)*

Scoulton
⊛ Melsop Farm Park
Melsop Farm, Ellingham Road
Tel: (01953) 851943

Farm park rare breeds centre. A 17thC thatched Listed house, set in 11 acres of rural Breckland countryside. *Open 29 Mar-29 Sep, Tue-Sun, Bank Hols, 1030-1700. £3.50/£2.50/£2.50. (H8)*

Snettisham
⊛ Park Farm Snettisham [Q]
Tel: (01485) 542425

Providing unique safari tours, a visitor centre, crafts centre, art gallery, tearoom and souvenir shop. Indoor and outdoor activities include farm animals and pets. *Open 1 Feb-1 Apr, daily, 1000-dusk; 2 Apr-1 Nov, daily, 1000-1700; 2 Nov-29 Dec, Fri-Sun, 1000-dusk. £4.25/£3.25. (D4)*

West Runton
⊛ Norfolk Shire Horse Centre
West Runton Stables
Tel: (01263) 837339

Shire horses are demonstrated working twice daily with native ponies and a bygone collection of horse-drawn machinery. There is also a children's farm. *Open 24 Mar-31 Jul, daily except Sat unless Bank Hol, 1000-1700; 1-31 Aug, daily, 1000-1700; 1 Sep-25 Oct, daily except Sat, 1000-1700. £5.00/£3.00/£4.00. (K2/3)*

Wroxham
⊛ Junior Farm at Wroxham Barns [Q]
Tunstead Road, Hoveton, Norfolk NR12 8QU
Tel: (01603) 783762

10 acres of converted barns and farmland with something for everyone. Meet, feed and learn about the friendly farmyard animals at Junior Farm. Williamson's Traditional Fair with swing boats, Ferris wheel, Merry-go-rounds, Peter Pan Railway and End of the Pier Old Penny Arcade. Also 13 resident craftsmen, gift and clothes shops, food and fudge shops and tearoom. *Open daily 10am-5pm except Dec 25 and 26 and January 1. Fair (seasonal). Free admission and parking. Junior Farm £2.25 per person (Under 3s free). Fair rides individually priced. See also our entry under Speciality Shopping page 214. (L/M6)*

Norfolk

Countryside

Nr Saxlingham

Country Parks and Nature Reserves

◈ Cley Marshes Nature Reserve

Cley-next-the-Sea Tel: (01263) 740008

Coastal nature reserve, with an international reputation. Popular with bird-watchers who come to see migrant and wading birds. Visitor centre overlooks the reserve. (NWT). *Reserve open all year, Tue-Sun, Bank Hol Mon, 1000-1700. Visitor centre open 1 Apr-31 Oct, daily, 1000-1700; 6 Nov-15 Dec, Wed-Sun, 1000-1600. Admission 50p. (I2)*

◈ East Wretham Heath Nature Reserve

Wretham Tel: (01953) 498339

A nature reserve with grassy heath, Pine plantation, meres and associated wildlife. There is also a self-guided nature trail and access to the hide. (NWT) *Open at any reasonable time. (G9/10)*

◈ Foxley Wood

Foxley Tel: (01603) 625540

The largest ancient woodland in the county with 3 nature trails existing around the site. The wood is well used by naturalists, the general public and schools. (NWT). *Open all year, daily, 1000-1700. (I7)*

◈ Fritton Lake Country World Q

Fritton Tel: (01493) 488208

A 250-acre centre with a children's assault course, putting, an adventure playground, golf, fishing, boating, wildfowl, heavy horses, cart rides, falconry and flying displays. *Open 23 Mar-29 Sep, daily, 1000-1730; 5-27 Oct, Sat, Sun, daily during half term, 1000-1730. £5.30/£3.90/£4.80. (O10)*

◈ Hickling Broad

Hickling Tel: (01692) 598276

A nature reserve with a broad, dykes, marshes, fens and woodland with a visitors centre and water trail. (NWT) *Open all year, daily, 1000-1700. Visitors' centre open, 1 Apr-30 Sep, daily, 1000-1700. £2.50. (N5)*

◈ High Lodge Forest Centre

Forestry Commission, Santon Downham, Brandon
Tel: (01842) 810271

High Lodge visitor centre houses a restaurant, gift shop and information. Other facilities include the maze, cycle hire and trails, walks and adventure play area. *Open Forest Centre 5 Jan-24 Mar, Sat, Sun, 1000-1600; 25 Mar-25 Oct, Mon-Fri, 1000-1700; Sat, Sun, 1000-1800; 2 Nov-22 Dec, Sat, Sun, 1000-1600; Forest Drive open all year, daily, 1000-dusk. Closed 25 Dec. Winter: car £1.50, Summer: £2.50. (F10)*

Holme Bird Observatory Reserve

Broadwater Road
Tel: (01485) 525406

Nature reserve with over 320 species of birds recorded since 1962. One of 18 bird observatories in the UK. Various species of dragonfly. Over 50 species of flora. *Open all year, Tue-Sun, Bank Hol Mons, 1000-1700, or dusk, if earlier. Please phone for Christmas closure. £2.00. (D2)*

Norfolk

Knettishall Heath Country Park
Knettishall Tel: (01953) 688265

Park with 375 acres of Breckland heath with access to the River Ouse along walks. Picnic areas, toilets and the start point for Peddars Way, Angles Way and the Icknield Way. *Open 2 Jan-31 Dec, 0900-dusk; closed 25, 26 Dec. (H11)*

⊛ Lynford Arboretum
Forestry Commission, East Anglia Forest District, Santon Downham
Tel: (01842) 810271

An important collection of over 100 species of trees represented by both broad leaves and conifers with a show of daffodils in spring and walks through the forest. *Open at any reasonable time. (F10)*

Natural Surroundings
Bayfield Tel: (01263) 711091

Eight acres of demonstration gardens, orchid meadow and woodland walk with a shop, sales area and light refreshments. *Open 10 Jan-31 Mar, Thu-Sun, Bank Hols, 1000-1600; 2 Apr-29 Sep, Tue-Sun, 1000-1700; 3 Oct-22 Dec, Thu-Sun, 1000-1600. Admission £2.25/£1.25/£1.75. (I3)*

⊛ Norfolk Wildlife Trust: Broads Wildlife Centre
Ranworth Tel: (01603) 270479

A nature trail and conservation centre with displays showing history and wildlife and a gallery with telescopes and binoculars over-looking the Ranworth Broad nature reserve. *Open 1 Apr-31 Oct, daily, 1000-1700. (M6)*

⊛ Pensthorpe Waterfowl Park Q
Pensthorpe, Fakenham
Tel: (01328) 851465

One of the largest waterfowl and wildfowl collections in the world with information centre, conservation shop, adventure play area, walks, nature trails and a licenced restaurant. *Open 6 Jan-17 Mar, Sat, Sun, 1000-1600; 23 Mar-31 Dec, daily, 1000-1700; closed 25 Dec. £5.00/£2.50/£4.40. (G4)*

⊛ RSPB Titchwell Marsh Nature Reserve Q
Tel: (01485) 210779

Nature reserve with 3 bird-watching hides and 2 trails. Visitor centre with large shop, food servery, large car park and toilets. (RSPB) *Open all year, daily, summer 1000-1700; winter 1000-1600. (D/E2)*

Norfolk Wildlife Trust: Broads Wildlife Centre, Ranworth

⊚ Sheringham Park
Sheringham Tel: (01263) 823778
Park with rhododendrons, woodland and spectacular views of the park and coastline. (NT) *Open all year daily, dawn-dusk. There is a car park charge. (J/K2/3)*

⊚ Strumpshaw Fen Nature Reserve
Strumpshaw Tel: (01603) 715191
Extensive trails take visitors through unspoilt broadland scenery and habitats - woodland, meadows, fens and reed beds. (RSPB). *Open at any reasonable time. Closed 25 Dec. £2.50/50p. (M7)*

⊚ Thetford Forest Park
Thetford Tel: (01842) 810271
Thetford Forest Park is a working forest as well as a place for relaxation and recreation. A haven for wildlife and there is a good chance of seeing deer, cross bills and more. *Open at any reasonable time. (F/G10/11)*

Wildlife Water Trail
How Hill, Ludham Tel: (01692) 678763
A water trail by electric launch, through the marshes and fens of How Hill Nature Reserve with a guide. Includes short walk to bird hide. *Open 29 Mar-26 May, Sat, Sun, Bank Hols, 1100-1500; 1 Jun-30 Sep, daily, 1000-1700; 5-27 Oct, Sat, Sun, 1100-1500. £3.00/£2.00/£2.00. (N6)*

DID YOU KNOW

The Norfolk Broads are Britain's biggest protected wetland. During medieval times peat was dug from the ground, and when the sea level rose, these became flooded to form shallow lakes - or the Broads. Only home of the largest butterfly in Britain - the rare Swallowtail.

Pensthorpe Waterfowl Park

⊚ Wolterton Park
Erpingham Tel: (01263) 584175
A beautiful Georgian house with lake and extensive parkland. Park has a playground, walks and orienteering. House with facinating history. *Park open all year, daily, 0900-dusk. Hall open 26 Apr-25 Oct, Fri, 1400-1700. Last admission 1600. £4.00. (K4)*

Naturalists' Organisations & Other Abbreviations used in this section

Broads Authority, 18 Colegate, Norwich, Norfolk NR3 1BQ. Tel: (01603) 610734

EN: English Nature: (Norfolk Team), 60 Brancondale, Norwich, Norfolk NR1 2BE. Tel: (01603) 620558

⊚ NT: The National Trust, Blickling, Norwich, Norfolk NR11 6NF. Tel: (01263) 738030

NOA: Norfolk Ornithologists' Association, Broadwater Road, Aslack Way, Holme-next- the-Sea, Hunstanton, Norfolk PE36 6LQ. Tel: (01485) 525406

⊚ NWT: Norfolk Wildlife Trust, 72 Cathedral Close, Norwich NR1 4DF. Tel: (01603) 625540. For a guide to all 37 NWT reserves, contact the above.

⊚ RSPB: Royal Society for the Protection of Birds, HQ: The Lodge, Sandy, Beds SG19 2DL. Tel: (01767) 680551 East Anglia Regional Office, Stalham House, 65 Thorpe Road, Norwich NR1 1UD. Tel: (01603) 660066

SSSI: Site of Special Scientific Interest

Norfolk

Activities & Sport

Boat Hire and Regular Excursions

Bank Boats
Staithe Cottage, Wayford Bridge, Stalham
Tel: (01692) 582457
All weather dayboats available on the beautiful River Ant, from 2 hours or more. Canoes are also available. *Open all year, daily, 0900-1700. Please contact for details of prices. (M/N5)*

⊛ Blakes Holiday Boating
Wroxham
Tel: (01603) 739400 (Reservations),
Tel: (01603) 739333 (Brochures)
NB Blakes are due to be relocating late 2001
The largest fleet of holiday yachts on the Norfolk Broads, a wide choice of quality rated cruisers and a few houseboats. Narrow boats on the Cambridgeshire waterways. Choose from a wide selection from 2-12 berth. *(L/M6)*

⊛ Broads Tours Ltd
The Bridge, Wroxham
Tel: (01603) 782207
Leading passenger boat company on the Norfolk Broads. *Open 23 Mar-31 Oct, daily 0900-1700. Closed 24-28, 31 Dec, 1 Jan. (L/M6)*

⊛ Broom Boats Ltd
Riverside, Brundall
Tel: (01603) 712334
Fax: (01603) 714803
2-9 berth boats. *Weekly hire and short breaks (M7)*

⊛ City Boats
Griffin Lane, Thorpe St Andrew, Norwich
Tel: (01603) 701701
Unique venues afloat, tour bus operators, private functions and scheduled river bus services throughout Norwich. *Open all year. Call for details. (K/L7)*

The Broads

⊛ Connoisseur
Porter and Haylett Limited, Wroxham
Tel: (01603) 782472
Email: info@connoisseurcruisers.co.uk
www.connoisseurcruisers.co.uk
and www.emeraldstar.ie
2-8 berth cruisers. Weekly hire and short breaks. *Breaks also available in France, Ireland, Belgium, Italy and Germany. (L/M6)*

⊛ Herbert Woods
Broads Haven, Potter Heigham
Tel: (01692) 670711
All-weather cabin-type day launches, either electric or diesel. Passenger boats make regular trips to Hickling Broad. *Over 100 hire cruisers for weekly hire or short breaks. Fleet of sailing yachts for weekly hire. (N5/6)*

⊛ King Line Cruisers & Cottages
Horning Tel: (01692) 630297
www.norfolk-broads.co.uk
Boats by the hour or by the day, plus a wheelchair accessible day boat. Riverside cottages with facilities for wheelchairs. *(M6)*

Mississippi River Boat
Lower Street, Horning
Tel: (01692) 630262
A large double-decker paddle steamer, sightseeing trips, weddings and private parties. Three public trips daily with excellent commentary. Full bar facilities, hot drinks, snacks, ample parking space and toilet. *Open 1 May-31 Oct, daily, 1030, 1300, 1500, Tue, Thu, 1930, 2130. Limited trips Mar, Apr, Dec. (M6)*

DID YOU KNOW
Cley Marshes was the first nature reserve in England - opened in 1926.

Norfolk

Brancaster

⊛ **Norfolk Broads Yachting Co Ltd**
Southgate Yacht Station, Lower Street, Horning
Tel: (01692) 631330
Email: info@nbyco.com
Norfolk Wherry Charter (skippered)-10 berth, 2-8 berth yachts. *By the day/short break/week. Day boats for hire by the hour or day. (M6)*

⊛ **Stalham Yacht Services**
Stalham Yacht Services, The Staithe, Stalham
Tel: (01692) 580288
2-10 berth Broads cruisers, houseboats, day launches. *Weekly, daily and hourly hire available. Holiday cottage also available, sleeps four. (M/N5)*

⊛ **Wherry Yacht Charter**
Barton House, Hartwell Road,
The Avenue, Wroxham
Tel: (01603) 782470
Broadland cruising on historic wherry yachts 'Olive' and 'Norada' and pleasure wherry 'Hathor'. *For groups of up to 12 on each. Days by arrangement. (L/M6)*

Golf Courses

⊛ **Barnham Broom Hotel**
Golf, Conference & Leisure
Barnham Broom, Norwich NR9 4DD
Tel: (01603) 759393 Fax: (01603) 758224
www.barnham-broom.co.uk
Extensive leisure facilities including - indoor swimming pool, sauna, steam room, squash, tennis, gymnasium, two 18 hole golf courses, 3 academy holes; 5 acre practice ground and tuition by PGA professionals of the Peter Ballingall Golf School. Situated 10 miles south west of Norwich off the A11 and A47. *(K/L7)*

Searles Golf Resort
South Beach Road, Hunstanton PE36 5BB.
Tel: (01485) 534211 Fax: (01485) 533815
www.searles.co.uk
9 hole par34 golf course designed in a links style with good large greens. Heacham river winds through the 3rd and 4th and environmental areas have been created to establish wildlife. 10 bay covered driving range is also now open and the clubhouse is opening Easter 2002. *(D3)*

Leisure Centres
and Indoor Activities

⊛ **Oasis Leisure Centre**
Central Promenade, Hunstanton
Tel: (01485) 534227
The Oasis is FUN for all, with indoor and outdoor pools 33m slide, catering facilities, squash, bowls, fast tanning sunbed, skating, fitness suite and aerobics classes, *call reception (01485) 534227. (D3)*

⊛ **The Splash Leisure Pool**
Weybourne Road, Sheringham
Tel: (01263) 825675
Giant waterslide and wave pool with children's paddling area. Health and fitness club. *Call 01263 825675 for opening times. (J/K2/3)*

Racing

⊛ **Horseracing at Fakenham**
Tel: (01328) 862388 *(G4)*

Specialist Holidays and Outdoor Activities

⊛ Anglia Cycling Holidays
87 Perth Street, Blairgowie, Perthshire PH10 6DT
Tel: (01250) 876100
Email: info@angliacycling.co.uk
www.angliacycling.co.uk
Leisurely cycle tours around the Suffolk Coast and Norfolk Broads. Comprehensive service, quality bikes, comfortable accommodation, detailed maps and routes. Optional luggage carrying. 7 night tours, Short Breaks or cycle hire only.

⊛ Awayadays
Stone Cottage, Front Road, Wood Dalling, Norwich NR11 6RN
Tel: (01263) 587005
www.awayadays.com
Personalised East of England and Norfolk tours for groups and people with special interests. All packages can include attractions, accommodation and luxury travel. No car needed. Awayadays, West End Farm, Ingworth, Norwich, Norfolk NR11 6PM. (K/L7)

⊛ Barford Lakes
Chapel Street, Barford, Norwich NR9 4AB
Tel: (01603) 759624
Course fishing lakes offering match fishing and fishing on a day ticket. Tuition, rod hire and rod licensing available. (J7/8)

⊛ Camp Beaumont
Runton Sands Tel: (0845) 6081234
Residential summer camp with climbing, archery, watersports, zip wire, caving system, swimming, motorsports, laser zone, big top circus and much more. Parents not accommodated. Camp Beaumont, Runton Sands, West Runton, Cromer, Norfolk NR27 9NF. (K/L2/3)

⊛ Hilltop
Outdoor Centre, Sheringham
Tel/Fax: (01263) 824514
http://www.hilltopoutdoorcentre.co.uk
Adventure activities including abseiling, aerial slides, air rifles, all terrain cycles, archery, assault course, climbing wall, heating outdoor swimming pool, crate stacking, bridges, high ropes, orienteering, team work problems, nature studies. Children's residential summer camps, adventure days and disabled groups catered for. (J/K2/3)

⊛ Searles Sea Tours
South Beach Road, Hunstanton
Tel: (07831) 321799 www.seatours.co.uk
2 hour sea tour to view the beautiful seals of the wash in the MFV Sealion. 30 minute coastal cruises on board the LARC, our Vietnam war amphibious landing craft. Also visit one of the Wash Sandbanks onboard the Wash Monster (LARC) walk down the ramp and explore this unique environment. (D3)

⊛ Suffolk Cycle Breaks
See entry on page 251.

⊛ West Hall Farm Holidays & Lakeside Caravan Park & Fisheries
West Hall Farm, Sluice Road, Denver, Downham Market, Norfolk PE38 0DZ
Tel: (01366) 387074 or (01366) 383291
Self-catering studio apartments in the quiet picturesque village of Denver in Norfolk. Fishing available in our private lakes. Caravan site with electric hook ups and toilets. Look at our website for more details: www.west-hall-farm holidays.co.uk or telephone for a brochure and price list. (C8)

Fishing by the River Thet, Thetford

DID YOU KNOW

Thetford Forest is the largest lowland pine forest in Britain, covering around 50,000 acres. Whilst Foxley Wood is Britain's largest stand of ancient woodland.

Norfolk

NEW HORIZON Holidays

Holidays to Remember

Boating Holidays
On the Norfolk Broads

Family Holiday Villages
Choose from 3 in Norfolk and the Isle of Wight

Over 50's Holiday Villages
On the Norfolk & Sussex Coasts and the Isle of Wight

Boating Holidays Brochure & Booking	Tel. No. 01692 582277	Fax No. 01692 581522
Family Holiday Villages Brochure & Booking	Tel. No. 01493 733610	Fax No. 01493 731239
Over 50's Holiday Villages Brochure & Booking	Tel. No. 01493 733610	Fax No. 01493 731239

For further information, please write to: New Horizon Holidays, The Staithe, Stalham, Norfolk NR12 9BX

Norfolk

Restaurants

Blakeney
◉ Morston Hall
Morston, Holt NR25 7AA
Tel: (01263) 741041
Fax: (01263) 740419
E-mail: reception@morstonhall.com
Internet: www.morstonhall.com
East Anglia Hotel of the Year 2000

Dating back to the 17th century, Deluxe Morston Hall is set in secluded gardens and retains its original charm and character. Six large bedrooms; restaurant with a set four course menu changing daily. Galton Blackiston the Chef-Patron is acknowledged as one of the best Chefs in the country. *(H/12)*

Blickling
The Buckinghamshire Arms
Blickling, Nr Aylsham NR11 2NF
Tel: (01263) 732133

Probably Norfolk's most attractive inn - standing next to the stunning Blickling Hall. Four poster beds, local produce in delicious dishes. Beautiful garden and log fire in the winter. *(K4/5)*

Burgh Castle
(Nr Great Yarmouth)
◉ Church Farm Public House
Church Road NR31 9QG
Tel: (01493) 780251

Church Farm nestles beside Breydon Water where the rivers Waveney and Yare meet opposite the Berney Arms Windmill, giving the most spectacular views of Norfolk. The towns of Gorleston and Great Yarmouth are 10 minutes drive away with their entertainments, beaches and shops. *(O8)*

Easton
Des Amis Restaurant
Dereham Road,
Easton, Norwich NR9 5EJ
Tel: (01603) 880966
(mobile 07771 537808)
www.desamis.co.uk

Patio dining and 60 seat non-smoking restaurant (smoking lounge). Full menu includes Creole, Cajun and French cooking. Outside catering available for Caribbean style weddings with steel band. Jazz Pianist Saturday nights. Lunch approx. £8, Dinner approx. £18. *Open: Tues-Sat 1800-1130, 1200-1500. Weekdays lunch bookings taken. (J7)*

Grimston (Nr. King's Lynn)
◉ The Orangery Restaurant
at Congham Hall Country House Hotel
AA Three Red Stars and Two Rosettes
RAC Gold Ribbon Award
ETC 3 Star Gold Award
Tel: (01485) 600250

The Orangery Restaurant has been carefully designed to retain a special intimate atmosphere allowing guests panoramic views of the gardens and parkland, which leads out onto an adjacent terrace which, is the ideal place to wile away a summers' afternoon. Breakfast, lunch and dinner are served daily to both residents and non-residents as to is morning coffee and afternoon tea. *Lunch from £11.50, Sunday lunch £18.50 and dinner from £27.50. (D/E5)*

DID YOU KNOW

Lord Nelson, England's greatest seafaring hero, was born in Burnham Thorpe on 29th September 1758.

Norwich
⊛ Boswells
24 Tombland
Tel: (01603) 626099

Open "all day, every day" Boswells is "continentally unique". At night, live jazz and blues and dancing until 2am. During the day a brasserie-style menu, varied and delicious, ranges from spectacular sandwiches to three-course meals served indoors or out on its fully licensed terrace overlooking Tombland. Situated along the forewall of the Cathedral, Boswells is a landmark in the historic heart of the city. *Open Monday to Saturday 12 noon to 2am, Sunday 12 noon to 6pm. Average price under £6. (K/L7)*

Norwich
⊛ Pizza One Pancakes Too!
24 Tombland
Tel: (01603) 621583

Norwich's first and oldest pizza restaurant, also serving delicious pastas and French crèperes. The produce is still homemade after twenty two years and is a favourite haunt for families, businessmen, students and tourists. Situated along the Cathedral wall in Tombland, the historic heart of the city, this atmospheric restaurant is the perfect spot for lunch or dinner at "best value for money" prices. *Average price is £8.00. Student discount on food available. (K/L7)*

Norwich

Norwich
⊛ The Trafalgar Restaurant
Swallow Nelson Hotel,
Prince of Wales Road
Tel: (01603) 760260

Offering a Table d' hôte and á la carte menus seven days a week, also a traditional Sunday Luncheon served in our fully air conditioned, non-smoking restaurant overlooking the River Wensum. *Light meals, snacks and informal dining is available in our Quarter Deck Restaurant open seven days a week. Average prices: Lunch from £6.40, table d' hôte from £16.95 and á la carte dinner from £17.90. (K/L7)*

Norfolk

West Runton
The Pepperpot Restaurant
Water Lane, West Runton NR27 9QP
Tel: (01263) 837578

The Pepperpot restaurant has gained a formidable reputation for its excellent standard of cuisine and service. Antoine's dishes are a joy to the eye and his flair for sauces, patés, and dessert arouse and excite the most tired of taste buds; Debbie is the charming hostess welcoming every guest in the warmest atmosphere. The restaurant itself has just been refurbished to give additional comfort. The menus and the wine list are extensive and are outstanding value for money. *Three course lunch £12.95, a la carte £20.00. Gardens open to diners, weather permitting. Car park to the rear. Open all year round. (K2/3)*

Wolterton (North Norfolk)
❀ The Saracen's Head 'With Rooms'
Tel: (01263) 768909

Only 20 minutes drive from Norwich, the Saracen's Head is a civilised free house without piped music or fruit machines. Built in the early 19th century as a coaching Inn. Impeccably maintained and run by chef/proprietor Robert Dawson-Smith. There are log fires and wicker chairs. It is more a restaurant than a pub. Typical dishes include braised local rabbit, grilled fillets of smoked mackerel, venison, duck and steaks. Desserts are traditional favourites such as bread and butter pudding and treacle tart. The wine list is from Australia, South Africa, Spain and France. *Open 7 days a week 1100-1500, 1800-2300. (K4)*

Local fishing boats, Cromer

Norfolk

afternoon teas

Bressingham
Into-Food Café
Blooms of Bressingham, Diss
Tel: (01379) 688585

Three miles west of Diss on A1066. This impressive building was completed in Spring 2000 and the Tea Rooms renamed. Distinctive daily menus all at a reasonable cost provide delicious snacks, lunches or tea-time treats in this unique setting with outside decking area an added attraction. *Open: Daily 0900-1730, March to October; 0900-1630 November to February except Christmas Day/Boxing Day. See also entry for Blooms of Bressingham under Nurseries & Garden Centres on page 190. (I/J11)*

Heacham
⊛ Norfolk Lavender Ltd. Q
Caley Mill, Heacham
Tel: (01485)571965/570384

Locally baked cakes and scones and cream teas a speciality. Lunches available all year and log fire October-April. Miller's Cottage Tearoom in the middle of lavender/herb gardens and fragrant meadow. *Seats: 120 all year, 88 in summer. Free admission, open daily 1000-1700 except Dec 25, 26 & Jan 1. Average price: £2.70. (D3)*

Thursford
⊛ The Thursford Collection Q
Thursford, Fakenham
Tel: (01328) 878477

Proprietor: Mr J Cushing Afternoon cream teas on the lawn served from our Garden Conservatory. Teas, light refreshments and hot meals also served in our 'Barn'. *Seats: 92 inside, 150 outside. Admission: £4.90/£2.40/£4.60. (H4)*

Walsingham
Sue Ryder
The Martyrs House, High Street
Tel: (01328) 820622 Fax: (01328) 820505

Retreat House Accommodation: bed & breakfast and evening meal (non-residents). Groups and individuals welcome. Open all year. Special functions at Easter and Christmas. Coffee Shop: Home-made cakes and light lunches. Seating up to 100. Gift Shop: Extensive range of carefully selected gifts. *(G/H3)*

Norwich Cathedral

VISIT

THE BLACK SHEEP SHOP AND
NEW COUNTRYWEAR COLLECTION
Aylsham
⚫ **Black Sheep Shop**
Black Sheep Jerseys,
9 Penfold Street, Aylsham NR11 6ET
Tel: (01263) 733142/732006
Email@blacksheep.ltd.uk
www.blacksheep.ltd.uk

The Black Sheep shop has always been known for the very best in naturally undyed and dyed knitwear, everything from jerseys and cardigans to hats, gloves, scarves and socks. Now we have added an extra dimension with our exclusive countrywear section. Only the best will do and we have introduced Sports and hacking jackets, casual coats and jackets as well as boots, belts and tweed caps and a wide range of gift items. If you cannot come and visit us then send for our free colour catalogue. *Open Mon-Fri 0900-17.50, Sat 1000-17.00, closed Sun. Free customer parking. (K4/5)*

DID YOU KNOW

The weather-boarded mill at Stoke Holy Cross (just to the south of Norwich) is the birthplace of Colman's, the world-famous mustard producers in 1823.

NORFOLK
CHILDREN'S
BOOK CENTRE

between Aylsham and Cromer
Norfolk Children's Book Centre
Surrounded by fields, the Centre displays one of the best collections of children's and teachers' books in East Anglia. Here you will find a warm welcome and expert advice. You can browse through the latest and the classics in both fiction and non-fiction. We also sell story cassettes, videos and cards. Find out more about the Centre on www.ncbc.co.uk or telephone 01263 761402. *Open daily, Mon-Sat, 1000-1700, closed Bank Hols. Teachers welcome anytime, please phone. Find us between Aylsham and Cromer just off the A140. Look out for the signposted turn 500 metres north of Alby Craft Centre. (K4)*

Cley-next-the-Sea
⚫ **Made in Cley**
High Street, Cley-next-the-Sea,
Holt NR25 7RF
Tel: (01263) 740134
Hand-thrown domestic and sculptural Pottery in stoneware, porcelain and raku, contemporary jewellery in silver and gold, prints and sculptures in marble and other stones. Everything is made on the premises and exhibited in a Regency shop which is itself of historical interest. *Open daily, closed Wednesdays October to June. (I2)*

Cromer
⚫ **Bond Street Antiques** (inc BRIGGS)
6 Bond Street, Cromer NR27 9DA
Tel: (01263) 513134
Goldsmiths, Silversmiths and Jewellers, Incorporating Gem Test Centre. Gems, jewellery, Amber, gifts and objets d'art. Top prices paid for gold, silver and antiques. Valuations for Insurance and Probate. Member of The National Association of Goldsmiths and Fellow of The Gemmological Association of Great Britain. *(K/L3)*

Erpingham
❀ Alby Crafts

Cromer Road, Erpingham, Nr. Norwich NR11 7QE
Tel: (01263) 761590

Alby Crafts is set amongst superb gardens and wooded areas with very easy parking and delightful Tea Rooms, Gallery and Gift Shop. The Centre itself is contained in beautifully converted farm buildings, which are now the workshops of some of Norfolk's finest crafts people. You will be able to watch work in progress and browse among the many quality items offered for sale. We are easy to find, on the main A140 between Aylsham and Cromer, next to the Horseshoes Pub. *Open 1000-1700, Tuesday to Sunday, mid March to mid December and weekends only mid January to mid March. Tel: 01263 761590. (K4)*

Great Walsingham
❀ Great Walsingham Barns

Great Walsingham, Fakenham NR22 6DR
Tel: (01328) 820900

An attractive range of converted barns comprising: **The Textile Centre Shop & Post Office** - Gifts, casual clothes with an excellent tea room providing light lunches and cream teas. **Great Walsingham Gallery** - Exhibitions of paintings, sculptures, woodcarving, fine-art cards, jewellery and Medici prints. **The Potting Shed** - Rustic garden equipment and basket-ware, pottery and crafts handmade on the premises. **Oriental Carpets and Rugs.** *Open: daily 0930 - 1700, weekends and Bank Holidays 1000-1700. (G/H3)*

Great Yarmouth
❀ Candlemaker and Model Centre

Mill Road, Stokesby
Tel: (01493) 750242

Situated 9 miles from Great Yarmouth on the banks of the River Bure, boasts England's largest variety of handcrafted candles, with many that are unique. The Centre also has a good selection of modelling kits. *The candle shop and workshop is open Easter to the end of October from 0900-1800, closed on Mondays, except Bank Holidays, and during Nov, Dec, Feb, March from Thu to Sun 1000-1600 with free admission. Free parking and river moorings. Coffee shop/restaurant now open. Riverside garden. (O/P7)*

Norfolk Lavender Ltd.

Heacham
❀ Norfolk Lavender Ltd. Q

Caley Mill, Heacham, King's Lynn
Tel: (01485) 570384

Set in the ground floor of Caley Mill, the Gift Shop contains a very wide range of gifts for all the family. There are items to suit every pocket, masses of choice and frequent new ideas. The Old Barn houses the Lavender Shop where you can buy Norfolk Lavender's fragrant products: The English Lavender, Rose, Night Scented Jasmine, Lily of the Valley and Lavender for Men. *Open daily 1000-1700 (closed Dec 25, 26 and Jan 1). (D3)*

DID YOU KNOW

The Hanseatic League were medieval trading links, forged with Northern European countries. These traders came in search of wool, and later some of Europe's finest cloth. King's Lynn was chosen as a base for many of their warehouses, and one of these survives today. It is the only remnant of the Hanseatic League left in Britain.

Norfolk

Holt
◉ **Bircham Contemporary Arts**
14 Market Place
Holt, Norfolk NR25 6BW
Tel: (01263) 713312
e-mail: Birchamgal@aol.com
www.bircham-arts.co.uk

Originally established in 1988, Bircham Contemporary Arts has developed a reputation as a leading independent gallery, exhibiting artists and craftspeople from East Anglia and beyond. Housed in a fine pink Georgian building in the historic market town of Holt, the gallery exhibits the finest contemporary paintings, prints, ceramics, sculpture, glass and jewellery and offers a lively and constantly changing display with seven to eight solo exhibitions a year. Crafts Council listed. Gallery shop selling magazines, cards etc. *Opening times: 9.00am to 5.00pm Monday to Saturday, 10.00am to 4.00pm on Bank Hols. Free Admission. (I/J3)*

King's Lynn
◉ **Caithness Crystal Visitor Centre** Q
8-12 Paxman Road,
Hardwick Industrial Estate,
King's Lynn PE30 4NE
Tel: (01553) 765111/765123
Fax: (01553) 767628

Glassmaking is a magical craft that can transform sand into exquisite glassware using only the heat of a furnace and the skill of hand and eye. Witness it for yourself at our King's Lynn Visitor Centre and marvel at the demonstration of the skills of glassmaking. Unique factory shopping experience, extensive selection of giftware - stemware paperweights and glass sculptures, as well as ceramics at bargain prices. *Open: seven days a week (Factory Shop/Restaurant); glass making Mon-Fri. Free admission. (C5/6)*

Wells-next-the-Sea

Norfolk

Langham
◎ Langham Glass Q
The Long Barn, North Street,
Langham, Holt NR25 7DG
Tel: (01328) 830511
E-mail: langhamglass@talk21.com
www.langhamglass.co.uk

In a large beautiful Norfolk barn complex, teams of glassmakers can be seen working with molten glass using blowing irons and hand tools that have been traditional for hundreds of years. There is an enclosed children's adventure playground, factory gift shops, museum, restaurant, video, rose & clematis walled garden. Pottery throwing, didgeridoo making and other crafts. *Open 7 days a week all year 1000-1700. Glassmaking Easter-31 October (everyday); 1 Nov-Easter (Mon-Fri). Group visits welcome. (H2/3)*

Sutton
◎ Sutton Pottery
Church Road, Sutton,
Norwich NR12 9SG
Tel: (01692) 580595
www.suttonpottery.com

1 1/2 miles southeast of Stalham, 3/4 mile east of A149 to Great Yarmouth (16 miles). Norwich 16 miles. Malcolm Flatman designs and produces a large range of wheel-made microwave- and dishwasher-safe stoneware tableware and decorative items in a choice of glazes. Special "one-off" orders and commissions willingly undertaken. Visitors are welcome in the small workshop to see work in progress and purchase from a wide selection of finished pieces. Price list available by post. Website catalogue and order form. Full postal service. *Usually open Mon-Fri 0900-1800, throughout the year. Please telephone before a special journey, and weekend visits. Free admission. (N5)*

Gentleman's Walk, Norwich

Cromer Pier

Taverham
⊛ Nursery Craft Centre
The Craft Units, Fir Covert Road, Taverham,
Norwich NR8 6HT
Tel: (01603) 860522

A purpose-built centre for the finest in traditional crafts, hand made on the premises by local crafts people. You'll find many different crafts, from embroidery and lacemaking to sugar craft, painting and framing. Watch crafts people at work, talk to them about their skills, and come away with a pretty and practical keepsake. Plus garden centre, coffee bar, pet food and corn stores. Facilities for the disabled: coach parties welcome. Free car parking for 1000 cars. *Open Mon-Sat, 1000-1700, Sun 1100-1700. Coaches very welcome (telephone for catering requirements). Please phone before calling for specific crafts and opening hours. (J6)*

DID YOU KNOW

Following a newspaper story in the London Evening News in the 1930's, Gimingham became known as the strangest village in England. The report remarked that the village had no butcher, baker, fishmonger, draper, tailor, boot-maker or policeman, and no resident named Smith, Brown, Jones or Robinson. There was no doctor, dentist or chemist. There was a railway but no station, no public house and though next to the sea, no sea view!

Holkham Hall Country Fair

THE ALTERNATIVE
SHOPPING™
GUIDES

Explore the Countryside

Discover quality and good value produces for sale in farm barns, stately homes, listed buildings and other unlikely locations.

Each full colour guide book contains an area map and regional information to help you plan a good day out or a short stay shopping break. Each entry has details of products, opening times, a location map, a description and photograph.

Plan a Shopping Adventure

There are Alternative Shopping Guides for: Central South and South West England; East of England - £3.50 each. Heart of England; Derbyshire, Staffordshire, Cheshire and North Shropshire; South East England; Lancashire and Lake District; Yorkshire - £3.95 each from bookshops. Add 50p (UK) and £1.00 (P&P overseas) direct from:

The Stable Publishing Company
Woolsthorpe by Belvoir, Grantham,
Lincolnshire NG32 1NT
Telephone: 01476 870770 Fax: 01476 870887
Website@ www.shopntour.co.uk

Wroxham
⊛ **Wroxham Barns** Q
Tunstead Road, Hoveton, Norfolk NR12 8QU
Tel: (01603) 783762
Email: info@wroxham-barns.co.uk

A delightful collection of beautifully restored 18th century barns, set in 10 acres of Norfolk countryside. 13 resident craftsmen. Botanical, paintings, model shipbuilding, pottery, stained glass, woodturning, patchwork and quilting, cider and apple juice pressing, minerals and jewellery and handmade children's clothes. All craftsmen produce items for sale and many take commissions. Handmade local crafts, pictures, paintings, greeting cards, children's books, toys, casual and country clothing also available in the gift and clothes shops. Food and fudge shops offer a fine selection of gourmet and hand made foods. Meet, stroke, feed and learn about the friendly farmyard animals at Junior Farm. Williamson's Traditional Fair with swing boats, Ferris wheel, Merry-go-rounds and Peter Pan Railway. Also features the End of the Pier Old Penny Arcade, with East Anglia's widest range of classic amusement machines. Enjoy traditional cream teas, snacks and home made lunches in the waitress-served tearoom and the coffee shop. Outside seating also available. *Open daily 10am-5pm except Dec 25 & 26 and Jan 1. Fair (seasonal). Free admission and parking. Junior Farm £2.25 per person. (under 3's Free). Fair rides individually priced.*

Norfolk

discovery tours

Family Favourites
Three ideas to keep dad, mum and the children happy in North and West Norfolk.

Tour 1
Starting point: Fakenham, Norfolk *(G4)*
Mileage: 14m/23km
Morning - take the A1067 to visit *Pensthorpe Waterfowl Park*, then retrace your steps to Fakenham and follow the A148 towards Cromer. After 4m, turn left (following signs) to the musical *Thursford Collection*.
Afternoon - return to the A148 and head to the pretty town of Holt. Jump aboard the *North Norfolk Railway* for a steam train ride to seaside *Sheringham*. Enjoy a walk along the prom with an ice cream!

Tour 2
Starting point: Wells-next-the-Sea, Norfolk *(G2)*
Mileage: 18m/29km
Morning - explore the quaint fishing town of *Wells*, then take the little steam railway to the pretty pilgrimage centre of *Little Walsingham*.
Afternoon - return to Wells, and take the A149 west to the magnificent *Holkham Hall*. End the day by continuing along the A149 to Hunstanton, and enjoy a watery tour of the *Sea Life and Marine Sanctuary*.

Tour 3
Starting point: Cromer, Norfolk *(K/L3)*
Mileage: 13m/21km (or 15m/24km with Langham Glass)
Morning - wander the streets of cliff-top *Cromer*, and enjoy a crab tea overlooking the famous pier.
Afternoon - leave Cromer on the A149 to Weybourne, where you can take a ride on the Gama Goat at *The Muckleburgh Collection*. Continue along the A149 to Blakeney, where there are two choices, either take a boat trip to see the seals on *Blakeney Point*. Or head south on the B1156 to the *Langham Glass* workshops.

Grimes Graves

Bloomin' Beautiful
Enjoy the spectacular colours and delicate fragrances of some of England's finest gardens.

Starting point: King's Lynn, Norfolk *(C5/6)*
Mileage: 23m/37km
Morning - take the A17 to Terrington St. Clement, and visit the *African Violet Centre*. Then retrace your steps to King's Lynn and take the A149 north. After 6m, turn right onto the B1439 to *Sandringham*.
Afternoon - enjoy the Queen's favourite blooms. Then take the B1440 to Dersingham. At the T-junction, turn right and follow the road to the A149. Join this north to *Heacham*, and the home of *Norfolk Lavender*.

Wells Walsingham Railway

From Dinosaurs to Dells
Discover the fauna and flora of the world - from the stone age to the present day.

Starting point: Norwich, Norfolk *(K/L7)*
Mileage: 46m/74km
Morning - follow the A1067 for 8 miles to *Morton*, then turn left to *Weston Longville*, and meet T-Rex at *The Dinosaur Adventure Park*. Head south to reach the A47, where you turn left back towards *Norwich*. After 8 miles, join the A11 towards Thetford. 12 miles later (at *Attleborough*), turn left onto the B1077 to Cake Street, then turn right along an unclassified road to reach the exotic animals of *Banham Zoo*.
Afternoon - take the unclassified road south via *North Lopham* to the A1066. Turn left here to reach the world-renowned *Dell Garden* at the *Bressingham Steam Experience and Gardens*.

Things that go Bump in the Night
Let us send a shiver down your spine with all things spooky and strange!

Starting point: Norwich, Norfolk *(K/L7)*
Mileage: varied (depending on tour taken)
Morning - wander *Norwich's* ancient streets and lanes, and visit the eerie dungeons of the *Castle Museum*.
Afternoon - take the A1151 to *Wroxham*, and enjoy a tour of the reed-fringed Norfolk Broads. Scare yourself silly with tales of black devil dogs and ghostly drummer-boys. End the day by leaving Wroxham on the B1354 (via Aylsham) to 17th C. *Blickling Hall*, haunt of Anne Boleyn.

Strange Tales and Curiosities
Discover the flipside of the east, its customs, stories and local characters.

Starting point: Thetford, Norfolk *(F/G10/11)*
Mileage: 42m/68km
Morning - head north on the A134. After 5m, turn left to explore the bat-infested flint mine at *Grimes Graves*. Continue on the A134/A1065 to *Swaffham*. Visit the church to see the memorial to the famous Pedlar.
Afternoon - take the B1077 to *Watton*, which is connected to the 'Babes in the Wood' story. Then follow the B1108 to *Hingham*, once home of Abraham Lincoln's descendants. Remain on the B1108/B1135 to *Wymondham*, where the abbey's twin towers came from an argument between the monks and townspeople.

Castle Acre Priory, Castle Acre

Seaside Special
Fun for all the family at one of Britain's most popular seaside resorts.

Starting point: Great Yarmouth, Norfolk *(O/P7)*
Mileage: 7m/11km
Morning - start the day with a trip underwater at the *Sea Life Centre*, and a ride on the rollercoaster at the *Pleasure Beach*. Before leaving, make a sandcastle on the beach, and enjoy a stroll along the prom.
Afternoon - head north along the A149/A1064 to either the giant crocodiles of *Thrigby Hall Wildlife Gardens (Filby)*, or the steam engines and fairground rides at *The Village Experience (Fleggburgh)*.

Saints and Sinners
Heavens above! - a tour of 'good versus evil', with naughty monks and devoted saints.

Starting point: King's Lynn, Norfolk *(C5/6)*
Mileage: 32m/51km
Morning - discover Lynn's infamous murderers, highwaymen and witches at *Tales of the Old Gaol House*. Then take the B1145 east for 16 miles, before turning right onto the A1065, to visit the 12th C. *Castle Acre Priory*. Here relics of godly saints once attracted pilgrims from all over Europe.
Afternoon - remain on the A1065 to Swaffham, then follow the unclassified road (via Cockley Cley) to Oxborough. Visit the 15th C. *Oxburgh Hall*, where you can peer into a Catholic priest's hole.

Suffolk

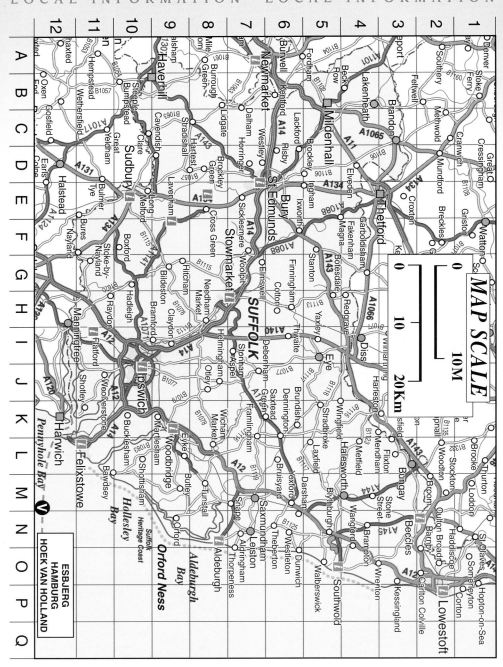

MAP SCALE

0 ... 10M

0 ... 10 ... 20Km

ESBJERG
HAMBURG
HOEK VAN HOLLAND

Suffolk

Suffolk

County Town: Ipswich
Population: 674,600 approx.
Highest Point: Rede 128m (420 feet).
Rivers: Alde, Brett, Deben, Dove, Gipping, Glem, Lark, Little Ouse, Orwell, Stour, Waveney, Yox.
Landmarks: 'Constable Country', Lowestoft Ness (the most easterly point in England), Minsmere Nature Reserve, Newmarket, Orford Ness, Port of Felixstowe, Sizewell Power Station, Suffolk Wool Towns, Thetford Forest Park.

Industry Past & Present

Suffolk has always been an *agricultural* county, growing rich from its variety of crops and produce. Wind and water mills dot the landscape, once busy with *corn grinding*. The Middle Ages saw the start of the prosperous *cloth/wool* trade. This reached its height in the late 15th C. when beautiful churches and timber-framed buildings were built. Flint has also played a major part in the county's past - extracted from mines since neolithic times, and used for tools and building. Brandon was the last British home of the *gun flint* industry. On the coast, the rich pickings of the sea saw busy ports appear at Aldeburgh, Orford and Southwold, but today only a handful of boats remain. Lowestoft, once one of the UK's major fishing (herring) centres, is now noted for North Sea *gas/oil production*. To the south is the imposing Sizewell Power Station, and the Port of Felixstowe, the UK's largest container terminal. Ipswich, a port since the 6/7th C. is home to *administration, financial and hi-tech companies*. While to the west of the county is Newmarket, world-famous centre for the *racing, breeding, sale and training of horses*. There are also four famous Suffolk brewers, Adnams, Greene King, St. Peter's and Tolly Cobbold. Famous names include - Birds Eye Walls, British Telecom, Haywards Pickles and Wisdom (toothbrushes).

Famous People:

Elizabeth Garrett Anderson *(England's first woman doctor)*, Robert Bloomfield *(poet)*, Benjamin Britten *(composer)*, Lord Byron *(poet)*, Thomas Cavendish *(second Englishman to sail around world)*, John Constable *(painter)*, Edward Fitzgerald *(author)*, George Crabbe *(poet)*, Charles Dickens *(author)*, King Edmund, Thomas Gainsborough *(painter)*, Rider Haggard *(author)*, M.R. James *(author)*, P.D. James *(author)*, Maria Marten and William Corder *(Red Barn Murder)*, Alfred Munnings *(painter)*, George Orwell *(author)*, Beatrix Potter *(author)*, Arthur Ransome *(author)*, Ruth Rendell *(author)*, Thomas Seckford *(benefactor)*, The Taylor Sisters *(authors)*, Robert Watson-Watt *(inventor of radar)*, Cardinal Wolsey *(Chancellor of England)*.

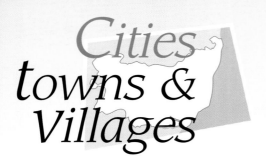

Cities
towns &
Villages

MD:	Market Day
EC:	Early Closing
i	Tourist Information Centre

Aldeburgh *(N8)*
Charming and sedate seaside town, which grew from an old medieval fishing and shipbuilding centre. The wide High Street has attractive Georgian shop-fronts. Historic buildings include the Moot Hall (c.1520) and the 15th C. church. Fishermen still pull their boats onto the steep shingle beach, and sell their catch each morning. The famous music festival is held in June. **EC**: Wed. **i**

Beccles *(N2/3)*
Set on the River Waveney, this fine market town was once a flourishing Saxon seaport. Red-brick Georgian houses and unusual 18th C. octagonal town hall. The magnificent 14th C. church has a detached bell tower. Long gardens run down to the river, now a major boating centre for the Broads. Nearby Roos Hall is one of England's most haunted houses. **MD**: Fri. **EC**: Wed. **i**

Brandon *(C/D3)*
Small town, set beside the Little Ouse River and surrounded by forest and heathland. Brandon stands on flint, is largely built from flint, and was for long the home of England's oldest industry, flint knapping. This provided decorative building materials and also gunflints for firearms. Heritage Centre and country park.
MD: Thurs and Sat. **EC**: Wed.

Bungay *(L3)*
Unspoilt market town, set beside a loop of the River Waveney. The Norman castle was rebuilt by the ruthless Bigod Family, but by the 14th C. it was in ruins. After a great fire in 1688, Bungay rebuilt itself as a Georgian town with red-brick facades and Dutch gables. The Butter Cross was built in 1689, while the church tower is noted for its four pinnacles. **MD**: Thurs. **EC**: Wed.

Bury St. Edmunds *(D/E6/7)*
Named after St. Edmund (the Saxon King of East Anglia), this ancient market town has played an important part in English history. For it was here in 1214, that the barons of England vowed to extract from King John the concessions set out in the 'Magna Carta'. The ruins of the 12th C. abbey (once one of the most powerful in Europe) are overlooked by the cathedral's new gothic tower. Bury is noted for its award-winning gardens, Georgian Theatre, and the smallest pub in Britain 'The Nutshell'. **MD**: Wed and Sat. **i**

Clare *(C9/10)*
Delightful small town, with colour-washed and timber-framed buildings, many decorated with pargetting. The 13th C. church is linked to the medieval family who founded Clare College in Cambridge. While the country park is dominated by the 100ft high motte of the former Norman castle. Close by is the 13th C. priory, the first Augustinian house in England. **MD**: Mon and Sat.

St. Edmundsbury Cathedral, Bury St. Edmunds

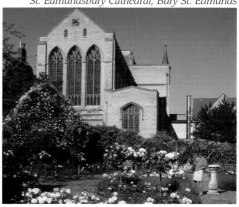

Eye *(I5)*

Retaining the peaceful atmosphere and character of a small 18th C. agricultural market town, Eye sits in the heart of the Suffolk countryside. The first definite evidence of a settlement dates from Roman times. The Norman castle mound, which dates back to 1156, affords panoramic views of the town. The west tower of the 15th C. church is one of the best in the county. **EC**: Wed.

Felixstowe *(L11)*

Edwardian resort, retaining much of its original charm, with beautiful south-facing gardens, paved promenade, leisure centre, pier and theatre. Its popularity began with the arrival of the railway in 1887, and a visit in 1891 by the Empress of Germany. The docks, Britain's leading cargo and container port, were developed on marshland in 1886. **MD**: Thurs and Sun. **EC**: Wed.

Framlingham *(K/L7)*

Ancient market town, which has been a major power in royal fortunes, and once held an important agricultural market. The triangular-shaped market place is bordered by attractive buildings. Framlingham is noted for its well-preserved 12th C. castle, built by the Bigod Family (Earls of Norfolk), and the church with its magnificent tombs and effigies. **MD**: Sat. **EC**: Wed.

Traditional pargetting, Ipswich

Hadleigh *(G10)*

Once a Viking Royal town, Hadleigh prospered through its wool and cloth trade in the 14th and 15th C. It is the reputed burial place of the Danish King Guthrum. The long High Street is lined with fine timber and plasterwork buildings, some with pargetting. St. Mary's Church with its tall spire is bordered by the 15th C. Guildhall and red-brick Deanery Tower. **MD**: Fri. **EC**: Wed.

Halesworth *(M4/5)*

Nestled in a curve of the River Blyth, Halesworth was a major centre for malting and brewing in the 19th C. There are many fine buildings, including the carved Gothic House, a Tudor Rectory and Elizabethan almshouses. St. Mary's Church has an unusual 18th C. altar, and a memorial to a local father and son who both became directors of Kew Gardens in London. **MD**: Wed. **EC**: Thurs.

Haverhill *(B9/10)*

Sits beside an old Roman road, its market dating from 1222. Fire destroyed many of the town's older buildings in 1665, although Anne of Cleves' House - reputedly built by Henry VIII in 1540, as his marriage settlement to her - has been restored. Good examples of Victorian architecture. **MD**: Fri, Sat. **EC**: Wed.

Ipswich *(I/J10)*

Dating back to Saxon times, Ipswich is one of England's oldest towns. Its streets are lined with historic buildings, such as the Ancient House, renowned for its plasterwork. Twelve medieval churches stand testimony to the importance of the town as it developed in the Middle Ages. Close by is 16th C. Christchurch Mansion, which stands in a beautiful landscaped park. Ipswich has a rich maritime heritage, its port founded in the 6/7th C. Visit the wet dock with its marina, restaurants and bars. **MD**: Tues, Fri and Sat. *i*

Lavenham

Lavenham *(E/F9)*

England's best-preserved medieval town. From the 14-16th C. it was a major wool and cloth-making centre. The wealth generated has left a beautiful legacy of timber-framed houses set along narrow streets and lanes, such as the Guildhall and Swan Hotel. The 13th C. church is noted for its magnificent 141 feet high tower. Numerous gift, craft and tea shops. **EC**: Wed. *i*

Leiston *(N7)*

Small, mainly modern town, whose prosperity grew in the 19th C. with the success of the Garrett engineering firm. They pioneered steam power in the area, building traction engines and road rollers. The parish church retains its medieval tower, and an unusual 13th C. hexagonal font. Close by is the romantic ruins of 14th C. Leiston Abbey.
MD: Fri. **EC**: Wed.

Long Melford *(E10)*

This former wool town is now the 'Antiques Capital of Suffolk'. Its wide, tree-lined High Street is full of antique shops and centres. At one of end of the village is the large green, dominated by Melford Hall (c.1550s) and the magnificent 15th C. church, built of carved stone and flint. Just beyond the church is moated Kentwell Hall, renowned for its annual recreations of Tudor life.

Lowestoft *(P2)*

Attractive seaside resort at Britain's most easterly point (Lowestoft Ness). It has one of Britain's best sandy beaches, backed by a long promenade. Once a flourishing fishing port, visitors can see the yacht harbour and neighbouring docks, with its small fleet of trawlers. Impressive, glass Edwardian-style pavilion and pedestrianised shopping centre.
MD: Tues, Fri and Sat. **EC**: Thurs. *i*

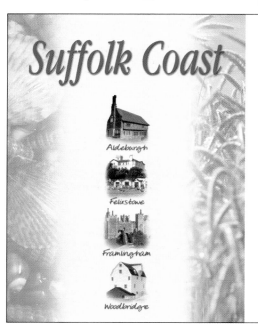

Mildenhall *(B5)*

Busy town, with a timbered 16th C. market cross and pump. The north porch of the 13th C. church is the largest in Suffolk. Mildenhall will be forever associated with a rich treasure of 4th C. Roman silverware which was unearthed in the area in 1942 (it is now in the British Museum). Close by is the large USAF air base (RAF Mildenhall), noted for its annual air fete. **MD**: Fri. **EC**: Thurs.

Needham Market *(H8)*

A small town set in the Gipping Valley. The High Street has many historic buildings, including a 17th C. Grammar School, the Friends' Meeting House, and numerous Georgian houses. The 15th C. church possesses one of the most superb hammerbeam roofs in England. Nearby Needham Lake offers walks, fishing and picnic sites. **EC**: Tues.

Newmarket *(A7)*

Associated with horses and royalty since Queen Boadicea's day, this is the only place in the world where every aspect of the horseracing industry is in evidence. Over 35 race days a year, two fine racecourses, The National Horseracing Museum, the heathland "gallops", training yards, studs, a horse hospital and Tattershall's sales rooms. **MD**: Tues and Sat. **EC**: Wed. *i*

Southwold

Orford

Orford *(N9)*

Steeped in history, this attractive small town is overlooked by its 12th C. castle keep built by Henry VII for coastal defence. From the top, there are panoramic views over the town and marshes. Brick and timber buildings line the streets to the little quayside, where there are boat trips to the mysterious Orfordness (a shingle spit). The town is noted for its oysters.

Oulton Broad *(O/P2)*

Forming the southern gateway to the Broads, this is one of the finest stretches of inland water in England. A haven for lovers of watersports, Oulton Broad is perfect for sailing, rowing or taking it easy on a modern cruiser. The Nicholas Everitt Park has bandstand concerts and children's play areas. Regular sailing regattas and speedboat racing events. **EC**: Wed.

Saxmundham *(M7)*

Small town dating from Saxon times, its market granted in 1272. Later it became a popular coaching stop. The 19th C. town hall displays the arms of the Longs family, who lived at nearby Hurts Hall, a Jacobean mansion. The church has a fine hammerbeam roof. **MD**: Wed. **EC**: Thurs.

Southwold *(O4/5)*

This charming town used to be renowned for its herring fishery. St. Edmund's Church is noted for its 15th C. pulpit. Nearby is another landmark, the white lighthouse built in 1890. Nine open greens are surrounded by period houses and fisherman's cottages. Picturesque harbour, colourful beach huts, specialist shops and real ale from the town's own brewery. **MD**: Mon and Thurs. **EC**: Wed. *i*

Suffolk

Stowmarket *(H7/8)*

At the centre of Suffolk, this bustling market town is set in the Gipping Valley. Its medieval heart lay around the parish church, and the area leading down to the river. The industrial growth of the town began in 1793 with the opening of the canal to Ipswich. Today Stowmarket is a popular shopping centre and home of the Museum of East Anglian Life. **MD**: Thurs and Sat. **EC**: Tues. *i*

Sudbury *(E10)*

Set on the River Stour, this ancient market town is surrounded by water meadows. Mentioned in the Domesday Survey of 1086, Sudbury has thrived on the textile industry, firsuy with wool, then silk. The famous painter Thomas Gainsborough was born here in 1727, and his statue stands on the Market Place, overlooked by the 15th C. church. **MD**: Thurs and Sat. *i*

Walberswick *(O5)*

Attractive seaside village at the mouth of the River Blyth. In the early 20th C. it attracted many painters. Tarred wooden huts overlook the river, while pebble, brick and flint houses surround the pretty green. It is best known for its annual crabbing contest.

Wickham Market *(L8)*

Bypassed by the busy A12, this quiet town has a little square, which was granted a market by Henry VI in about 1440. Georgian and timber-framed buildings. All Saints' Church mainly dates from 1299, but was extensively restored in the 19th C. Quilter's Haven features patchwork and quilts in a 16th C. beamed setting. **EC**: Wed.

Woodbridge *(K9)*

Set on the River Deben, this attractive market town was once a port, noted for its shipbuilding and sail-making industries. Narrow streets hide many historic buildings, including fine examples of Georgian architecture. On the quayside is the famous Tide Mill, and on the opposite bank of the river, Sutton Hoo, the burial site of Anglo-Saxon kings. **MD**: Thurs and Sat. **EC**: Wed. *i*

Pick of the villages

1 **Bildeston** - large former wool town. Half-timbered houses and Victorian clock tower. *(G9)*
2 **Blythburgh** - overlooks Blyth estuary. Magnificent church with tales of Black Shuck. *(N5)*
3 **Cavendish** - picture postcard village, with green, almshouses and church. *(D9)*
4 **Chelsworth** - pretty houses and 18th C. humpbacked bridge. Annual gardens open day. *(G9)*
5 **Dalham** - set beside River Kennett. Thatched/plastered cottages and little footbridges. *(B7)*
6 **Debenham** - former court of East Anglia's Saxon kings. Several historic buildings. *(J7)*
7 **Dunwich** - former capital of East Anglia, but after centuries of coastal erosion, now just a village. *(O6)*
8 **East Bergholt** - birthplace of painter John Constable. Unusual wooden bell cage. *(H11)*
9 **Easton** - estate village, noted for its pretty cottages and crinkle-crankle wall. *(K8)*
10 **Euston** - estate village, seat of the Dukes of Grafton. Thatched and flint houses. *(E4)*
11 **Felixstowe Ferry** - hamlet on River Deben. Weather-boarded houses and fish for sale. *(L11)*
12 **Haughley** - green and castle remains. The post office is one of the earliest recorded in the UK. *(G7)*
13 **Hoxne** - bridge where King Edmund met his death at the hands of the Vikings (c.870). *(J5)*
14 **Ixworth** - attractive main street with ancient buildings and listed petrol pumps. *(F6)*
15 **Kersey** - one of the prettiest villages in England. Lovely ford with ducks. *(G10)*
16 **Moulton** - pretty village beside River Kennett, with 15th C. packhorse bridge. *(B7)*
17 **Nayland** - narrow streets, 16th C. Guildhall and milestone obelisk. *(F11/12)*
18 **Pakenham** - last parish in England with working water mill and windmill. *(F6)*
19 **Peasenhall** - main street with little watercourse and colour-washed houses. *(L6)*
20 **Pin Mill** - tiny riverside hamlet with quay. Connections to author Arthur Ransome. *(J11)*
21 **Polstead** - noted for its cherries and notorious Victorian 'Red Barn Murder'. *(G11)*
22 **Santon Downham** - set in Thetford Forest. Built on shifting sands. Norman church. *(D3)*
23 **Somerleyton** - Victorian estate village, with cottages grouped around a wide green. *(OI)*
24 **Stoke-by-Nayland** - hilltop village with superb church tower and 16th C. Guildhall. *(G11)*
25 **Thornham Magna** - seat of Lord Henniker. Old houses and parkland with walks. *(I5)*
26 **Thorpeness** - former fantasy holiday village. House in Clouds and boating lake. *(N/O7)*
27 **Ufford** - set amongst water meadows. Whipping post/stocks. Amazing church font cover. *(L8)*
28 **Walsham Le Willows** - main street with little stream. Weather-boarded/timbered houses. *(G5)*
29 **Woolpit** - Georgian brick and Tudor-style houses, covered pump and splendid church. *(F7)*
30 **Yoxford** - former coaching centre. Variety of architecture styles. Cast-iron signpost. *(M6)*

Suffolk

Tourist Information Centres

With so much to see and do in this area, it's impossible for us to mention all of the places you can visit. You will find Tourist Information Centres (TICs) throughout Suffolk, with plenty of information on all the things that you can do and the places you can visit. TICs can book accommodation for you, in their own area, or further afield using the 'Book A Bed Ahead Scheme'. They can be the ideal place to purchase locally made crafts or gifts, as well as books covering a wide range of local interests. A list of the TICs in this area can be found below, together with a map reference to help you locate them.

* Not open all year.

Aldeburgh *(N8)*, 152 High Street,
Tel: (01728) 453637
Email: atic@suffolkcoastal.gov.uk
Web: www.suffolkcoastal.gov.uk
* **Beccles** *(N2/3)*, The Quay, Fen Lane,
Tel: (01502) 713196
Bury St. Edmunds *(D/E6/7)*, 6 Angel Hill,
Tel: (01284) 764667
Email: tic@stedsbc.gov.uk
Web: www.stedmundsbury.gov.uk
Felixstowe *(L11)*, The Seafront
Tel: (01394) 276770
Email: ftic@anglianet.co.uk
Web: www.suffolkcoastal.gov.uk
* **Flatford** *(I11)*, Flatford Lane, East Bergholt,
Tel: (01206) 299460
Email: flatfordvic@babergh.gov.uk
Web: www.babergh-south-suffolk.gov.uk
Ipswich *(I/J10)*, St Stephens Church, St Stephens Lane, Tel: (01473) 258070
Email: tourist@ipswich.gov.uk
Web: www.ipswich.gov.uk
* **Lavenham** *(E/F9)*, Lady Street,
Tel: (01787) 248207
Email: lavenhamtic@babergh.gov.uk
Web: www.babergh-south-suffolk.gov.uk
Lowestoft *(P2)*, East Point Pavilion, Royal Plain,
Tel: (01502) 533600
Email: touristinfo@waveney.gov.uk
Web: www.visit_lowestoft.co.uk
Mid Suffolk *(H7/8)*, Wilkes Way, Stowmarket,
Tel: (01449) 676800
Email: tic@midsuffolk.gov.uk
Web: www.heritage-suffolk.org.uk

Newmarket *(A7)*, Palace House, Palace Street,
Tel: (01638) 667200
Email: newmarket.tic@forest-heath-dc.demon.co.uk
Southwold *(O5)*, 69 High Street,
Tel: (01502) 724729
Email: southwoldtic@waveney.gov.uk
Sudbury *(E10)*, Town Hall, Market Hill,
Tel: (01787) 881320
Email: sudburytic@babergh.gov.uk
Web: www.babergh-south-suffolk.gov.uk
Woodbridge *(K9)*, Station Buildings,
Tel: (01394) 382240
Email: wtic@suffolkcoastal.gov.uk
Web: www.suffolkcoastal.gov.uk

Blue Badge Guides:

There are also experts available to help you explore some of our towns and cities. These Registered Blue Badge Guides have all attended a training course sponsored by the East of England Tourist Board. Below are some of the tours offered by these Guides - you can obtain further information by contacting the appropriate Tourist Information Centre, unless otherwise indicated. Some Blue Badge Guides have a further qualification to take individuals or groups around the region for half day, full day or longer tours if required.

Ipswich
● **Regular Town Tours:** Individuals may join the tours, lasting approximately 90 minutes, leaving from the Tourist Information Centre. May-Sep, Tue, Thu, 1415. Contact Ipswich TIC Tel: (01473) 258070
● **Group Tours:** Tours can be arranged for groups anytime all year round Contact Ipswich TIC Tel: (01473) 258070.

Bury St. Edmunds
● **Regular Town Tours:** Tours with Blue Badge Guides, lasting 1.5 hours, leave from the Tourist Information Centre. Tickets can be purchased in advance or on the day. Tours run daily in the summer, except Sat at 1430; Also available themed walks on summer evenings. Tel: (01284) 764667. Comprehensive leaflet from T.I.C.
● **Tours for Groups:** Guides can be arranged for groups at any time if enough notice is given. Special themes also available. Tel: (01284) 764667.

Suffolk

historic houses

Flatford
⊚ Bridge Cottage
East Bergholt Tel: (01206) 298260
A 16thC building with a tea garden, shop and a Constable exhibition set in a part of the Dedham Vale with many walks. *Open 5 Jan-24 Feb, Sat, Sun, 1100-1530; 1-31 Mar, Wed-Sun, 1100-1700; 1 Apr-31 Oct, daily, 1100-1730; 1 Nov-15 Dec, Wed-Sun, 1100-1530. (I11)*

Hadleigh
Guildhall
Market Place Tel: (01473) 823884
A medieval timber-framed complex, Grade I Listed (with a Victorian addition) dating from 14th-15thC. *Open 9 Jun-22 Sep, Thu, Sun, 1400-1700. Garden open for teas Sun-Fri 1430-1700. £1.50/free/£1.00. (G10)*

Haughley
Haughley Park
Tel: (01359) 240701
A Jacobean manor-house with gardens and woods set in parkland. *House by appointment only. Open 28 Apr, 5 May, Sun, 1430-1730; 7 May-24 Sep, Tue, 1430-1730. £3.00/£3.00. (H7)*

Hengrave
Hengrave Hall Centre
Tel: (01284) 701561
Hengrave Hall stands in 44 acres with a lake, varied gardens and parkland. This unique Tudor house is renowned for its oriel above the gatehouse and stained glass window. *Open by appointment only, please phone for details. (D6)*

Ickworth
⊚ Ickworth House, Park and Gardens
Tel: (01284) 735270
An extraordinary oval house with flanking wings, begun in 1795. Fine paintings, a beautiful collection of Georgian silver, an Italian garden and stunning park land. *Please contact for details of opening times and admission prices. (D7)*

Ipswich
The Ipswich Unitarian Meeting House
Friars Street
A Grade I Listed building, built 1699 opened in 1700. One of the finest surviving meeting houses and one of the most important historic structures in Ipswich. *Open 2 May-28 Sep, Tue, Thu, 1200-1600, Sat, 1000-1600. (I/J10)*

Lavenham
⊚ Lavenham Guildhall of Corpus Christi
Market Place Tel: (01787) 247646
An impressive timber-framed building dating from the 1530s. Originally the hall of the Guild of Corpus Christi, now a local museum with information on the medieval wool trade. *Open 2-31 Mar, Sat, Sun, 1100-1600; 3 Apr-31 May, Wed-Sun, Bank Hols, 1100-1700; 1 Jun-30 Sep, daily,1100-1700; 2-31 Oct, Wed-Sun, 1100-1700; 2-30 Nov, Sat, Sun, 1100-1600. £3.00/free/£3.00. (E/F9)*

Otley Hall

Lavenham
⚜ Little Hall
Market Place Tel: (01787) 248179

A 15thC hall house with a crown-post roof which contains the Gayer-Anderson collection of furniture, pictures, sculpture and ceramics. There is also a small walled garden. *Open 6 Apr-27 Oct, Wed, Thu, Sat, Sun, 1400-1730, Bank Hols, 1045-1730. £2.00/£1.00/£2.00. (E/F9)*

Long Melford
⚜ Kentwell Hall
Tel: (01787) 310207

A mellow redbrick Tudor manor surrounded by a moat, this family home has been interestingly restored with Tudor costume displays, a 16thC house and mosaic Tudor rose maze. *Please contact for details of opening times and prices. See page 228 for more information. (E10)*

Long Melford
⚜ Melford Hall
Tel: (01787) 880286

Turreted brick Tudor mansion with 18th C and Regency interiors. Collection of Chinese porcelain, gardens and a walk in the grounds. Dogs on leads where permitted. *Open 30 Mar-28 Apr, Sat, Sun, Bank Hol Mon, 1400-1730; 1 May-29 Sep, Wed-Sun, Bank Hol Mon, 1400-1730; 5-27 Oct, Sat, Sun, 1400-1730. £4.50/£2.25. (E10)*

Ickworth House, Park and Gardens

Otley
⚜ Otley Hall
Hall Lane Tel: (01473) 890264

A 15thC moated medieval hall, rich in architecture and family history, set in 10 acres of garden including a canal, mount, nuttery, herbacious and rose garden. *Open 31 Mar, 1 Apr, 5, 6, 27, 28 May, 25, 26 Aug, Sun, Bank Hol Mon, 1230-1800. Gardens 22 Apr-25 Sep, Mon, Wed, 1400-1700. £4.50/£2.50. (J8)*

Somerleyton Hall and Gardens

Suffolk

Somerleyton
⬤ **Somerleyton Hall and Gardens** Q
Tel: (01502) 730224

Anglo Italian-style mansion with state rooms, a maze, 12-acre gardens with azaleas and rhododendrons, miniature railway, shop and tearooms. *Open 31 Mar-30 Jun, Thu, Sun, Bank Hol Mon, 1230-1730; 2 Jul-29 Aug, Tue-Thu, Sun, Bank Hol Mon, 1230-1730; 1-29 Sep, Thu, Sun, 1230-1730. Please contact for Oct opening times and admission prices. (O1/2)*

South Elmham
South Elmham Hall
St Cross
Tel: (01986) 782526

South Elmham Minster, a ruined Norman chapel in fortified enclosure. *Open 6 Jan-24 Mar, Sun, 1000-1700; 29 Mar-31 Oct, Thu, Fri, Sun, Bank Hol Mon, 1000-1700; 3 Nov-29 Dec, Sun, 1000-1700. £6.00. (L/M 3/4)*

Wingfield
⬤ **Wingfield Old College**
Tel: (01379) 384888

Medieval house with gardens offering unique combination of arts and heritage. Award-winning College Yard galleries exhibit contemporary arts and are home to Wingfield Arts. *Open 23 Mar-29 Sep, Sat, Sun, Bank Hol Mon, 1400-1600. Please contact for details of admission prices. (J/K4/5)*

DID YOU KNOW

Borley Rectory was once the most haunted house in Britain, until it was destroyed by fire in 1939.

Suffolk

ancient
monuments

Bury St Edmunds
Saint Edmundsbury Cathedral
The Cathedral Office, Angel Hill
Tel: (01284) 754933
Building of magnificent gothic-style lantern tower will mark the millennium and complete the 16thC nave. Restaurant, shop and exhibitions. *Please contact for details of opening times. (D/E6/7)*

Clare
Clare Castle Country Park
Malting Lane
Tel: (01787) 277491
A small country park incorporating the remains of a castle and a Victorian railway station in a 30-acre site fronting onto the River Stour. *Open all year, daily, dawn-dusk. (C9/10)*

Bungay
Bungay Castle
Tel: (01986) 893148
The remains of an original Norman castle with Saxon mounds. The visitor centre with model of Bungay area in 1350 is in the centre of a fine market town. *Please contact for details of opening times. £1.00/50p/50p. (L3)*

Bury St Edmunds
⊛ Bury St Edmunds Abbey
The remains of a Benedictine abbey in beautifully kept gardens. The 2 great gateways (one being 14thC) are the best preserved buildings. There is also a visitor's centre. *Open all year, Mon-Fri, 0730-dusk; Sat, Sun, Bank Hol Mon, 0900-dusk; for opening hours of visitors centre, please telephone (01284) 763110. (D/E6/7)*

Eye
Eye Castle
Castle Street
Tel: (01449) 676800
A Norman motte-and-bailey with medieval walls and a Victorian folly. The Castle has always had close associations with royalty since the Norman conquest. *Open 18 Mar-30 Sep, daily, 0900-1900/or dusk if earlier. (15)*

Felixstowe
⊛ Landguard Fort
An ancient monument, a 1744 fort with 1875 modifications and additions in 1890, 1901 and 1914. *Please contact for details of opening times. £2.50/£2.00. (L11)*

Leiston Abbey

Suffolk

Framlingham
⊛ Framlingham Castle Q
Tel: (01728) 724189

A castle with 12thC curtain walls, 13 towers, Tudor-brick chimneys and a wall walk, built by the Bigod family, the Earls of Norfolk. The home of Mary Tudor in 1553. *Open 2 Jan-28 Mar, daily, 1000-1600; 1 Apr-30 Sep, daily, 1000-1800; 1-31 Oct, daily, 1000-1700; 1 Nov-31 Dec, daily, 1000-1600. Closed 24-26 Dec, 1 Jan. £3.70/£1.90/£2.80. (K/L7)*

Herringfleet
⊛ Saint Olave's Priory
Priory remains with an early 14thC undercroft and a brick vaulted ceiling. See also the nearby windmill. *Open at any reasonable time, for key telephone (01493) 488609. (O1/2)*

Leiston
⊛ Leiston Abbey
The remains of a 14thC abbey for premonstratensian canons including the transepts of the church and a range of cloisters and a restored chapel. *Open at any reasonable time. (N7)*

Lindsey
Saint James's Chapel
A small 13thC medieval chapel once attached to the nearby castle. *Open all year, daily, 1000-1600. (G10)*

Orford Castle, Suffolk

Framlingham Castle
(© English Heritage Photographic Library)

Orford
⊛ Orford Castle
Tel: (01394) 450472

A 90-ft high keep with views across the River Alde to Orford Ness, built by Henry II for coastal defence in the 12thC with a local topographical display and sculpture. *Open 2 Jan-28 Mar, Wed-Sun, 1000-1300, 1400-1600; 1 Apr-30 Sep, daily, 1000-1800; 1-31 Oct, daily, 1000-1700; 1 Nov-29 Dec, Wed-Sun, 1000-1300, 1400-1600. Closed 25, 26 Dec, 1 Jan. £3.10/£1.60/£2.30. (N9)*

West Stow
⊛ West Stow Anglo-Saxon Village
The Visitor Centre, Icklingham Road
Tel: (01284) 728718

Reconstructions of 8 pagan Anglo-Saxon buildings on original site and an information centre with displays of excavated finds. *Open all year, daily, 1000-1700; last admission 1600; closed 24-26 Dec. £4.50/£3.50/£3.50. (D5/6)*

Woodbridge
Sutton Hoo Burial Site
Sutton Hoo

An Anglo-saxon royal burial site. Sutton Hoo is a group of low grassy burial mounds overlooking the River Deben in south east Suffolk. New exhibition, The Story of Sutton Hoo. *Please contact for details of opening times. £3.50/£2.00/£1.50. (K9)*

Suffolk

museums, heritage & Craft Centres

Aldeburgh
Moot Hall Museum

A 16thC Listed ancient building with a museum displaying items of local interest such as photographs and artefacts depicting life in Aldeburgh. *Open 30 Mar-27 May, Sat, Sun, Bank Hol, 1430-1700; 1-30 Jun, daily, 1430-1700; 1 Jul-20 Aug, daily, 1030-1230, 1430-1700; 1-22 Sep, Sat, Sun, 1430-1700. 80p/free. (N8)*

Beccles
Beccles and District Museum

Leman House, Ballygate
Tel: (01502) 715722

A Grade I Listed building concerning printing, Waveney, agricultural costumes, cultural and domestic items. Also a model of the town in 1841 and a natural history diorama. *Open 1 Apr-31 Oct, Tue-Sun, Bank Hol Mon, 1430-1700. (N2/3)*

Moot Hall, Aldeburgh

Suffolk

Brandon
⊛ Brandon Heritage Centre

George Street Tel: (01842) 813707

The centre gives details of the flint, fur and forestry industries in the Brandon area, together with a local interest section housed in the former fire station premises. *Open 30 Mar-27 Oct, Sat, 1030-1700, Sun, 1400-1700, Bank Hol Mon, 1030-1700. 50p/40p/50p. (C/D3)*

Bredfield
The Soap Shop

The Forge Tel: (01394) 386161

A soap shop with exhibits of our hand-made soaps and toiletries and historical features. *Open all year, Mon-Sat, 1000-1600. (K8/9)*

Bungay
Bungay Museum

Waveney District Council Office,
Broad Street Tel: (01986) 892176

The museum consists of 2 small rooms upstairs which are inter-connecting. These contain showcases of general items from Norman to Victorian periods. *Open 1 Jan-31 Jul, Mon-Fri, 0915-1300, 1400-1615; 1-30 Aug, Mon-Fri, 0915-1300, 1400-1615, Sat, 1400-1630; 2 Sep-31 Dec, Mon-Fri, 0915-1300, 1400-1615. 60p/30p/30p. (L3)*

Bury St Edmunds
Bury St Edmunds Art Gallery

Cornhill Tel: (01284) 762081

Housed at Market Cross, Robert Adam's only public building in Eastern England, originally designed as a playhouse. The upper floor is now used for changing exhibitions. *Open all year, Tue-Sat, 1030-1700. £1.00/free/50p. (D/E6/7)*

Bury St Edmunds
⊛ Manor House

5 Honey Hill Tel: (01284) 757072

A collection of clocks, watches, costumes and textiles with fine and decorative arts of national importance in a magnificent 18thC building. *Open all year, Sat, Sun, Tue, Wed, 1000-1700; closed 25, 26 Dec. £3.00/£2.00/£2.00. (D/E6/7)*

Bury St Edmunds
⊛ Moyse's Hall Museum

Cornhill Tel: (01284) 757488

Dating back over 800 years, Moyse's Hall contains local history collections, Murder in the Red Barn and highlights from the Suffolk Regiment. *Please phone for details of opening times and prices. (D/E6/7)*

Long Shop Steam Museum, Leiston

Bury St Edmunds
Theatre Royal
Westgate Street
Tel: (01284) 769505
An historic building. Built in 1819 by William Wilkins, a rare example of a late Georgian playhouse. Presenting a full programme from drama to comedy and dance. Theatre tours available by appointment. *Please contact for details of admission prices. (D/E6/7)*

Cavendish
Sue Ryder Foundation Museum
Tel: (01787) 282591
Displays showing the reason for establishing the Sue Ryder Foundation and its work. Past, present and future. *Open all year, daily, 1000-1700; closed 25 Dec. 80p/40p/40p. (D9/10)*

Debenham
☺ Carter's Teapot Pottery
Low Road   Tel: (01728) 860475
World-renowned pottery designing and making collectable teapots. There's a viewing area and pottery shop with prices to suit all pockets and a tea and coffee area. *Open all year, Mon-Fri, 0900-1730, Sat, Bank Hol Mon, 1030-1630, Sun, 1400-1700. Please phone for Christmas closing times. (J7)*

Dunwich
☺ Dunwich Museum
St James's Street   Tel: (01728) 648796
A museum showing the history of Dunwich from Roman times, chronicling its disappearance into the sea and local wildlife. *Open 2-31 Mar, Sat, Sun, 1400-1630; 1 Apr-30 Sep, daily, 1130-1630; 1-31 Oct, daily 1200-1600. (N/O5/6)*

Felixstowe
Felixstowe Museum
Landguard Point, Viewpoint Road
Tel: (01394) 672284
The museum is housed in the Ravel in block adjacent to Landguard Fort. There are 12 rooms covering history of the Felixstowe area. *Open 31 Mar-2 Jun, Sun, Bank Hol Mon, 1300-1730; 5 Jun-29 Sep, Wed, Sun, Bank Hol Mon, 1300-1730; 6 Oct-27 Oct, Sun, 1300-1730. (L11)*

Framlingham
Lanman Museum
Framlingham Castle
Tel: (01728) 724189
A museum with rural exhibits relating to everyday life in Framlingham and the surrounding area including paintings and photographs. *Open 2 Jan-31 Mar, daily, 1000-1600; 1 Apr-31 Oct, daily, 1000-1800; 1 Nov-31 Dec, daily, 1000-1600. Closed 25 Dec, 1 Jan. (K/L7)*

Halesworth
Halesworth and District Museum
The Railway Station, Station Road
Tel: (01986) 873030
A museum housed in the 19thC railway station building. Displays of local geology and archaeology. Also railway, local history and rural life exhibitions. *Open 5 Feb-30 Apr, Tue, Thu, 1000-1230; 1 May-28 Sep, Tue, Wed, 1000-1230, 1400-1600, Thu, Sat, 1000-1230, Bank Hol Mon, 1400-1600; 1 Oct-28 Nov, Tue, Thu, 1000-1230. (M4/5)*

Haverhill
**Haverhill and District
Local History Centre**
Town Hall, High Street
Tel: (01440) 714962
A collection of over 4000 items relating to Haverhill and district. There is also a vast collection of photographs. *Open all year, Tue, 1900-2100; Wed, Thu, 1400-1600; Fri, 1400-1600, Sat, 1030-1530; closed 29, 30 Mar, 22 Dec-3 Jan. (B9/10)*

Ilketshall St Lawrence
The Cider Place
Cherry Tree Farm
Tel: (01986) 781353
Traditional apple pressing equipment can be seen ready for use. Explanations given on its use and quality single apple juices and ciders can be sampled and brought. *Open all year, Mon, Tue, 0900-1300, 1400-1800; Thu-Sat, 0900-1300, 1400-1800, Sun, 1400-1800. Closed 25, 26 Dec. (M3)*

Suffolk

Snape Maltings

Ipswich
◉ Christchurch Mansion
Christchurch Park Tel: (01473) 433554
Fine Tudor mansion built between 1548/50, collection of furniture, panelling, ceramics, clocks and paintings from the 16th-19thC. Art exhibitions in Wolsey Art Gallery. *Open all year, Tue-Sat, 1000-1700, Sun, 1430-1630, in winter, or dusk, if earlier. (I/J10)*

Ipswich
◉ Ipswich Museum and Gallery
High Street Tel: (01473) 433550
Displays of Roman Suffolk, Suffolk wildlife, Suffolk and world geology, the Ogilvie bird gallery, People of the World and Anglo-Saxons come to Ipswich displays. *Open all year, Tue-Sat, 1000-1700; closed 29 Mar, 24-26 Dec, 1 Jan. (I/J10)*

Ipswich
The John Russell Gallery
4-6 Wherry Lane Tel: (01473) 212051
Eighteenth-century wharf in the oldest and most historic part of the docklands of Ipswich. *Open all year, Mon-Sat, 0930-1700; closed Bank Hol Mon, 29 Mar, 12-26 Aug, 25 Dec-25 Jan. (I/J10)*

Ipswich
Tolly Cobbold
Brewery and the Brewery Tap
Cliff Road Tel: (01473) 231723
Taste the malt and smell the hops on a fully-guided tour of this magnificent Victorian brewery. Also visit the new brewhouse and bottlers' room. *Open 1 Jul-30 Aug, Mon, Fri, 1430. Other times by appointment. £4.90. (I/J10)*

Ipswich
Wattisham Airfield Museum
Wattisham Airfield
Tel: (01449) 728207
Wattisham Airfield Museum houses an extensive photographic record, models, artefacts and memorabilia depicting the history and squadrons based at the station. *Open 7 Apr-27 Oct, Sun, 1400-1630. (H10)*

Kentford
Animal Health Trust Visitor Centre
Lanwades Park Tel: (01638) 751000
The John MacDougall Visitor Centre gives an insight into the veterinary work of the Animal Health Trust charity. Coffee shop serves light refreshments and tours available. *Open all year, Mon-Fri, 0900-1700. (B/C6)*

Suffolk

Kersey
Kersey Pottery
The Street   Tel: (01473) 822092
Hand-made stoneware pottery, all made and fired in Kersey, using all the processes of making craft pottery including throwing, turning and decorating. *Open all year, Tue-Sat, 1000-1730, Sun, 1100-1700. (G10)*

Laxfield
Laxfield and District Museum
The Guildhall, High Street
Museum is housed in the early 16thC guildhall opposite church in Laxfield. Displays relate to the domestic and working life of the village in the 19th/20thC. *Open 4 May-29 Sep, Sat, Sun, Bank Hol Mon, 1400-1700. (L5)*

Leiston
Long Shop Steam Museum
Main Street Tel: (01728) 832189
Award-winning museum, Grade II* listed Long Shop. Leiston's unique history and home of the Garrett collection. First production line to the 1st woman doctor. *Open 1 Apr-1 Nov, Mon-Sat, 1000-1700; Sun, 1100-1700. £3.00/70p/£2.50. (N7)*

Lowestoft
Lowestoft and East Suffolk Maritime Museum
Sparrows Nest Park, Whapload Road
Tel: (01502) 561963
The museum houses models of fishing and commercial ships, shipwrights' tools, fishing gear, a lifeboat display, an art gallery and a drifter's cabin with models of fishermen.' *Open Easter (29 Mar-1 Apr), 28 Apr-6 Oct, daily, 1000-1630. 75p/25p/50p. (P2)*

Lowestoft
Lowestoft Museum
Broad House, Nicholas Everitt Park
Tel: (01502) 511457
A museum housing displays on local history, Lowestoft porcelain, fossils, flint implements, medieval artefacts from local sites and domestic history. *Please contact for details of opening times. (P2)*

Lowestoft
Royal Naval Patrol Service Association Museum
Sparrows Nest Tel: (01502) 586250

A museum with photographs of models of World War II officers and crews, minesweepers and anti-submarine vessels. *Open 20 May-18 Oct, Mon, Wed, Fri, 1000-1200, 1400-1630; Sun, 1400-1630, 30, 31 Mar, 1000-1200, 1400-1630. Closed 29 Mar. (P2)*

Mildenhall
Mildenhall and District Museum
6 King Street Tel: (01638) 716970

A local voluntary museum housed in early 19thC cottages with modern extensions. Displays include RAF Mildenhall, Fenland and Breckland local archaeology and local history. *Open 1 Mar-20 Dec, Wed, Thu, Sat, Sun, 1430-1630; Fri, 1100-1630. Closed 29 Mar. (B5)*

Needham Market
Alder Carr Farm
Tel: (01449) 720820

Courtyard craft centre, by the river on a pick-your-own fruit and vegetable farm with farm shop in traditional barn. Tearoom, restaurant and monthly farmer's market. *Open 8 Jan-30 Apr, Tue-Sat, 1000-1600; 1 May-29 Sep, Tue-Sun, 1000-1700; 1 Oct-21 Dec, Tue-Sat, 1000-1600. Closed 24 Dec-7 Jan. (H/18)*

Newmarket
⊛ National Horse-Racing Museum and Tours
99 High Street Tel: (01638) 667333

Award-winning display of the people and horses involved in racing's amazing history. Minibus tours to gallops, stables and equine pool. Hands-on gallery with horse simulator. *Open 29 Mar-30 Jun, Tue-Sun and Bank Hol Mon, 1000-1700; 1 Jul-31 Aug, daily, 1000-1700; 1 Sep-31 Oct, Tue-Sun, 1000-1700. £4.50/£2.50/£3.50. (A7)*

Orford
Dunwich Underwater Exploration Exhibition
The Orford Craft Shop
Tel: (01394) 450678

Exhibits show progress in the underwater exploration of the former city and underwater studies off the Suffolk coast. Attraction is not suitable for small children. *Open all year, daily, 1100-1700. 50p. (N9)*

Shotley Gate
HMS Ganges Association Museum
Old Sail Loft, Shotley Marina
Tel: (01473) 684749

The history of HMS Ganges contained in 1 large room, museum with photographs, artifacts and documentation. *Open 6 Apr-27 Oct, Sat, Sun, Bank Hol Mons, 1100-1700. (K11)*

Snape
⊛ Snape Maltings
Tel: (01728) 688303

Maltings on the banks of the River Alde with shops, galleries, restaurants, river trips, painting and craft courses in the summer and a world-famous concert hall. *Open all year, daily, 1000-1700; closed 25, 26 Dec. (M7)*

Southwold
Alfred Corry Museum
Ferry Road
Tel: (01502) 722103

The old Cromer lifeboat station transported by sea to Southwold. Restored and now houses the old Southwold lifeboat. One hundred and eight years old. *Open all year, Mon-Fri, 1400-1630, Sat, Sun, 1000-1230,1400-1700, Bank Hol Mon, 1000-1630. (O4/5)*

Southwold
The Amber Museum
15 Market Place
Tel: (01502) 723394

A purpose-built museum telling the story of amber. The precious gem found on the Suffolk shores. From how it is formed through historical uses to spectacular modern pieces. *Open 3 Jan-30 Jun, Mon-Sat, 0900-1700, Sun, 1100-1600; 1 Jul-30 Sep, Mon-Sat, 0900-1700, Sun, 1100-1600; 2 Oct-30 Dec, Mon-Sat, 0900-1700, Sun, 1100-1600. Closed 24-26 Dec, 1 Jan. (O4/5)*

South Elmham
⊛ Saint Peter's Brewery Ⓠ and Visitor Centre
St Peter's Hall, St Peter
Tel: (01986) 782322

A small brewery in the grounds of a 13thC hall with a 17thC barn containing the visitor centre. *Open all year, Fri-Sun, Bank Hols, 1100-2300. £5.00/50p. (L/M3/4)*

Southwold
Southwold Lifeboat Museum
Gun Hill Tel: (01502) 722422
A museum with RNLI models, photographs of lifeboats and relics from old boats. *Open 25 May-29 Sep, daily, 1430-1630. (O4/5)*

Southwold
Southwold Museum
9-11 Victoria Street
Tel: (01502) 723374
Museum housing local history, archaeology, natural history, exhibits relating to Southwold railway and The Battle of Sole Bay and domestic bygones. *Open 29 Mar-31 Jul, daily, 1400-1600; 1-31 Aug, daily, 1100-1200, 1400-1600, 1 Sep-31 Oct, daily, 1400-1600. (O4/5)*

Steeple Bumpstead
Steeple Bumpstead Pottery and Gallery
Church Street
Tel: (01440) 730260
Traditional working pottery set in a Victorian village school. With gallery displaying the pots made here. *Open all year by appointment only, Mon-Sat, 1000-1800, Sun, 1400-1800. (B10)*

Stowmarket
Museum of East Anglian Life
Tel: (01449) 612229
East Anglia's open-air museum, set in 70 acres of Suffolk countryside. Museum displays and special events to interest visitors of all ages. *Open 1 Jan-29 Mar, Mon-Fri, 1000-1500; 1 Apr-31 Oct, Mon-Sat, 1000-1700; Sun, 1100-1700; 1 Nov-31 Dec, Mon-Fri, 1000-1700. Closed 25 Dec-2 Jan. Please contact for details of admission prices. (H7/8)*

Lowestoft Museum

Sudbury
⊛ **Gainsborough's House** [Q]
46 Gainsborough Street
Tel: (01787) 372958
The birthplace of Thomas Gainsborough. An elegant townhouse with paintings by Gainsborough, a garden, print workshop and a programme of temporary exhibitions. *Open 2 Jan-31 Mar, Tue-Sat, 1000-1600; Sun, 1400-1600; 1 Apr-31 Oct, Tue-Sat, 1000-1700; Sun, Bank Hol Mon, 1400-1700; 1 Nov-22 Dec, Tue-Sat, 1000-1600; Sun, 1400-1600. £3.00/£1.50/£2.50. (E10)*

Weston
Home and Garden at Winter Flora
Hall Farm
Tel: (01502) 713346
Garden closely planted with unusual plants. Many varieties featured for sale. Spacious shop reflects current trends. Topiary, silk flowers, exotics and stylish pots. *Open all year, Mon-Sat, 1000-1700, Sun 1100-1700. Closed 31 Mar, 24-29 Dec, 1 Jan. (N3)*

Woodbridge
Suffolk Horse Museum
The Market Hill Tel: (01394) 380643
An indoor exhibition about the Suffolk Punch breed of heavy horse. *Please contact for details of opening times and admission prices. (K9)*

Woodbridge
Woodbridge Museum
5a Market Hill Tel: (01394) 380502
A museum with exhibits on Sutton Hoo and Burrow Hill. Exhibits reflect the life of Woodbridge and its people. *Open 30 Mar-28 Oct, Thu-Sat, Bank Hol, 1000-1600; Mon, Tue in school hols, 1000-1600; Sun, 1430-1630. £1.00/30p/£1.00. (K9)*

Woolpit
Woolpit and District Museum
The Institute Tel: (01359) 240822
A 17thC timber-framed building with one permanent display of brickmaking and other displays, changing yearly, depicting the life of a Suffolk village. *Open 30 Mar-29 Sep, Sat, Sun, Bank Hol Mon, 1430-1700. (G7)*

DID YOU KNOW

Bawdsey Manor is the birthplace of radar. It was developed here in the 1930's by Sir Robert Alexander Watson-Watt.

Suffolk

machinery
& transport

Carlton Colville
East Anglia Transport Museum
Chapel Road
Tel: (01502) 518459

A working museum with one of the widest ranges of street transport vehicles on display and in action. Developing street scene and a 2-ft gauge railway. *Open 29 Mar-1 Apr, daily, 1400-1700; 5 May-29 Sep, Sun, Bank Hol Mon, 1100-1730, Wed, 1100-1730; 5 Jun-10 Jul, Wed, 1400-1700; 15 Jul-30 Aug, Mon-Fri, 1400-1700. Last admission 1 hour before closing. £4.50/£3.00/£3.00. (O2/3)*

East Anglia Transport Museum, Carlton Colville

Cotton
Mechanical Music Museum & Bygones Trust
Blacksmith Road
Tel: (01449) 613876

A selection of fairground organs, pipe organs, street pianos, music boxes, polyphons and many other musical items. *Open Suns Jun-Sept, 1430-1730. Weekday groups by arrangement. Fair Organ Enthusiasts Day 6 Oct 1000-1700. £4.00/£1.00. (H6)*

Flixton
Norfolk and Suffolk Aviation Museum
East Anglia's Aviation Heritage Centre,
The Street
Tel: (01986) 896644

A museum with 30 aircraft on display together with a large indoor display of smaller items connected with the history of aviation. Donations are encouraged. *Open 15 Jan-31 Mar, Tue, Wed, Sun, 1000-1600; last admission 1500; 1 Apr-31 Oct, Sun-Thu, Bank Hol Mon, 1000-1700; last admission 1600; 3 Nov-15 Dec, Tue, Wed, Sun, 1000-1600; last admission 1500. (L3)*

Ipswich
Ipswich Transport Museum
Old Trolleybus Depot, Cobham Road
Tel: (01473) 715666

The museum features over 100 vehicles built or operated in and around Ipswich, together with examples from local engineering companies. *Open 31 Mar-24 Nov, Sun, Bank Hol Mon, 1100-1630; Please ring for school holiday openings. £2.50/£1.50/£2.00. (I/J10)*

Suffolk

Ipswich
Wattisham Airfield Museum
See entry under Museums section.

Lowestoft
Lydia Eva Steam Drifter/Mincarlo Trawler
Yacht Basin, Lowestoft Harbour
Tel: (01603) 782758
Mincarlo was launched in 1962. Both vessels are preserved by the Trust as museums of the local fishing industries. Lydia Eva Steam Drifter currently out of service. *Open 29 Mar-13 Oct, daily, 1000-1630; please phone Great Yarmouth Tourist Information Centre on 01493 842195 or Lowestoft Tourist Information Centre on 01502 533600. (P2)*

DID YOU KNOW

When completed in 1982, The Orwell Bridge, Ipswich, had the longest, pre-stressed concrete span (190 metres/623 feet) of any bridge in Britain.

Parham
390th Bomb Group Memorial
Air Museum
Parham Airfield
Tel: (01728) 621373
A museum housed in the original control tower with a refreshment, sales hut and an archive building. *Open 3 Mar-2 Jun, Sun, Bank Hol Mon, 1100-1800; 5 Jun-28 Aug, Wed, 1100-1600, Sun, Bank Hol Mon, 1100-1800; 1 Sep-27 Oct, Sun, 1100-1800. (L7)*

Stowmarket
Museum of East Anglian Life
See entry in Museums section.

Wetheringsett
Mid-Suffolk Light Railway Museum
Brockford Station
Tel: (01449) 766899
A re-created Mid-Suffolk light railway station with exhibits relating to Mid-Suffolk Light Railway and restoration of the station and trackwork on part of the original route. *Open 29 Mar-29 Sep, Sun, Bank Hol Mon, 1100-1700. £1.50/50p/£1.50. (I6)*

Ipswich Transport Museum

mills

DID YOU KNOW

The post-mill at Friston is the tallest in Europe at 55 feet/17 metres high. Built in 1811, it is now being restored.

Stanton
Stanton Postmill
Mill Farm, Upthorpe Road
Tel: (01359) 250622
A postmill dating from 1751. In working order with an exhibition of postmills in the United Kingdom and other local mills. Flour available. *Open at any reasonable time. Please phone (01359) 250622 for view inside the mill. £2.00/50p. (F5)*

Thelnetham
Thelnetham Windmill
Mill Road Tel: (01359) 250622
A tower windmill, built in 1819 with 4 very large patent sails driving 2 pairs of millstones. In full working order with flour available for sale. *Open 31 Mar, 1 Apr, 5, 6 May, 2, 3 Jun, 25, 26 Aug, Sun, Bank Hol Mon, 1100-1700; 7 Jul-8 Sep, 2nd Sun in month, 1100-1800. £1.50/25p. (G4)*

Herringfleet
Herringfleet Marshmill
Tel: (01473) 583352
The last surviving smock drainage mill in the Broads area; the last full-size working windmill in the country with 4 common sails and a tailpole. *Open 12 May, 1300-1700; also open for 2 further Sun in the year. (O1/2)*

Holton St Peter
Holton Saint Peter Postmill
Mill House Tel: (01986) 872367
A restored 18thC post windmill with 4 sails and a working fantail. *Open 27 May, 26 Aug, Bank Hol Mon, 1000-1800. (M4/5)*

Pakenham
Pakenham Water Mill
Mill Road
Tel: (01359) 270570
An 18thC working watermill on a Domesday site with an oil engine, mill pool, short river walk, picnic and barbecue area. *Open 1 Apr-29 Sep, Wed, Sat, Sun, Bank Hols, 1400-1730. £2.00/£1.20/£1.75. (F6)*

Saxtead Green
Saxtead Green Postmill
The Mill House Tel: (01728) 685789
An elegant white windmill, dating from 1776. A fine example of a traditional Suffolk postmill. Climb the stairs to the 'buck' to see the machinery, all in working order. *Open 1 Apr-30 Sep, Mon-Sat, 1000-1300, 1400-1800; 1-31 Oct, Mon-Sat, 1000-1300, 1400-1700. Please check with regional office before your visit. £2.20/£1.10/£1.70. (K6/7)*

Thorpeness
Thorpeness Windmill
Tel: (01394) 384948
A working windmill housing displays on the Suffolk Coast and Heaths, Thorpeness village and information on the workings of the mill. *Please contact for details of opening times. (N/O7)*

Woodbridge
Buttrums Mill
Burkitt Road Tel: (01394) 382045
A fine 6-storey towermill which is now fully restored with sails and machinery. There is also a display on history and machinery. *Open 31 Mar-28 Apr, Sun, Bank Hol Mon, 1400-1730; 4 May-31 Aug, Sat, Sun, Bank Hol Mon, 1400-1730; 1-29 Sep, Sun, 1400-1730. £1.50/25p/£1.50. (K9)*

Woodbridge
Woodbridge Tidemill
Tidemill Quay Tel: (01473) 626618
A completely restored 18thC tidalmill. The machinery works at varying times, subject to tides. *Open 6-28 Apr, Sat, Sun, 1100-1700; 1 May-30 Sep, daily, 1100-1700; 5-26 Oct, Sat, Sun, 1100-1700. £1.50/free/£1.00. (K9)*

Suffolk

gardens & Vineyards

Ashbocking
James White Cider and Apple Juice Co.
White's Fruit Farm, Helmingham Road
Tel: (01473) 890202
Apple juice and bottling along with farm shop selling apple juice and ciders produced on site. Herb garden and pick-your-own soft fruit. Free tastings are given. *Shop open all year, daily, 1000-1700; Production Tue-Fri, 1000-1500; closed 25, 26 Dec. (J8)*

Benhall
The Walled Garden
Park Road
Tel: (01728) 602510
A retail nursery and garden selling almost 1500 varieties of plants nestles in the warmth of the high wall of an old kitchen garden. *Open 2 Jan-16 Feb, Tue-Sat, 0930-dusk; 19 Feb-30 Nov, Tue-Sat, 0930-1700; 3-20 Dec, Tue-Sat, 0930-dusk. (M7)*

Bruisyard
⊛ **Bruisyard Wines** [Q] **and Herbs**
Church Road Tel: (01728) 638281
A 10-acre vineyard showing summer work and maintenance of the vines, a tour of the winery and herb garden. *Open 16 Jan-21 Dec, Tue-Sat, summer, 1030-1700. Winter 1100-1600. £4.00/£2.50/£3.50. (L6)*

Coddenham
Shrubland Gardens
Shrubland Park
Tel: (01473) 830221
Extensive Italianate Victorian garden laid out by Sir Charles Barry in historic parkland. *Open 31 Mar-1 Sept, Sun, Bank Hol Mon, 1400-1700. £3.00/£2.00/£2.00. (I8)*

East Bergholt
⊛ **East Bergholt Place Garden**
East Bergholt Place
Tel: (01206) 299224
The Place Garden was laid out at the turn of the century and covers 15 acres with fine trees, shrubs, rhododendrons, camellias and magnolias. *Open 1 Mar-30 Sep, daily, 1000-1700; closed 31 Mar. £2.50. (H11)*

Flatford
⊛ **Bridge Cottage**
See entry in Historic Houses section.

Framlingham
⊛ **Shawsgate Vineyard**
Badingham Road Tel: (01728) 724060
An attractive 15-acre vineyard with a modern, well-equipped winery, vineyard walk, guided tours, wine tasting all day, a picnic area, children's play area and shop open all year. *Open 1 Feb-24 Dec, daily, 1030-1700; please phone for weekend opening during winter. £4.00/free/£3.50. (K/L7)*

Hadleigh
Guildhall
See entry in Historic Houses section.

Hartest
⊛ **Giffords Hall Vineyard and Sweet Pea Centre**
Tel: (01284) 830464
A 33-acre vineyard with vines, a winery, rare breeds of sheep, pigs, free-range chickens, a rose garden, wild flower meadows and a sweet pea centre. *Open 29 Mar-30 Sep, daily, 1100-1800. £3.50/ free/£3.00. (D8/9)*

Haughley
Haughley Park
See entry in Historic Houses section.

Helmingham Hall Gardens

Helmingham
⊛ Helmingham Hall Gardens
Estate Office Tel: (01473) 890363

A moated and walled garden with many rare roses and possibly the best kitchen garden in Britain. Also highland cattle and safari rides in the park to view the red and fallow deer. *Open 28 Apr-8 Sep, Sun, 1400-1800. £3.75/£2.00/£3.75. (J8)*

Ickworth
⊛ Ickworth House, Park and Gardens
See entry in Historic Houses section.

Kelsale
⊛ Laurel Farm Herbs
Main Road (A12)

Tel: (01728) 668223

Well established herb garden to view. Specialist herb grower with a large range of culinary and medicinal pot grown plants. Established since 1985. *Open 2 Jan-28 Feb, Wed-Fri, 1000-1500; 1 Mar-31 Oct, daily except Tue, 1000-1700; 1 Nov-27 Dec, Wed-Fri, 1000-1500. (M6)*

Lavenham
⊛ Lavenham Guildhall of Corpus Christi
See entry in Historic Houses section.

Lavenham
⊛ Little Hall
See entry in Historic Houses section.

Long Melford
⊛ Kentwell Hall
See entry in Historic Houses section.

Long Melford
⊛ Melford Hall
See entry in Historic Houses section.

Otley
⊛ Otley Hall
See entry in Historic Houses section.

Somerleyton
⊛ Somerleyton Hall and Gardens Q
See entry in Historic Houses section.

Stanton
Wyken Hall Gardens and Wyken Vineyards
Tel: (01359) 250287

Seven acres of vineyard, 4 acres of garden, woodland walks and a 16thC barn containing restaurant, cafe and shop. *Open 7 Jan-24 Dec, daily, 1000-1800; Gardens 1 Apr-1 Oct, daily except Sat, 1400-1800. £2.50/free/£2.00. (F5)*

Thornham Magna
The Thornham Walled Garden
Thornham Field Centre Trust, Red House Yard

Tel: (01379) 788700

Restored Victorian glasshouses in the idyllic setting of a 2-acre walled garden with fruit trees, wide perennial borders and collection of East Anglian geraniums. *Open summer, 1000-1800; winter, 1000-dusk. Please phone to check Oct-Mar openings. Closed 25 Dec. (H/I 5/6)*

Wingfield
⊛ Wingfield Old College
See entry in Historic Houses section.

Suffolk

nurseries & garden centres

Aldeburgh
The Exotic Garden Company
Hall Farm, Saxmundham Road,
Aldeburgh, Suffolk
Tel: (01728) 454456

Visit our tropical surroundings where you can purchase hardy exotic plants from around the world. We specialise in hardy palms, bamboos, tree ferns, bananas and many other Mediterranean varieties. *Opening times: 10.00-5.00pm Monday-Saturday. 10.00-4.00pm Sunday. (N8)*

East Bergholt
⊛ The Place For Plants
East Bergholt Place Garden,
Suffolk CO7 6UP
Tel: (01206) 299224

Plant Centre and Garden for specialist and popular plants, voted 7th most recommended nursery in the Country (Gardeners' Favourite Nurseries, by Leslie Geddes-Brown). A plant centre has been set up in the Victorian Walled Garden at East Bergholt Place stocked with an excellent range of plants, shrubs, trees, climbers, herbaceous plants, ferns, grasses, bamboo's, herbs etc. and a selection of terracotta pots. Situated 2 miles east of the A12 on B1070, on the edge of East Bergholt. *Plant Centre opens daily 10.00-17.00. (Closed Easter Sunday). Garden open - please see entry in Gardens and Vineyards section on page 240. (H11)*

Seafront Gardens, Felixstowe

Dunwich
Bridge Nurseries & Café Tea Room
Bridge House, Dunwich, Suffolk IP17 3DZ
Tel: (01728) 648850   www.fiskclematis.co.uk

Situated in the coastal village of Dunwich, just a few miles off the A12. Bridge Nurseries supply a wide-range of plants, including the world-famous Fisk's Clematis collection, featuring hundreds of varieties. Our award-winning hanging baskets and containers are a major attraction. The café-tea room serves light meals and home made cakes all day. The terrace overlooks the church and is a natural sun trap. Clematis catalogues available on our website or via the post. We operate a mail order service for clematis only. *Open every day throughout the year - summer 9.00am - 5.00pm and winter 10.00am - 4.00pm. (N/O5/6)*

Woodbridge
⊛ Notcutts Garden Centres
Ipswich Road, Woodbridge, Suffolk
Tel: 01394 445400

Discover a world of ideas and inspiration around every corner for you, your home and your garden. From fabulous plants to gifts and treats galore, there's so much to see. Gift ideas from around the world, houseplants, books, fresh cut & silk flowers, 3,000 varieties of hardy plants (with a 2 year replacement guarantee), restaurant, expert friendly advice about seasonal and bedding plants, garden furniture and barbecues. Keep an eye open for regular offers on key garden products. *Notcutts open 7 days a week, free car-parking plus children's play area. (K9)*

Flatford Mill

Kelsale
⊛ Laurel Farm Herbs
Main Road, Kelsale,
Saxmundham, Suffolk IP17 2RG
Tel: (01728) 668223
Email: seagontheherbman@aol.com
www.theherbfarm.co.uk

Laurel Farm Herbs, on the main A12 between Saxmundham and Yoxford, is one of Suffolk's longest established herb nurseries. We offer an extensive range of culinary and medicinal plants, including a variety of larger specimens for those who want 'instant' results. In addition to our three sales areas we have a 1,800 sq foot garden, which allows you to see plants as they will be, once they have matured. Hard paths and ramps offer good access to all areas. *Open 10.00am to 5.00pm, closed Tuesdays. (M6)*

Suffolk

Felixstowe
Manning's Amusement Park
Sea Road   Tel: (01394) 282370
A traditional amusement park with rides and attractions, a children's park, a nightclub, sportsbar, quasar arena and Sunday market. *Open 13 Apr-29 Sep, Sat, Sun and School Hols, please phone for further details. (L11)*

Kessingland
Suffolk Wildlife Park **Q**
Tel: (01502) 740291
Discover the ultimate African adventure set in 100 acres of coastal parkland. Experience close encounters with rhino, lions, giraffes, hyenas, zebras and many more. *Please contact for details of opening times. £7.50/£5.50/£5.50 (O3)*

Kentwell
Kentwell Hall
Rare breeds farm.
Also see entry on page 227/228.

Baylham
Baylham House Rare Breeds Farm
Mill Lane   Tel: (01473) 830264
A rare breeds farm, visitor's centre, riverside walk and a Roman site. *Open 21 Mar-29 Sep, Tue-Sun, Bank Hol Mon and Oct school hols, 1100-1700. £3.50/£1.75/£2.50. (H/18/9)*

Earsham
Otter Trust
Tel: (01986) 893470
A breeding and conservation headquarters with the largest collection of otters in the world. There are also lakes with a collection of waterfowl and deer. *Open 1 Apr-30 Sep, daily, 1030-1800. £5.00/£3.00/£4.00. (L3)*

Felixstowe
Golf FX
Manning's Amusement Park,
Sea Road
Tel: (01394) 282370
Indoor adventure golf with 13 holes of skill, fun and surprises. Suitable for all the family. *Open all year, daily, summer, 1000-2130, winter, 1000-1800. Closed 25 Dec. Admission over 1m tall £2.00, admission under 1m tall £1.50. (L11)*

Suffolk

Lowestoft
⊛ East Point Pavilion Visitor Centre Ⓠ
Tel: (01502) 533600

A glass, all-weather Edwardian-style structure with a large indoor play platform called Mayhem. Small souvenir shop, restaurant and tearooms. *Open 2 Jan-30 Mar, daily, 1030-1700; 1 Mar-30 Sep, daily, 0930-1730; 1 Oct-31 Dec, daily, 1030-1700. Closed 25, 26 Dec, 1 Jan. Child from £2.50. (P2)*

Lowestoft
⊛ New Pleasurewood Hills Theme Park
Leisure Way, Corton
Tel: (01502) 586000

Tidal wave watercoaster, log flume, chairlift and 2 railways, pirate ship, Aladdin's cave, parrot and sealion shows, megaspin rollover, go-karts and rattlesnake coaster. *Please contact for details of opening times and admission prices. (P2)*

Newmarket
⊛ National Stud
Tel: (01638) 663464

A visit to the National Stud consists of a conducted tour which will include top thoroughbred stallions, mares and foals. *Open 1 Mar-30 Sep, Mon-Sat, tours 1115, 1430, Sun, 1430. £4.50/£3.50/£3.50. (A7)*

Historic recreation at Kentwell Hall, Long Melford

Southwold Pier

Southwold
⊛ Southwold Pier
Tel: (01502) 722105

Pier and amusements. *Amusements open 5 Jan-22 Jun, Sat, Sun, from 1000; 22 Jun-7 Sep, daily, from 0900; 7 Sep-22 Dec, Sat, Sun, from 1000. (O4/5)*

Stonham Aspal
⊛ Stonham Barns Leisure Complex
See entry under Museums, Heritage and Craft Centres section.

Stonham Aspal
⊛ Suffolk Owl Sanctuary
Stonham Barns
Pettaugh Road
Tel: (01449) 711425

An outdoor flying arena featuring frequent demonstrations of birds of prey in flight with many aviaries, information centre and shop. *Please contact for details of opening times. Donations appreciated. (17)*

Stowmarket
Playworld Ocean Adventure
Mid-Suffolk Leisure Centre, Gainsborough Road
Tel: (01449) 674980

A children's indoor play area facility for the under 12's with a wide range of inflatables, aerial runway, grand prix cars, bikes and more. *Open all year, Mon-Fri, 0930-1900; Sat, Sun, 0900-1800; closed 25, 26 Dec, 1 Jan. Child £2.85. (H7/8)*

Suffolk

Pleasurewood Hills Theme Park, Corton, Lowestoft

Wickham Market
⚙ **Easton Farm Park** Q
Easton Tel: (01728) 746475

A Victorian farm setting for many breeds of farm animals. Children can touch and feed the animals. Free pony rides at weekends and holidays. *Open Feb school hols, 1 Apr-30 Jun, Tue-Sun, Bank Hol Mon, 1030-1800; 1 Jul-31 Aug, daily, 1030-1800; 1-29 Sep, Tue-Sun, 1030-1800; Oct school hols. Please contact for details of admission prices. (L8)*

Wickham Market
Valley Farm Camargue Horses
Valley Farm Riding and Driving Centre
Tel: (01728) 746916

Britain's only herd of breeding Camargue horses as featured on television. Also the white animal collection including Camelot, the Camel. *Open all year, daily, 1000-1600. Closed 25, 26 Dec. (L8)*

DID YOU KNOW
The Otter Trust at Earsham is the world's largest collection of otters.

Countryside

Country Parks and Nature Reserves

⚜ Alton Water
Holbrook Road, Stutton, Ipswich.
Tel: (01473) 589105.
Water park with sailing, rowing, fishing, nature reserves and extensive walks. Visitor centre, cycle hire and catering. *Open at any reasonable time. (I11)*

River Stour, Sudbury

⚜ Brandon Country Park
Tel: (01842) 810185
Thirty acres of landscaped parkland with a tree trail and forest walks. Visitor centre open daily. Play area, orienteering course and road cycle loops totalling 20.75km. *Park open all year, daily, dawn-dusk; Visitor Centre 1 Jan-31 Mar, daily, 1000-1600; 1 Apr-30 Sep, daily, 1000-1700; 1 Oct-31 Dec, daily, 1000-1600; closed 25, 26 Dec, please telephone for Christmas closure. (C/D3)*

⚜ Minsmere Nature Reserve
Westleton   Tel: (01728) 648281
RSPB reserve on Suffolk coast with bird-watching hides and trails, year-round events and guided walk and visitor centre with large shop and welcoming tearoom. (RSPB) *Open Reserve all year, daily except Tue, 0900-2100/dusk; Visitor Centre 2-31 Jan, daily except Tue, 0900-1600; 1 Feb-31 Oct, daily, except Tues, 0900-1700; 1 Nov-30 Dec, daily except Tue, 0900-1600; closed 25, 26 Dec. Please contact for details of admission prices. (N6)*

Needham Lake and Nature Reserve
Needham Market Tel: (01449) 676800
A large man-made lake and nature reserve with picnic and educational facilities on the outskirts of Needham Market with a gravel pathway around the lake. *Open at any reasonable time. (H/18)*

Suffolk

Minsmere Bird Reserve

Naturalists' Organisations & Other Abbreviations used in this section

⊚ **NT:**   The National Trust, Blickling, Norwich, Norfolk NR11 6NF. Tel: (01263) 738030

⊚ **RSPB:**   Royal Society for the Protection of Birds, HQ: The Lodge, Sandy, Beds SG19 2DL. Tel: (01767) 680551 East Anglia Regional Office, Stalham House, 65 Thorpe Road, Norwich NR1 1UD. Tel: (01603) 660066

⊚ **SWT:**   Suffolk Wildlife Trust, Brooke House, The Green, Ashbocking, Ipswich. Suffolk IP6 9JY. Tel: (01473) 890089

SSSI: Site of Special Scientific Interest

Nowton Park
Bury St Edmunds Tel: (01284) 763666
Previously a country estate with 170 acres of woodland and pasture. Some formal recreation. All-weather pitch and 2 football pitches. Park Centre open weekends. *Open all year, daily, 0830-dusk. (D/E6/7)*

⊚ Orford Ness
Orford Tel: (01394) 450900
A 10-mile-long vegetated shingle spit stretching from Aldeburgh to Shingle Street. It is a Grade I Site of Special Scientific Interest. (NT) *Open 30 Mar-29 Jun, Sat, 1000-1700; 2 Jul-28 Sep, Tue-Sat, 1000-1400; 5-26 Oct, Sat, 1000-1400; ferries return on demand, last return 1700. Admission members of National Trust: £3.60/£1.80. Admission Non-members : £5.60/£2.80. (N9)*

⊚ Thornham Walks
Thornham Magna Tel: (01379) 788345
Twelve miles of walks through parkland, woods, meadow and farmland. *Open all year, daily, 0900-1800. (I5/6)*

⊚ West Stow Country Park
West Stow Tel: (01284) 728718
Country park with nature trail, paths and bird hides. Large car park with picnic area. Visitor centre with displays, cafeteria and shop. *Open all year, daily, 0900-1700. (D5/6)*

DID YOU KNOW

Orfordness is the largest vegetated shingle spit in Europe. Formerly a top secret military testing site during both World Wars, it is now a haven for bird lovers.

West Stow Anglo Saxon Village

Suffolk

Activities & Sport

Boat Hire and Regular Excursions

⊛ Deben Cruises

The Quay, Waldringfield, Woodbridge
Tel: (01473) 736260

The M.V. Jahan. Two hour cruises on the River Deben. Group parties 36-54; commentary, toilet, bar and meals. Lunchtime cruises with sherry/ploughmans £9.95pp. Afternoon cruise with set tea £8.75pp or just £5.00pp. Bookings by appointment only (CORPORATE catered for). *(K/L9)*

⊛ The Excelsior Trust

Lowestoft Tel: (01502) 585302
www.excelsiortrust.co.uk

A charitable trust ensuring historic sailing vessels are restored and continue to provide traditional sailing experience for people from all walks of life. *(P2)*

⊛ Lady Florence River Cruises

Orford Tel: (07831) 698298
Email: lady-flo@keme.co.uk

Based at Orford Quay. River cruise for 4 hours with lunch or dinner within the Rivers Alde and Ore. Cruise passes Aldeburgh, National Trust's Orford Ness and Havergate Island. *Open all year, daily, brunch 0900-1130; lunch 1200-1600; dinner daily, 1600-2000; champagne high tea, 1 Sep-31 Oct daily, 1600-1830. Times may vary due to sunset. Please phone for a leaflet, details or prices. (N9)*

Orwell River Cruises

Ipswich Tel: (01473) 692255

The only river cruise on the historic and beautiful Orwell, Stour and Harwich harbour. Recommended after a break of 50 years.

Golf Courses

⊛ Ufford Park Hotel, Golf & Leisure

Yarmouth Road, Ufford, Woodbridge IP12 1QW
Tel: (01394) 383555 Fax: (01394) 383582
Web: www.uffordpark.co.uk

Offering a wide range of top quality facilities, Ufford Park is set in 120 acres of historic parkland with 50 en-suite bedrooms, full wedding packages and 8 air-conditioned conference rooms. Par 71, 18 hole golf course, excellent natural drainage, and purpose built golf academy with expert PGA tuition. 2 restaurants, bar meals, light lunches & afternoon teas. Swimming pool, gymnasium, spa, steam/sauna rooms, solarium, beauticians and hairdressers. 1 1/2 miles from Woodbridge, on the river Deben, and within a few minutes drive from our heritage coastline. Access off the A12 past Woodbridge, with 200 parking spaces. Open all year round. OPEN TO NON-RESIDENTS AND NON-MEMBERS. *(K/L9)*

Sailing at Blythburgh

Leisure Centres and Indoor Activities

◉ Felixstowe Leisure Centre
Undercliff Road West, Felixstowe
Tel: (01394) 670411

Features include leisure swimming pool, learner pool, sauna, sunbeds, bowls hall, multi-purpose entertainment and conference hall, children's indoor adventure play area, creche, fitness and health suite. *(L11)*

◉ Lowestoft Family Bowl
Unit 11 Capital Trading Estate, Rant Score,
Whapload Road, Lowestoft
Tel: (01502) 519200

A family entertainment centre comprising 14 lanes of tenpin bowling, children's play area, video games, function room, diner and fully licensed bar. *(P2)*

Outdoor Activities

◉ Alton Water Sports Centre
Alton Water, Stutton
Tel: (01473) 328408

RYA approved centre: sailing, canoeing and windsurfing. Tuition and equipment hire. Café. *Open everyday except Christmas/Boxing Day from 10.00-20.00 weekdays, 10.00-18.00 weekends. (I11)*

◉ Byways Bicycles
Darsham, near Yoxford
(sign-posted from the A12)
Tel: (01728) 668764
www.bywaysbicycles.co.uk

A choice of cycles for hire - follow a planned route or choose your own. *(M7)*

◉ Horseracing at Newmarket
Tel: (01638) 663482 *(A7)*

Saxmundham Angling Centre
Rear of Market Place, Saxmundham
Tel: (01728) 603443

Fishing tackle and baits for coarse, sea and game anglers. Local club memberships and day tickets plus advice on local venues, tackle and tactics. Also trophies and engraving for all activities. *(M7)*

Suffolk

Lowestoft

Specialist Holidays and Activities

Anglia Cycling Holidays
see entry on page 203.

⊛ Byways Bicycles
Tel: (01728) 668764
www.bywaysbicycles.co.uk
A choice of new bikes for sale and for hire, to suit all ages. Also cycle repairs. Follow a planned route showing you local places of interest. Pubs, tea-rooms, picnic places or choose your own. Cycling holidays also arranged. Byways Bicycles, Darsham, near Yoxford, Suffolk IP17 3QD. (Sign-posted from the A12). *Open Easter and May-Oct 1000-1800. At other times by appointment. Closed Tue. (M7)*

⊛ Equine Tours
Tel: (01638) 667333
Tailor made tours behind the scenes of the horseracing industry with experienced guides. Can include horses on gallops, their swimming pool, a trainer's yard, the National Stud, Animal Health Trust, Royal Newmarket, the museum and a visit to the races. Equine Tours, 99 High Street, Newmarket, Suffolk CB8 8JL. *Open Easter-end October. Closed 24 Dec-6 Jan. (A7)*

⊛ Kids Klub
Tel: (01449) 675907
Email: info@kidsklub.co.uk www.kidsklub.co.uk
Easter and summer multi-activity holidays for children and teenagers. Also group programmes available all year round. Choose from four centres and over 50 activities. Call for a brochure. Kids Klub, The Lodge, Great Finborough, Stowmarket, Suffolk, IP14 3EF. *(H7/8)*

The National Horseracing Museum Minibus Tours
Tel: (01638) 667333
Privileged tours behind the scenes of Newmarket's racing industry. Our regular tour (departs 9.20am daily except Sundays and Mondays) takes you to see horses training on the gallops and in their swimming pool, before going to one of a number of trainers' yards where you will meet staff and their horses. These yards are not normally open to the public. We also have a programme of special tours including our famous all-day Introduction to Racing - our expert will take you racing and explain how it works, including a trip to the start and a visit to the jockey's weighing room. *(A7)*

⊛ Snape Maltings
Tel: (01728) 688305
Maltings on the banks of the River Alde with shops, galleries, restaurants, river trips, painting and craft courses in the summer and a world-famous concert hall. Snape Maltings, Snape, Saxmundham, Suffolk IP17 1SR. *(M7)*

⊛ Suffolk Cycle Breaks
Tel: (01449) 721555
www.cyclebreaks.co.uk
www.walkingbreaks.co.uk
Gentle cycling and walking holidays in Suffolk and Norfolk. Luggage transfer and accommodation pre-arranged. Suffolk Cycle Breaks, Bradfield Hall Barn, Alder Carr Farm, PO Box 82, Needham Market IP6 8BW. *(H/18)*

Suffolk

Tug-o-war, Felixstowe

⊛ Wildtracks
Wildtracks Limited, Chippenham Road,
Kennett, Newmarket
Tel: (01638) 751918
An activity park embracing all kinds of activities for children and adults including military vehicles, karting, quad bikes, motor cross, four-wheel driving and instruction. *(A7)*

⊛ Thornham Field Centre
Tel: (01379) 788153
Email: Info@thornhamfc.fsnet.co.uk
www.thornhamfieldcentre.org
Private country estate with residential field centre with shop, cafe and a network of footpaths. Thornham Field Centre, Thornham Magna, Eye, Suffolk IP23 8HH. *(I5)*

DID YOU KNOW

Thorpeness is the East of England's most eccentric village, home of probably the most unusual (former) water tower in Britain - the House in the Clouds.

Snape

⊛ Thorpeness Village
Tel: 01728 452176
This fascinating seaside village on the Suffolk coast was built in the 1920's. Thorpeness Hotel and Golf Club offers three crown accommodation and a superb 18 hole golf course. The "Dolphin Inn" offers bed and breakfast and the best of pub food and restaurant facilities, ideal for families visiting the village. In the summer there is an outside bar and BBQ area. The Country Club has seven tennis courts available for hire. The original wings have been sympathetically converted into apartments, with function and bar facilities. Guests staying in our village accommodation enjoy a variety of holiday packages all year round. *(N/O7)*

Suffolk

Restaurants

Bungay
⊛ St. Peter's Hall
St. Peter South Elmham
St. Peter's Brewery Co Ltd
Tel: (01986) 782322
Fax: (01986) 782505
Email: beers@stpetersbrewery.co.uk
Website: www.stpetersbrewery.co.uk

Among the Saints, in this beautiful part of Suffolk, enjoy a meal or a drink in the Great Hall of St. Peter's. For lunch try freshly made soup or beef casserole; a chocolate gateau for tea. In the evening a seafood chowder, Tournedos Rossini and a Treacle and Ginger Tart feature on the menu. Traditional English Ales brewed on the premises. Marriages may be solemnized in the chapel. *Average prices: lunch £6, dinner (3 courses) £20. Open Fri & Sat 1100-2300, food 1200-2100 (1830 dinner); Sun 1200-1900 both menus and roast. Also open Bank Holiday Mondays. (L3)*

Bury St Edmunds
⊛ The Angel Hotel
Angel Hill
Tel: (01284) 714000

This historical hotel with its Dickensian connections is owned and run by the Gough family. With two dining areas, the magnificent Abbeygate Restaurant overlooking the square and the Vaults Brasserie, a medieval undercroft, dating back to the 12 Century. The food ranges from homely venison sausages to confit of duck. Adnams and Greene King supply the beers. *Special weekend rates offered from £69.00 per person per night which includes, full English breakfast and 3 course dinner (£20.00 allowance). Conference, banquets and weddings ranging from an intimate dinner for 6 to an extravaganza wedding for 60. (D/E6/7)*

Bury St Edmunds
⊛ Linden Tree
7 Out Northgate
Tel: (01284) 754600

An established Pub/Restaurant, well known for plentiful portions of home-made food and fast service. Reservable non smoking conservatory restaurant plus table service throughout. Families welcome. Large mature gardens with facilities for children. *Average prices: £2-£10 (Lunch). Two courses £10 (evenings). Food served: 1200-1400 (1500 Sundays) and 1800-2130. 7 days. (D/E6/7)*

DID YOU KNOW

The Nutshell pub in Bury St Edmunds is reputedly the smallest pub in Britain. It's bar measures just over 5 metres by 2 metres. Whilst the 19th C. Theatre Royal is one of the oldest and smallest (capacity of just 352) in Britain.

Ramsholt

Hadleigh
The Marquis of Cornwallis
Upper Street, Upper Layham, Hadleigh, Ipswich
IP7 5JZ Tel: (01473) 822051

Nestled in Constable countryside, the Marquis of Cornwallis offers a truly traditional welcome. The candle-lit ambience provides the perfect atmosphere for sampling and enjoying its real ales, country wines and traditional English country menu. Perched on the rim of the valley, the Marquis' garden rolls down to the River Brett and provides the perfect location to watch the sun set over the vale. *Open daily, we have no petty restrictions with patrons able to sit in one of the bars, the dining room or the garden. (G10)*

Nayland
The White Hart Inn
11 High Street, Nayland CO6 4JF
Tel: (01206) 263382 (reservations)
Fax: (01206) 263638
Email: Nayhart@aol.com
Website: www.whitehart-nayland.co.uk

A restaurant with guestrooms located in an old coaching house in the heart of Constable country. Rustic countryside-style with French flair cooking. Wedding Licence. Private function room and terrace available.*Light fare lunch menu with á la carte in the evenings. Closed on Monday all day, except Bank Holidays. Six bedrooms with en-suite facilities available seven days a week. (F/G11/12)*

Newmarket
⊛ The National Horseracing Museum
99 High Street, Newmarket CB8 8JL
Tel: (01638) 677333

Popular licensed café serving home-cooked light meals and teas using local ingredients. Daily specials include two vegetarian dishes. Three types of scone baked daily, plus our famous Newmarket sausage rolls. Garden, marquee, highchairs, good wheelchair/pushchair access. *Open all year, closed Sundays, Christmas and New Year. (A7)*

Kersey

DID YOU KNOW

The Ship Inn at Dunwich is said to be one of the first inns in England to be licensed. It has stood here since Tudor times. Nearby Aldeburgh was the childhood home of Elizabeth Garrett Anderson (1836-1917), the first woman doctor in Britain in 1870. She retired to Aldeburgh, and in 1908 became Britain's first woman's mayor.

Suffolk

Polstead
⊛ The Cock Inn
The Green, Polstead
Tel: (01206) 263150

Open Tuesday-Sunday. Situated in a peaceful village in the heart of Constable country, a seventeenth century inn with Victorian restaurant extension, recently extended to meet growing demand for their award winning traditional home made food. Lunchtime menus include a choice of traditional hot meals and salads. Also available are "Suffolk Huffers" with a variety of fillings. The elaborate evening menu includes a wide variety of starters and main courses incorporating meat, fish, and vegetarian dishes. The home made desserts are a speciality. As well as real ales, the bar also stocks a vast selection of fine wines and malt whiskies. *(G10)*

Oulton Broad
⊛ The Crooked Barn
Ivy House Farm (hotel), Ivy Lane, Oulton Broad,
Lowestoft NR33 8HY
Tel: (01502) 501353/588144
Fax: (01502) 501539

In extensive grounds on the tranquil south-west shores of Oulton Broad stands an 18th century thatched barn now converted to The Crooked Barn Restaurant. Not only do we serve delicious light lunches with a choice of large or small portions but also scrumptious cream teas after which you can ease your conscience with a stroll round the delightful country garden! The Crooked Barn menu which is offered at lunch and dinner features a variety of fish, meat, game and vegetarian dishes such as shredded smoked chicken baked in a paper bag! - Suffolk pork marinated in oriental spices served with stir fried vegetables and crispy egg noodles. *Open: daily. Lunch from 1200-1345 and dinner 1900-2130. Average prices: bistro lunch £8.95; à la carte £23.00 (3 courses). (O/P2)*

Coddenham

Suffolk ——————————————————

afternoon teas

Debenham
☙ Carters Teapot Pottery
Low Road, Debenham,
Suffolk IP14 6QU
Tel: (01728) 860475
Fax: (01728) 861110
www.cartersteapots.com

Whilst visiting the Teapot Pottery you may like to be served tea from one of our unusual teapots! Tea, coffee, orange juice and light refreshments served in our delightful conservatory. *Open: Mon-Fri, 0900-1730; Sat & Bank Hols 1030-1630; Sun 14.00-1700 all year. (J7)*

Monks Eleigh
☙ Corn-Craft Tearoom & Coffee Shop
See entry on page 259.

Newmarket
☙ The National Horseracing Museum
99 High Street, Newmarket
Tel: (01638) 667333

Popular licensed café serving home-cooked light meals and teas using local ingredients. Daily specials include two vegetarian dishes. Three types of scone baked daily, plus our famous Newmarket sausage rolls. Garden, marquee, highchairs, good wheelchair/pushchair access. *Open all year, closed Sundays and Christmas – New Year. (A7)*

Southwold
☙ Sarah's of Southwold
51A High Street, Southwold, Suffolk IP18 6DJ
Tel: (01502) 724077

Sarah's of Southwold is a small but charming teashop with an attractive patio garden situated in the High Street at Southwold. Delicious home-made cakes and scones baked on the premises. Do call in and sample our delights. We also have an interesting selection of gifts and preserves. *(O4/5)*

Walberswick
☙ The Parish Lantern
On the Village Green,
Walberswick IP18 6TT
Tel: (01502) 723173

Visit our celebrated tea room and courtyard garden. Enjoy morning coffee, light lunches, cream teas and home-baked cakes. Original crafts, gifts, clothes and pictures. Set in the unspoilt beauty of the fishing village of Walberswick. *Open: Daily from 1000 April-Dec; Fri, Sat, Sun only Jan-March. (O5)*

Cavendish

DID YOU KNOW
The Tolly Cobbold Brewery in Ipswich has the oldest working brewing vessel in Britain, dating from 1723. It is also home to Britain's largest collection of commemorative bottled beers.

Suffolk

regional produce

Bungay

⊛ **St Peter's Brewery Co Ltd** Ⓠ

St Peter's Hall, St Peter
South Elmham, Bungay NR35 1NQ
Tel: (01986) 782322
Fax: (01986) 782505
Email: beers@stpetersbrewery.co.uk
Website: www.stpetersbrewery.co.uk

The brewery was built in 1996 within converted farm buildings adjacent to St Peter's Hall. The site was ideal because of excellent water quality from a deep bore-hole. Locally malted barley, together with Kentish hops produces a range of classical English cask-conditioned ales. We also have a range of superb bottled beers. Visitor Centre, Restaurant, Bar and Shop. St Peter's Brewery also has a selection of other prestigious establishments; De La Pole Arms, Wingfield, The Jerusalem Tavern, Clerkenwell, London *Open: Brewery tours available every Friday, Saturday and Sunday. Telephone for details. (L2/3)*

Suffolk

Aldringham

Aldringham Craft Market
Aldringham, Near Leiston,
IP16 4PY Tel: 01728 830397

Family business, established 1958. Three relaxed and friendly galleries offering wide and extensive ranges of British craft products, original paintings, etchings and prints; studio, domestic and garden pottery, wood, leather, glass, jewellery, toys, kites, games, books, maps and many other good things including dolls houses and furniture, ladies' clothes, toiletries and hardy perennial plants. We only stock sensibly-priced, high quality products   Easy car parking; children's play area; coffee shop in season.

Open Mon to Sat 10.00-5.30.
Sun 2.00-5.30 (all year),
10.00-12.00 (Spring and Summer) (N7)

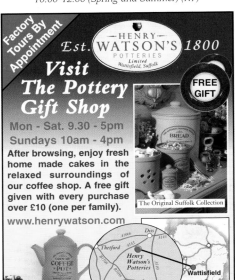

Beccles
⊛ **The Parish Lantern**
Exchange Square,
Beccles, Suffolk NR34 9HH
Tel: (01502) 711700

A rich mix of crafts, gifts, clothes, pictures and jewellery housed in this part 17th century listed building. Set in the historic market town of Beccles, which features a wealth of period buildings leading down to the River Waveney, 'Gateway to the Broads'. *Open Monday to Saturday 9am to 5pm. (N2/3)*

NURSEY & SON LTD

Bungay
⊛ 12 Upper Olland St, Bungay
Tel: (01986) 892821
Email: tnursey@aol.com
Web: www.nurseyleather.co.uk

Established 1790. Jerkins, gilets, jackets, leather and suede jackets, leather trousers, sheepskin coats, slippers, gloves, hats, rugs etc. The factory shop has a good selection especially for Gifts, handbags, wallets, purses, also a wide variety of sub-standard Products and Oddments. *Open Mon-Fri 1000-1300, 1400-1700, closed last week July and first week August. Nov, Dec, Jan open 6 days a week. Access, Visa. (L3)*

Hoxne

Suffolk

Debenham
⊛ **Carters Teapot Pottery**
Low Road, Debenham, Suffolk IP14 6QU
Tel: (01728) 860475 Fax: (01728) 861110
Email: info@cartersteapots.com
www.cartersteapots.com

It doesn't have to be tea time to visit this Pottery making highly collectable teapots, in the beautiful village of Debenham. Visitors can see from the viewing area how these world renowned teapots are made and painted by hand. Pottery shop selling teapots, mugs and quality seconds. Situated just off the High Street, follow the teapot signs. Parking available. Tea, coffee and light refreshments in the conservatory. *Open Mon-Fri 9-5.30, Sat & Bank Hols 10.30-4.30, Sun 2-5pm. (J7)*

Long Melford
Persian Carpet Studio
The Old White Hart, Long Melford,
Sudbury, Suffolk CO10 9HX
Tel: (01787) 882214
www.persian-carpet-studio.net

The Persian Carpet Studio is one of the UK's largest showrooms dedicated to antique and new decorative Oriental rugs and carpets. A kaleidoscope of colour and pattern await visitors to this 18th century former coaching inn.   Within a spacious, relaxed setting flooded with natural light, visitors can enjoy and examine the range of sensuous textiles, superb colours and exquisite patterns of the carefully selected stock. Visit our Restoration Workshop and see our team of highly skilled restorers carrying out a whole range of repairs, from simple fringes to extensive rebuilding where carpets have been badly damaged. *Open Mon - Sat 1000 - 1730. Car Parking. (E10)*

Suffolk

Monks Eleigh
⊛ **Corncraft**
Bridge Farm, Monks Eleigh
Tel: (01449) 740456 E-mail: rwgage@lineone.net
www.corncraft.co.uk

In the heart of the Suffolk countryside between Hadleigh and Lavenham, Corn Craft specialise in growing and supplying corn dollies and dried flowers. A wide range of their own products, along with an extensive selection of other British crafts is available from the craft shop and new flower shop. Coffee, cream teas, home made cakes and other light refreshments are served in the converted granary adjoining the shop. Ample space and easy parking. Evening demonstrations of corn dolly making are given by arrangement. Contact Mrs Win Gage. *Open every day throughout the year from 1000-1700, Sunday 1100-1700. (F/G9)*

Newmarket
⊛ **The National Horseracing Museum**
99 High Street, Newmarket
Tel: (01638) 667333

An amazing array of horseracing and horse-based gifts, ranging from jewellery, clothing, games and furnishings. Good choice of gifts for horse-mad children, and racing-obsessed adults, and very useful for finding presents for men. Books, videos and lots of soft toys. *Open all year, closed Christmas week and Sundays in winter. (A7)*

Stoke by Nayland

Snape
⊛ Snape Maltings
Nr. Saxmundham IP17 1SR
Tel: (01728) 688303/5

Snape Maltings is a unique collection of 19th century granaries and malthouses set on the banks of the River Alde. These historic buildings now house a variety of excellent shops and galleries including House & Garden (for furnishings, kitchenware and fine foods), Snape Craft Shop, Books & Cards and Countrywear and Little Rascals. The Granary Tea Shop offers light refreshment and the Plough & Sail pub specialises in modern British food in a relaxed contemporary setting. Holiday cottages are available to let all year, and painting and craft courses run during the summer months. *No admission charge. Free car parking. (M7)*

Walberswick
⊛ The Parish Lantern
Tel: (01502) 723173

Set in a grade II listed Georgian building with courtyard garden, the Parish Lantern offers good quality crafts, gifts, clothes and pictures, as well as delicious cream teas and light lunches. The unspoilt sea-side village of Walberswick, with it's picturesque harbour and sandy beach, has long attracted writers and artists, and was once the home of architect and designer Charles Rennie Mackintosh. Close to Minsmere R.S.P.B. Reserve and Dunwich Heath, and just a short ferry ride (in summer) or a pleasant walk from Southwold. *Open daily from 1000. Fri, Sat & Sun only during Jan and Feb. (O5)*

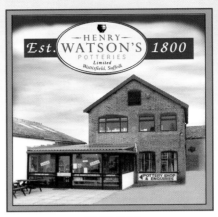

Wattisfield
⊛ Watson's Potteries
Wattisfield, Suffolk IP22 1NH
(A143 between Bury and Diss)
Tel: (01359) 251239
www.henrywatson.com

Henry Watson's Ltd. has been manufacturing pottery for over 200 years. Our country gift shop offers a wide choice of excellent quality seconds including the famous 'Original Suffolk Collection' of terracotta kitchenware & giftware at factory shop prices. See the original kiln and view our craftsmen at work on a guided factory tour by appointment. After browsing, enjoy light refreshments in the relaxed surroundings of our coffee shop. *Open Mon-Sat 0930-1700 & Sundays 1000-1600. Find us: On the A143 between Bury St Edmunds & Diss. (G5)*

DID YOU KNOW

The village of Long Melford has the longest High Street in Britain, at over a mile (1.6km) in length.

Suffolk

Woolpit
⬡ Elm Tree Gallery
The Old Bakery, Woolpit,
Nr Bury St. Edmunds IP30 9QG
Tel/Fax: (01359) 240255

An Aladdin's cave of attractive, good quality crafts and gifts, housed in The Old Bakery, a timber-framed building dating from c.1550. The extensive range includes jewellery, textiles, wood, ceramics - including locally crafted Clarecraft figures, Moorcroft pottery and Harmony Kingdom and one of the best selections of greetings cards in the region. Children's gifts include Ty Beanie Babies. Light refreshments available all day but limited seating available. *Open: All year, Mon-Sat 1000-1800 (inc. Bank Holidays 2-5pm) Open on Sundays in Dec until Christmas 10.00-18.00. (G7)*

Buttermarket Shopping Centre, Ipswich

Woodbridge Tidemill

Suffolk

discovery tours

Race day at Newmarket

Spinning Yarns
Weave your way through the land of the medieval wool industry.

Starting point: Lavenham, Suffolk *(E/F9)*
Mileage: 10m/16km
Morning - explore Britain's best preserved medieval town, and learn about the wool industry at the Guildhall. Then take the unclassified road to *Long Melford*, now the 'antiques capital of Suffolk'.
Afternoon - visit *Kentwell Hall*, to hear yarns of Tudor times, at one of the annual recreations. End the day by taking the A1092 to the pretty little town of *Clare*. Enjoy the views from the castle mound.

Historic Lavenham

Salty Tales of the Sea
Discover the maritime heritage of the East Coast.

Starting point: Lowestoft, Suffolk *(P2)*
Mileage: 21m/34km
Morning - visit the harbour, the historic *Lydia Eva Steam Drifter*, and the *Maritime Heritage Museum*.
Afternoon - take the A12/B1127 to *Southwold*, and enjoy a pint of ale from the town's own brewery. End the day by taking the A1095 to the A12. Head south, and after 2 miles, turn left to *Dunwich*, a former city lost to the sea. Visit the *Museum* and enjoy some of the best fish and chips in Britain.

Under Starter's Orders
Explore the horseracing capital of the world.

Starting point: Newmarket, Suffolk *(A7)*
Mileage: varied (depending on tour taken)
Morning - go 'behind the scenes' of racing establishments on a unique 'equine tour', including *The National Stud*. Then explore racing history and ride a horse simulator at the *Horseracing Museum*.
Afternoon - enjoy an exciting afternoon at the races, where you can cheer your favourite to the winning post!

Bloomin' Beautiful
Discover the spectacular colours and delicate fragrances of some of England's finest gardens.

Starting point: Bury St. Edmunds, Suffolk *(D/E6/7)*
Mileage: 3m/5km
Morning - explore historic *Bury St. Edmunds*, renowned for its beautiful gardens and parks. The town has twice won the Nations in Bloom 'green oscar'.
Afternoon - take the A143 south west to Horringer, and enjoy the stunning parkland and Italian garden of *Ickworth House*.

A Painter's Inspiration

Visit the places and landscapes which inspired two of Britain's greatest painters.

Starting point: Ipswich, Suffolk *(I/J10)*
Mileage: 21m/34km
Morning - visit *Christchurch Mansion* to see the Constable and Gainsborough paintings. Then take the A12 south for 6m to *East Bergholt*, where John Constable (1776-1837) was born. Continue to nearby *Flatford Mill*, scene of his most famous work "The Haywain".
Afternoon - return to the A12. Head south for ½ mile, then take the B1068 (via Stoke-by-Nayland) to the junction with the A134. Turn right to *Sudbury*, and visit the birthplace of Thomas Gainsborough (1727-88).

Strange Tales and Curiosities

Discover the flipside of the east, its customs, stories and local characters.

Starting point: Woodbridge, Suffolk *(K9)*
Mileage: 26m/42km
Morning - visit the unique *tide mill*, and *Sutton Hoo's* treasure-filled burial site. Then take the A1152/B1094, via UFO country (Rendlesham Forest) to *Orford*. Climb the 12th C. castle and discover the merman story.
Afternoon - take the B1084/B1078 to Tunstall, where you turn right onto the B1069. At Snape, turn right onto the A1094 to the unspoilt seaside town of *Aldeburgh*. Hunt out the little 'Snooks' statue, then follow the coast road north to eccentric *Thorpeness*, and its 'House in the Clouds' and storybook mere.

Milling Mayhem

Discover the turning sails and waterwheels of historic mills. Climb their towers and buy freshly milled flour.

Starting point: Stowmarket, Suffolk *(H7/8)*
Mileage: 15m/24km
Morning - start at the *Museum of East Anglian Life*, with its reconstructed water mill and wind pump. Then take the A14 west for 5 miles, to join the A1088 north to Ixworth. Just to the south west is *Pakenham*, the last parish in England with a working wind and water mill.
Afternoon - take the A143 to *Stanton*, where the windmill has an exhibition on post mills. End the day at *Wyken Hall* (just to the south along an unclassified road). Explore the gardens and enjoy a cream tea.

Fortresses and Fighters

From ancient fortresses to airborne fighters, this is an intriguing insight into the defence of the realm.

Starting point: Bungay, Suffolk *(L3)*
Mileage: 28m/45km
Morning - explore the remains of the Norman castle at *Bungay*, then take the B1062 to Flixton, and the *Norfolk and Suffolk Aviation Museum*, with its historic aircraft and exhibitions.
Afternoon - take the B1062/A143 to Harleston, where you join the B1116 south to *Framlingham*. Visit the magnificent 12th C. castle. Then continue on the B1116 to Parham, and visit the *390th Bomb Group Memorial Air Museum*, housed in an original wartime control tower.

Animal Magic

Discover British wildlife at its best - owls, horses and avocets.

Starting point: Needham Market, Suffolk *(H8)*
Mileage: 36m/58km
Morning - leave the town on the B1078. Then take the A140 north for 3 miles to join the A1120 to *Stonham Aspal*. Enjoy the flying displays at the *Suffolk Owl Centre*. Remain on the A1120 to *Earl Soham*, then follow the signs to *Easton Farm Park*. You can watch the cows being milked here!
Afternoon - head south east to *Wickham Market*, and join the A12 north for 12 miles. Just beyond *Yoxford*, turn right (following signs) to visit the famous *Minsmere Nature Reserve*.

Stanton Post Mill

Take time out to visit our website

www.eastofenglandtouristboard.com

... and discover some great deals on short breaks and holidays, as well as information on places to visit and events taking place throughout this picturesque corner of England.